REPORTS ON EUROPEAN EDUCATION

# McGRAW-HILL EDUCATION CLASSICS

EDWARD H. REISNER, *General Editor*

REPORTS ON EUROPEAN EDUCATION

# McGRAW-HILL EDUCATION CLASSICS

EDWARD H. REISNER, *General Editor*

*Luther, Calvin and Other Protestant Educators*
*Edited by* FREDERICK EBY

*Comenius*
*Edited by* M. W. KEATINGE

*Locke*
*Edited by* W. E. SEALOCK

*French Liberalism and Education in the Eighteenth Century*
*Edited by* F. DE LA FONTAINERIE

*Thomas Jefferson and Education in a Republic*
*Edited by* C. F. ARROWOOD

*Pestalozzi*
*Edited by* L. F. ANDERSON

*Reports on European Education*
*Edited by* EDGAR W. KNIGHT

*Horace Mann*
*Edited by* A. O. NORTON

*Henry Barnard*
*Edited by* JOHN S. BRUBACHER

*Pioneers of Women's Education*
*Edited by* WILLYSTINE GOODSELL

*Francis W. Parker*
*Edited by* EDWARD H. REISNER

*All in press or in preparation, July, 1930*

C. E. Stowe.

# REPORTS ON
# EUROPEAN EDUCATION

By
John Griscom
Victor Cousin
Calvin E. Stowe

Edited by

EDGAR W. KNIGHT

Professor of Education
University of North Carolina

McGRAW-HILL BOOK COMPANY, INC.

NEW YORK: 370 SEVENTH AVENUE
LONDON: 6 & 8 BOUVERIE ST., E.C.4.

1930

To

A. T. K.

# ACKNOWLEDGMENT

I am indebted to Mrs. V. A. Hill, Dr. William E. Drake, and Mr. W. W. Smiley for assistance in the preparation of the manuscript for publication.

EDGAR W. KNIGHT

*Chapel Hill, N. C.*

# CONTENTS

# REPORTS ON EUROPEAN EDUCATION

## The Influence on the United States of Reported Observations of European Education

THE American public school had its origin, in part at least, in conflicts which grew out of contending economic interests. Some of these conflicts led to the removal of religious and property restrictions on the ballot, to an increase in the number of elective offices, to the abolition of imprisonment for debt, to the betterment of the conditions surrounding the laboring classes, as well as to other reforms which were likewise humanitarian and social in nature. These evidences of the democratic awakening which marked the second quarter of the nineteenth century served to prepare the way for education as an important concern of the state.

While these reforms were being worked out, other influences were making themselves felt in the movement for public education in the United States, a movement which gained so increasingly as to give to the last two decades of the *ante-bellum* period the character of an educational and social awakening. One of these influences may be seen in the development of educational journalism. Before 1830, educational journals appeared in rather large numbers, beginning with the work of Albert Picket and his son, John Picket, in *The Academician*, in New York in 1818; and, by 1861, the list of those known to have been published had grown to 121 of general, local, and specialized educational interests. Another influence may be seen in the numerous educational conventions which were held in all parts of the country. The lyceum movement began, springing from democratic and spontaneous influences, and developed into a considerable force in the cause of universal education. Progressive educational sentiment was reflected also in and through official educational surveys in several states, in reports and memorials to state legislatures, and especially through the work of intelligent, fervid, and industrious leaders such as James G. Carter, Horace Mann, Henry Barnard, Joseph Caldwell, Calvin H. Wiley, Caleb Mills, Samuel Lewis, Samuel Galloway, and others who helped to remove some of the obstructions in the way of public education.

One of the most influential forces of all those at work in behalf of public education in the United States during the second quarter of the last century, however, arose out of reports on education in Europe. These came in the form of impressions which education there had made upon travelers, in the observations which they reported, and in official reports which served to acquaint educational leaders in this country with conditions elsewhere. One of the earliest of such reports, although quite local in effect but showing European influence, was that made in 1817 to the Legislature of North Carolina by Archibald D. Murphey, who revealed considerable acquaintance with conditions in Europe, especially in France, and some familiarity with Lancasterian and Pestalozzian methods, although Murphey had not gained his information by a first-hand study. His plan for a school system in North Carolina, however, resembled Condorcet's proposed plan for education in France in 1792; and, although Murphey's proposal for a public-school system was too Utopian and too advanced for the time and a slave-holding, aristocratic state, it nevertheless later became the basis on which North Carolina built, before 1860, a fairly creditable public-school system.

William C. Woodbridge, of New England, was in Europe in 1820 and for a considerable time during the years 1825 to 1829, and he published in William Russell's *American Journal of Education* important letters on European conditions and especially on the work of Pestalozzi and Fellenberg. A few Americans had studied at the University of Göttingen before 1820, and Joseph Neef, one of Pestalozzi's instructors, had come to this country in the early years of the nineteenth century and had taught in Philadelphia, Louisville (Kentucky), and New Harmony

(Indiana). These contacts between the United States and educational thought and practice in Europe had some influence upon educational development in this country, even though it was indirect and slight.

Contacts with Europe which had a much wider influence upon public education in the United States in the nineteenth century were those made by the small group of observers of European education immediately to be named. Important observations and impressions were reported by John Griscom, in 1819, on his year in Europe; by the translation of the report of the Frenchman, Victor Cousin, in 1831, to the French government, on education in Prussia; by Calvin E. Stowe, in 1837, to the Legislature of Ohio, on education in Europe; by A. D. Bache, in 1839, to the trustees of the Girard College for Orphans, on conditions surrounding the education of orphans in Europe, especially in Holland and Germany; and by Horace Mann, in 1843, to the state board of education in Massachusetts, of which he was then secretary, on conditions in England, Scotland, France, Germany, Belgium, and Holland. Henry Barnard visited Europe during the years 1835 to 1837 and later described in his publications the educational conditions which he found and, in 1854, published under the title *National Education in Europe* his own observations and those of other visitors abroad. The importance of the observations of Mann and of Barnard upon European conditions, is pointed out in other volumes

4

in this series.[1] The present volume treats only of the work of Griscom, Cousin, and Stowe.

The influence of these various reports on educational conditions in Europe during the second quarter of the nineteenth century was evident, particularly in the development of the principles of state control and state support of education, compulsory school attendance, and the training of teachers.

New York had taken the lead in the creation of state school supervision, as early as 1812, when, by an act of that year, provision was made for a chief state school officer. Gideon Hawley was the first appointee to the office, in January, 1813. Maryland created the office in 1826, Michigan followed a few years later, Louisiana and Pennsylvania in the early 'thirties, Tennessee in 1836, Ohio and Massachusetts in 1837, Kentucky in 1838, and by 1850 thirty-one states and three territories had provided for some form of state supervision. State boards of education were created during these years, and the beginnings of taxation for schools by general state legislation were made. Compulsory attendance legislation was enacted later, but the idea that the state had the right to compel parents to send their children to school began to grow slowly in the *ante-bellum* period. Massachusetts, in 1852, made a gesture toward compulsory attendance legislation, and, by 1897, thirty of

[1] See NORTON, ARTHUR O., *Horace Mann;* and BRUBACHER, JOHN S., *Henry Barnard.*

the states had enacted laws on the subject, but it was not until 1918 that the last state committed itself to the policy of requiring children between certain ages to attend school for all or some part of the school term. Legislation of this sort was viewed for a long time in this country as un-democratic. Like many other extensions of public educa-tional effort now common in the United States, laws com-pelling children to attend school had to wait upon the awakening of a livelier educational conscience than the American public developed before the Civil War.

Educational leaders in this country also derived some inspiration on the subject of teacher training through con-tact with the reports on European practices. Attempts to train teachers had been privately made by Samuel McCorkle, in North Carolina, before the close of the eighteenth century, in his academy known as Zion Par-nassus. Samuel R. Hall, as early as 1823, had used his school in Vermont for the purpose of training teachers through a three-years' course in which were taught the subjects given in the common schools, and, in 1829, Hall published his *Lectures on Schoolkeeping*.[1] Three years earlier, Governor DeWitt Clinton had urged upon the legislature of New York the importance of establishing a

[1] An exact reproduction of the first (1829) edition of this book has been made by Arthur D. Wright, of Dartmouth Col-lege, and George E. Gardner, of the Graduate School of Educa-tion of Harvard University. The Dartmouth Press, 1929.

school for the training of teachers. Teacher-training features were found in some of the academies of New York in 1831. In the eighteen-twenties, James G. Carter had urged the establishment of public normal schools for Massachusetts, making his appeal chiefly through his "Essays on Popular Education" which appeared in the *Boston Patriot* in 1824 to 1825, and, by 1836, the establishment of normal schools had become a practical issue in Massachusetts. As a result of the work of Carter, Rev. Charles Brooks, Horace Mann, Edward Dwight, and other influential people, the first state normal school in the United States was opened at Lexington, Mass., July 3, 1839, and by September of the next year two other schools for training teachers had been opened in that state. Other states followed, and by 1870 the idea of separate and distinct schools for the professional or special preparation of teachers had been generally accepted (in theory at least) in the United States, and provision for such schools had been made by twenty-two states. Beginning with Pestalozzianism, however, which spread in part through the reports considered in this volume and especially through the Oswego Movement, after 1860, the normal school idea grew rapidly after 1870.

Although the influence of these European reports was most conspicuous in matters of state control and state support, compulsory education, and teacher training, it was evident also in educational journalism and educational associations which developed rapidly during the *ante-*

*bellum* period. Through these and other forces educational opportunity was slowly widened, many obstacles which had stood so stubbornly in the way of the democratic principles of education were removed, and this country came finally to accept these principles as sound. State school systems were organized, state taxation measures were adopted, state school laws were improved, localism weakened, and the way of public education seemed brighter as the public mind became enlightened on the benefits of public schools.

# 1. JOHN GRISCOM

## Selections from

## *A YEAR IN EUROPE*

Comprising a Journal of Observations in England, Scotland, Ireland, France, Switzerland, the North of Europe, and Holland. In 1818 and 1819. By John Griscom, Professor of Chemistry and Natural Philosophy in the New York Institution; Member of the Literary and Philosophical Society of New York, &c. In Two Volumes. New York: 1823.

## I. JOHN GRISCOM (1774–1852)
### and
## A YEAR IN EUROPE [1]

JOHN GRISCOM was born at Hancock's Bridge, near Salem, N. J., September 27, 1774, of Quaker parentage. His early education was received in a primitive rural school in the neighborhood which had a bewildering succession of teachers, one of whom, a Hungarian, had come to New Jersey as a Hessian soldier. Notwithstanding the difficulties in his way, young Griscom made some progress and gained the confidence of his neighbors as a student and for his love of learning. When he was only sixteen, they persuaded him to open a school in the neighborhood, in a log house about three miles from Salem. During this first session, he divided his time between the school and his father's farm, where he worked in the early mornings and late afternoons. Later he began to devote all of his time to teaching, which he found a very congenial occupation. In 1793, he entered the Friends' Academy in Philadelphia, which was then under the direction of William Waring, an able mathematician, but four months later an epidemic of yellow fever invaded the school and caused the death of Waring. Griscom was himself stricken,

[1] This report was made in two volumes running to 520 and 562 pages, respectively. Only brief selections are reprinted here. The original punctuation and spelling are followed.

but soon recovered, and the following year accepted a school at Burlington, where he remained as teacher for several years. During that period he organized a reading circle, whose members subscribed to many of the best English scientific and literary periodicals, and began, for himself, the study of chemistry in which he instructed some of his advanced students, and in 1806 he gave a series of public lectures on the subject.

In the spring of 1807, Griscom went to New York to take charge of a school at a salary of $2,250 for the year, and the following winter he delivered a successful course of chemistry lectures in that city. The supporters of the school had financial reverses, however, and were unable to renew the contract with Griscom, and in the winter of 1808 he began his own school with which he continued until 1818, when he made his trip to Europe.

Griscom had married, in 1800, the daughter of John Hoskins, a leading member of the Friends' denomination. His wife died in 1816 and left him with a family of eight children. These he placed in school and with relatives and, early in April, 1818, left for Europe in an effort to regain his health. He arrived about the first of May, and visited England, France, Switzerland, Italy, Belgium, Holland, Scotland, and Ireland, inspecting prisons, hospitals, manufactories, charitable institutions, and schools of all kinds. He returned to New York in June, 1819. The story of his trip, published in two volumes under the title of *A Year in Europe,* gives an interesting account of life and manners abroad. The work went through two editions and was quite popular. The profits from its sales were sufficient to pay the expenses of the trip.

Griscom seems to have engaged in a wide range of activities of an educational and charitable nature. He had been an influential member of the Literary and Philanthropic Society of New York, which DeWitt Clinton served as president, and he had been active also in the establishment in New York of the Society for the Prevention of Pauperism, which he served many years as secretary. Upon his return from Europe, he resumed his duties as secretary of that organization; and his observations of similar institutions in Europe revived the active interest of the members of the New York society. In 1823, he was chairman of a committee which led to the establishment of the House of Refuge for Juvenile Delinquents, which opened about two years later. Within a short time, institutions of this kind were established in many places in the United States. Griscom also led in a movement to establish in New York a monitorial high school, which opened in 1825 with a large number of students and continued until about 1831, when the trustees sold the institution to the Society of Mechanics and Tradesmen.

In 1827, Griscom was appointed professor of chemistry in the Rutger's Medical College. Five years later, he became principal of the Yearly Meeting Boarding School of Providence, R. I., where he remained for two or three years exercising general supervision over the school and lecturing meantime here and there before societies on his favorite subject of science. As a result of interest in his lectures, a lyceum was established in Burlington, N. J., where, after 1841, he spent the remainder of his life. During these last years he was not regularly employed, but his interest continued in educational and charitable causes.

He served as a member and took a deep interest in the work of the school board of Burlington for nearly a decade. He met Horace Mann at a convention of county school officers at Utica, N. Y., in 1842, and seems to have been in close touch with other educational leaders of the time. His last effort as a lecturer was made in his home town of Salem, New Jersey, at the request of his many friends there. He died February 26, 1852, and the tributes paid him at the funeral services revealed the high esteem in which he was held.

Most of the reports on European schools during the period considered in this volume were official or semi-official. But the report by Griscom was unofficial in character, although it was very influential. His observations were made with great diligence and generally with considerable skill and judgment, and Henry Barnard believed that this work had a wider influence than any other similar report "on the development of our educational, reformatory, and preventative measures, directly and indirectly."

Griscom was very enthusiastic for the monitorial system of Lancaster. The use of the Lancasterian methods in the elementary schools of New York impressed him and he highly praised its use in the high school of Edinburgh, Scotland. This school, he said, was "eminent almost to a proverb for the elevated tone of its classical attainments." Its students, who numbered 150, "made a more rapid progress, were more thoroughly taught, and pursued their studies with more vigor and alacrity, than in any institution in which the monitorial system was not adopted."

A rather lengthy review of Griscom's work appeared in

## JOHN GRISCOM

*The North American Review* for January, 1824 (Vol. XVIII, pp. 178–192), and concluded as follows:

"Professor Griscom seems to have gone to Europe in order to be able more effectually to do good, after his return home. His book, therefore, is simply a useful book, rendered very interesting by its relation to the present state of our own country. Its literary execution is not remarkably good. Its notices of society and manners are necessarily superficial and imperfect; and the accounts of individuals are sometimes more free, perhaps, than they themselves would think judicious. But, there is nothing in it to gratify scandal or spleen; no exhibition or excitement of party feelings and passions in religion or politics, or anything else. It is chiefly filled with accounts of what he himself saw; the manufactories, mines, prisons, hospitals, public schools, and other similar establishments, which he visited; and consists, therefore, in a great measure, of what may be called the statistics of the benevolent and useful institutions, by which misery and guilt are diminished, and knowledge and power diffused in Europe. It is a book, which, in all respects, does credit to its author, as a member of the Society of Friends, and can, therefore, hardly fail of being interesting and useful to the public."

## *A YEAR IN EUROPE*
### Preface [1]

THE relations between America and Europe are becoming every day more interesting and important.
The unexampled rapidity with which the commerce, agriculture, and arts of the United States are extending and
increasing; the extraordinary facilities now given to the
social intercourse between the new and the old world; and
the unabated spirit of enterprize and industry, which prevails in many parts of Europe; conspire to render these
relations a concern of the greatest moment,—as tending,
in no inconsiderable degree, to influence the tranquillity
and happiness of a larger portion of the civilized globe.

Under such circumstances, it must be considered, by
persons conversant with human nature, as extremely desirable, that the people on each side of the Atlantic, should
become more intimately and perfectly acquainted with
each other; for it may, perhaps, be stated as a political, as
well as social axiom, that the greater the intimacy, the
greater probability of a cordial and pacific union; that
many of the rancorous jealousies and deep rooted prejudices, which are so apt to prevail between nations, as well
as sects and neighbourhoods, would soften into kindness,
were opportunities afforded of studying the bright as well
as the dark sides of each other's character. And it requires

[1] To Vol. I.

but little ingenuity to perceive, that were there between nations a pervading sense of each other's merits, and a just feeling of each other's prosperity, it would be infinitely more difficult for the disaffected to bring about that condition of things, which is the most disastrous to human improvement, a state of open warfare,—infinitely more easy to suppress the evil when it did prevail.

From these considerations it will be admitted, that books of travels, when written under the proper qualifications, are among the most useful kinds of literature; that they furnish the principal means by which distant communities and nations become acquainted with each other's peculiarities, by which the useful arts are extended, and morals and manners are rendered more diffused and impressive.

It will be admitted also, that however beaten the track over which travellers may have passed, it is impossible to exhaust the stores of useful illustration, or to overcharge the picture of national and local representation, as long as truth and feeling guide the hand and qualify the pencil. It can never be said of the describer of nature, and more especially of human nature, as it may of the orator, who confines himself to some particular topic, that he has left nothing to be desired. So vast is the field of humanity, and so infinite are the shades which diversify the moral condition of the human race, that it is scarcely possible for two individuals to follow each other in the same, precise track of description. Not only do different observers see the same thing in different points of view, but each one has his particular sphere of observation, and will almost unavoidably throw some new light upon the subjects he attempts to elucidate. Hence every person who visits a foreign country will at once perceive, that, how diligent soever he may have been in studying that country through the medium of books,—there is a continual variety of untouched description, and that a small part only of the whole has been laid before him.

But notwithstanding these obvious truths, the Author cannot assure himself, that, even by the most reflecting and liberal-minded readers, he will be deemed to have acted wisely in exposing his sheets to the public eye. His journey was by no means undertaken with a fixed intention of exhibiting its occurrences beyond the circle of his family and friends. The motives to the voyage, were the renovation of impaired health, and the hope of spending a short time in Europe, both profitably and agreeably. The rapidity with which the journey was performed, and the multiplicity of objects which engaged his attention, prevented him from doing little more, while travelling, than to bestow a faithful attention to his note book; and since his return, other unavoidable avocations have delayed the filling up of the outline; but this delay, he trusts, has not been without its benefit, in the further development which time has given to some features of the narrative.

The writer is aware that "A Year in Europe," in two volumes, thick octavo, may possibly startle the cautious reader, and induce him to infer, that it either contains a great deal of fanciful speculation, upon things hastily seen; or that it consists of a prosing detail of what most persons already know. He also recollects the jocose threat of a venerable philosopher in Milan, who, in pleasantly reproaching him for staying so short a time in that city, and

in adverting to the superficial habits and statements of
many travellers, said: "If you go home and make a book, I
will publish in the journals of Italy, that you were in the
city of Milan only three days!" But notwithstanding the
danger on both hands,—of being either too dull or too
fanciful,—the Author would suggest to those who think
that the size of the work is disproportionate to the period
of the journey, the reflection, that in nothing is it possible
to avail one's self of the advantages of industry, to a
greater extent, than in travelling:—that, as it is very easy
to spend months, and even years, in a single place, without
exhausting the subjects of inquiry,—so is it possible by
activity and diligence, to see and learn much in a very
limited time.

The objects which primarily engaged the writer's attention, were literary and benevolent institutions, prisons,
manufactories, and distinguished works of art; and, as
far as opportunities were afforded, *characters* connected
with such labours of utility and philanthropy. Morals and
religion were topics at all times interesting, and were not
overlooked, when occasions presented for observation and
inquiry. On the subject of institutions, the Author believes
he has been more full than any preceding American traveller in Europe. This part of his descriptions may appear
to some readers, to have introduced a tautology of narra-
tion that had better been avoided. But, regarding public
institutions, as among the most intelligible evidences of
the genius and character of a people, he thought it right
to omit nothing in the details to the reader, which he
deemed it important to notice in order to satisfy his own
inquiries. He has only to express the hope, that the pecu-

liarities both of subject and of style, which may be perceived
to have arisen from the nature of his associations, will be
readily excused by the candid reader.

Having a letter to W. Roscoe, Esq., a gentleman well
known in the literary world, and deservedly esteemed here
and every where for his learning and philanthropy, *****
accompanied me to his office. He received me with great
urbanity. He is a banker, and a man of business. The
coldness and reserve of the mere scholar, are completely
worn off by his business habits, while the contracted
"single aim" of the merchant, is softened, dignified, and
expanded by letters and an extensive intercourse with
literary men. He has been a member of parliament, and as
such was an active and enlightened promoter of measures calculated to advance the interests of general humanity. . . .

It gave me pleasure to find in a conversation with W.
Roscoe, at his office, that the subject of an amelioration
of the penal code of England, had engaged his active attention, and aroused his warm and generous sympathies.
He wished to obtain further information relative to our
penitentiaries: I freely communicated what I knew; and
put him in the way of receiving from New York, a further
account of them. He almost despairs of any important
change in the British laws within a reasonable time, on
account of the strong prejudices of the nation, and the
fears of the government in the adoption of alterations in
their long established usages. As an evidence of the severity of the present laws, and the arbitrary manner in which
they are executed, he stated to me, that some time ago, a

man was taken up for writing a song which was thought to have a dangerous tendency, tried, thrown into prison, and kept there more than *two years,* in a narrow miserable place, where he could use no exercise. When finally liberated, he was emaciated, feeble, and scarcely able to walk. R. knowing him to be a man of talents and education, and destitute of support, procured for him a situation as tutor to the children of a gentleman; which duty he fulfilled to satisfaction.

A town meeting was called, sometime ago, to celebrate the fiftieth year of the reign of the present king. It was proposed, that the money raised on the occasion, should be employed in an illumination. R. moved that instead of wasting it in a blaze, it should be employed in liberating all the prisoners who were confined for debt. This motion, though much opposed, prevailed, and the prisoners, about seventy in number, were discharged. There was a balance left of £800 sterling. This was invested in stock, and the interest goes to the employment of a solicitor, whose duty it is, to inquire into the detention of every prisoner for debt, and to see that no frauds are practised upon him. A great number of unjust exactions, and vexatious proceedings, are doubtless prevented by this salutary and humane regulation.

We were conducted to Chetham's Hospital, more commonly called the college. This is a charity school, founded about the year 1650 by Humphrey Chetham, a wealthy individual of Manchester. The building which it occupies, formerly belonged to the collegiate church, and is curiously antiquated in its appearance, both within and without. About eighty poor boys are here lodged, fed, clothed and

instructed. They are to be the "children of honest, industrious, and pains-taking parents, and not of wandering
or idle beggars, or rogues." They are clothed uniformly in
a costume extremely *outré* in its appearance, and ridiculous
in its form. Instead of pantaloons, they wear blue cloth
petticoats, a yellow under petticoat, blue worsted stockings,
and blue cloth caps. The little fellows are fed with a plain
but wholesome diet, and have a very healthy and contented
look. The building contains also a library, founded by
the same benevolent individual, "for the use of scholars, and
all others well affected, to resort unto." None of the books
were to be taken out of the library, but "fixed or chained
as well as may be." This library has become very valuable,
and now contains 18,000 volumes. In the gallery are
several specimens of natural history, and other curiosities,
by way of museum. These were explained to us by one of
the boys, as a matter of course, in a tone and manner that
might have done credit to a well trained parrot. . . .

Manchester is distinguished by its charities, and more
especially that noblest of all charities, a liberal instruction
of the children of the poor. This town was among the
first to adopt the plan of the benevolent RAIKES, in the
organization of Sunday schools. Nearly 8,000 children attend the schools, supported by members of the established
church, and about 5,000 those for other denominations.
What an aggregate of charity is here presented to the
mind! This benevolence goes far to remedy the evils arising from the severe task imposed upon the children in
the manufactories, and which are so justly condemned by
Southey in the letters of Espriella. There is no doubt, however, that a further amelioration of the condition of these

infant labourers, is still called for by the soundest dictates of humanity. The subject is before parliament, and hopes are entertained that a law will be passed, giving every child a right to a certain portion of education, and restricting them to 10 or 11 hours of confinement in the manufactories, instead of 15 or 16 as now practised. . . .

We arrived at Oxford at half past six; and the evening being pleasant, I immediately engaged a guide, and spent two hours and a half in exploring the wonders, the curiosities, and the beauties, of this ancient and renowned seat of learning. If any thing in art and antiquity, in Great Britain, can strike an American eye with delight and surprise, it will here be met with, probably, in its greatest perfection. The exterior of the colleges, presents an imposing aspect of antique greatness. The massy structure of the buildings, the number of statues, and the quantity of carved work within and without, would seem to require the labour of ages. Every thing I saw was in a style of neatness. The yards, the gardens, the interior of all the apartments, are kept in the greatest cleanliness and order. The walks are highly beautiful. A broad, gravelled pathway, with rows of high and majestic elms on each side, extends, in some cases, a mile in length, winding along the margin of a river or canal, and surrounding a beautiful meadow. The rooks build their nests on the tops of the trees, and fly about the college buildings, in great numbers, unmolested. The painted or stained glass in the chapels, the tesselated pavements, the carved ceilings, and the numerous fine paintings with which they have been ornamented, hold the eye and the mind long in admiration. I was in the theatre, or rather amphitheatre, in which the emperor of

Russia, and king of Prussia, received their honorary degrees, sitting on each side of the prince regent. In the library the sovereigns dined. On the table of this room, was an engraved figure, exhibiting the arrangement of the seats at the dinner. From the top of this building, I had a fine panoramic view of the city. The students were seen walking every where. Their dress, to a stranger, appears very singular. It consists of a black gown, worn over their other garments, and a cap of black cloth fitting the head closely, and to the top of which is fastened a flat square board, which they call a trencher, covered with the same substance as the cap, and resting horizontally on the head, with one corner in front, to which is suspended a few tassels. Its appearance is rather picturesque and tasteful.

Of the morality of some of the collegians, I had a most unfavourable specimen. Four or five of them came in the evening to the inn where I had taken up my quarters, in the principal street in the town. They entered the coffee room, where two or three travellers and myself were sitting, engaged in conversation. After surveying us and the room for some time, they went out, but shortly after returned, seated themselves in one of the recesses, into which one side of the room is divided, and ordered supper and drink. Their conversation soon assumed a very free cast, and eventually took such a latitude, as I should suppose would set all Billingsgate at defiance. They abused the waiter, broke a number of things, tore the curtains that enclose the recesses—staid till near twelve o'clock, and then went off, thoroughly soaked with wine, brandy, and hot-toddy. I was told the next morning that two of them were noblemen! Alas! for such an education as this. What can Latin and Greek, and all the store of learning and science have, to make amends, in an hour of retribution, for a depraved heart, and an understanding debased by such vicious indulgence? I cannot but cherish the hope, that this incident does not furnish a fair specimen of morals of the students. It will doubtless happen, that in so large a number as that here collected in the various colleges, many will bring with them habits extremely unfavourable to morality and subordination. But from the information derived from my guide, who was a moderate man, and certainly well informed with respect to the habits of the place, and from the observations which forced themselves upon me, in my walk through the streets and gardens this evening, I am obliged to deduce the lamentable conclusion, that the *morals* of the nation are not much benefited by the *direct* influence of this splendid seat of learning. . . .

17th. My excellent friend, W. A. took me to-day to the Borough-road School, where we spent an hour, in observing the operations of this improved and most important method of conveying instruction to the children of the poor. This school is intended as a model for others, both in the construction of the building, and in the management of the classes. I can only say, that we were highly gratified with the indications of neatness, order, and skill, in its appearance, and in the performance of the scholars. The Lancasterian principles of instruction, or the art of managing large schools at a very small expense, is evidently gaining ground, not only in England, but in other countries; and it may doubtless be regarded, as the most valuable practical discovery, in relation to human happiness with which the world has been recently blessed. Great credit is certainly due to Joseph Lancaster, for the extraordinary ingenuity which he displayed in the mechanism of his system, and the still more extraordinary perseverance with which he urged the adoption of his mode of instruction, throughout the kingdom. Had there been as much discretion in his subsequent deportment, as there was of talent and benevolence in the early part of his career, he might still be entitled to the high eulogium once bestowed upon him by the Prince Regent, that "he was doing more good than any man alive." But, whatever may have been his merits, scarcely less is due to my friend A. and his deceased coadjutor, Dr. Fox, for their disinterested and noble efforts to preserve the Lancasterian system from sinking beneath the pressure of pecuniary embarrassment, in the early stages of its advancement. The former has long served as treasurer to the British and Foreign School Society; and to no individual, perhaps, is the general extension of this invaluable system more deeply indebted. . . .

25th. With one of my London acquaintance, I visited this morning some of the charitable institutions on the south side of the river. Our first object was the asylum for the "Deaf and Dumb." It happened to be the period of vacation, and but a small proportion of the pupils were in the house. We were, however, kindly received by Dr. Watson, who has long been at the head of this establishment; and whose intelligent efforts to promote the welfare of the unfortunate subjects of his daily care, have received the plaudits of the society and the public. The house is large and convenient. Several of the pupils were exercised before us, and they furnished decisive evidence, that the power of speech and articulation, sufficiently distinct to be understood, as well as the ability to comprehend, from the motion of the lips, what others say, may be conferred upon them by instruction. To whatever perfection the language of signs may be brought, it is impossible that a stranger should converse with a deaf and dumb person, in any way so easy, and with so little effort to himself, as by the motion of the lips: and as the intellectual improvement of this class of pupils, so essentially depends upon the ideas communicated by others, it appears to me important that they should be thoroughly practised in this easy mode of conducting a conversation. I once knew an interesting female, entirely deaf, with whom I could sit and converse with so much ease, that a stranger would not discover, excepting from the peculiar intonation of her voice, that there was any thing unusual in the conversation. She had entirely lost her hearing, if I recollect rightly, about the age of 19. Articulation was, of course, more easy to her, than to one who had never practised it, except by the aid of mechanical instruction. But the facility with which she acquired the power of comprehending from the motion of the lips, was such, that, in a place of worship, she could comprehend nearly the whole of a sermon, from the inaudible repetition of it by the lips of a friend who sat near her. In the mode of teaching the deaf and dumb, adopted by the Abbé Sicard, and now practised in America, articulation and the language of the lips, are, I believe, entirely discarded. I have not been able, however, to discover the wisdom of obliging every person who would wish to converse with one who is deaf and dumb, to learn to spell words with his fingers, or to write at full length all that he wishes to say: much of the pleasure and profit of conversation must be excluded from so circuitous and troublesome a procedure.

This highly useful charity is under the direction of a society of which the Duke of Gloucester is president.

The school for the indigent blind is situated near that of the deaf and dumb. The pupils are here taught, as in Liverpool, such useful arts as will enable them either wholly or in part to support themselves. They are retained in the school no longer than is sufficient to become skilful in the employments assigned them. Basket and rope making are practised with great advantage. In one room, in which a great number of women were spinning, they began, from a hint given to them by my companion, to sing together in concert, and in a strain of no unfeeling harmony. To see so many blind and indigent human beings singing at their work, and with countenances expressive of content, was to me novel and affecting. This extensive school is supported by donations and annual subscriptions.

I am not aware that any attempts have been made in the United States to establish schools for this class of the poor, so deserving of the sympathy and kindness of their fellow creatures. A prosperous commencement has been made with the deaf and dumb. The blind, it is to be hoped, will not long be forgotten.

Our attention was next directed to the buildings and work shops of the Philanthropic Society. With this establishment every friend to humanity, who visits it, must be highly pleased. The plan of it was first suggested to the

public by Robert Young, Esq. Dr. Sims, the learned president of the Medical Society, was its first chairman and
vice president. Its great object is to afford an asylum to the
children of convicts, and those who are trained to vicious
courses, public plunder, infamy and ruin. It is the peculiar
distinction of this society, to seek for children in the
nurseries of vice and iniquity, in order to draw them away
from further contamination, and to bring them up to the
useful purposes of life. Prisons, bridewells, and courts of
justice, afford the materials upon which this society dis-
plays its bounty. They are seldom taken younger than eight
or nine, or older than twelve. Within the buildings of the
society, are more than sixty different wards. The apartments of the girls are separated from those of the boys,
by a high wall which prevents all intercourse. The boys
receive a sufficient share of school learning, and are placed,
on their admission, in one of the various manufactories or
work shops, which are conducted by master workmen and
journeymen. The principal trades pursued, are printing,
copper-plate printing, bookbinding, shoemaking, tailoring,
rope-making, and twine spinning. A portion of each boy's
earnings goes to his credit, and is given to him at his
discharge. Besides receiving those poor juvenile offenders
in their establishment, the committee have adopted the
plan of apprenticing out some of the best behaved boys,
to tradesmen of good character, with a sufficient premium;
but they are still considered as under the care of the
society. The girls make their own clothing, and shirts for
the boys; wash and mend for the manufactory; and, in
short, are educated so as to qualify them for useful and
respectable service. About one-hundred and fifty boys are

within the walls, and more than fifty girls. The society has a house, in another part of the town, called the Reform, where the most hardened offenders are first introduced, and where they are carefully instructed in the obligations of morality and religion, and in school learning. When out of school, they are here employed in picking oakum. In passing through the work shops of this beneficent institution, where industry and skill were apparent, it was cheering to find that so many wretched children were "snatched as fire brands" from criminality and ruin, and restored to the prospects of respectable and honourable life. The chapel of the establishment is remarkable for its neatness. It serves for a considerable auditory, in addition to that of the institution.

Taking a boat at Vauxhall bridge, we proceeded up the river to Chelsea, and looked into the large hospital there. This is a royal establishment for invalid soldiers, as that of Greenwich is for seamen. The whole front of the building is 804 feet. Next the river, it forms three sides of a hollow square. The hospital with the gardens, (which are laid out in a stiff, bad taste,) covers about forty acres of ground. The rooms of the house contain 500 persons; but the number of out door pensioners is no less than 50,000! What a tax is this upon martial glory! and what, to an independent and honest mind, is a daily ration of soup and potatoes, in comparison with the loss of a leg or arm; or a constitution physically and morally diseased! How incalculable are the mischiefs and the miseries of war, the deepest of all stains upon the history of *Christians!* The out door pensioners reside mostly in the town of Chelsea; and its appearances are such as might be supposed to result from such a population,—the reverse of cleanliness and comfort. . . .

I ought not to leave Cornwall without an acknowledgment, that the inhabitants appeared to me, as far as my intercourse with them extended, to possess rather an unusual degree of intelligence and hospitality. If personal beauty, too, be necessarily connected with rosy cheeks and florid complexions, the females of this part of England are entitled to a preëminence in personal charms. Every traveller must be struck with the appearance of almost universal bloom, even among the inhabitants of mud cottages, the female inmates of which, scarcely fail to place themselves at the door, from motives of curiosity, (I can hardly think of vanity,) when the passage of the stage coach is announced by the rattle of the wheels or the sound of the driver's bugle. Education is an object of pointed attention and zeal, in many parts of the country. Sir Humphrey Davy [1] is a native of the western part of Cornwall, and there received those early impulses which have placed him in so high a rank in the science of his country. . . .

13th. I called to-day, with *****, of Philadelphia, recently arrived in Paris, on the Abbé Gaultier, and found him with a class of boys, composed of the monitors of different schools. This excellent man is a warm friend and promotor of the system of mutual instruction, as they here call the plan, which, in England, is denominated Lancasterian. The boys were undergoing, in his presence, an examination in grammar. To no person perhaps, in France, is the erection of schools, and the extension of education among the poor, more highly indebted. Besides

[1] Now President of the Royal Society.

his exertions, in common with others, to establish schools on the improved system, he has published a variety of books adapted to that system, which are now in use in the schools. The mildness of his manners, and the benevolence of his countenance, impressed me very agreeably. . . .

27th. I went, with some friends, to see a gymnastic school, kept by Amonton. The boys were exercised in jumping, climbing, walking on stilts, and other bodily manoeuvres. A systematic course of instruction, with proper exercises, on the right use of their limbs, I have long thought, would be very advantageous to boys. The person, who gives this instruction, endeavoured, some time ago, to establish a school at Madrid, on the plan of Pestalozzi; but the effort was not very successful. . . .

On our return, we attended an examination of the pupils of a school, entitled *"L'Institut Academique des nations Européens."* Neither the appearance of the room, nor the exercises of the boys, had much to correspond with this pompous title. A considerable audience of male and female visitors was present, mostly relations of the scholars. Two of the boys answered questions in logic, and recited each a portion of a sermon. Several of them construed a page or two of Greek, Latin, English, and German, and one performed an exercise in Mathematics. One of the instructors read an address to the scholars and to the audience, and to make it more emphatical, it was written in verse, and delivered with strong gesture. My friend*******, who sat near me, and who is a French writer of some note, told me the poetry was not good. The prizes were then delivered agreeably to a written statement of the progress of the scholars, read by one of the teachers. They consisted of books, very handsomely bound. When the boy's name was pronounced, he came to the table, the prize was delivered to him by an elderly gentleman, and a wreath of flowers put on his head. A band of music then cheered him to his seat. Those of the boys who had female relations present, went to them and received a kiss before they sat down.

4th. I visited this morning several persons, prior to my departure for Switzerland. Among them were Count Lasteyrie, Bishop Gregoire, and the Abbé Gualtier with whom I had much interesting conversation relative to schools and to the prejudices of the clergy and people of this country. These gentlemen are all influenced, I believe, by benevolent motives, and are remarkably free from prejudice. The two former exert themselves notably in the cause, and rejoice in the success, of the system of mutual instruction.

A large proportion of the schools in France, are taught by a fraternity, styled "Les Frères de la Religion Chrétienne." They assume a peculiar dress, and from long custom, consider it their privilege, (as it has become their means of support,) to educate the youth of the country. These men have, of course, opposed the new system with great zeal. It is nevertheless making its way with rapidity, and even the "Frères" find that their custom, instead of diminishing, is increased by the general stir. The schools, however, of the new system, are still confined to the children of Catholics. The influence of the priests is so great, it is thought necessary to conform to the prejudice, and the Protestants are, accordingly, obliged to open separate schools for their own youth.

Count Lasteyrie is one of the first who embarked in

this concern, and who advised the formation of a society for the promotion of education, upon the new plan. If this had not been done prior to the king's restoration, it is doubtful whether the system could have gained admission into the country; and were it not for the weight and influence of the society, it would still have to struggle with difficulties almost insurmountable. . . .

In our walks we stopped at the School *d'Enseignment Mutuel*.[1] It was not the day of admission to visitors, but we apologised, and were let in. It is a new establishment; and the room is arranged in the usual Lancasterian manner. The number of scholars is about eighty, and the system pursued appeared to be very similar to that of the schools in England. . . .

Dr. V******, took us to the School *D'Enseignment Mutuel*. The building is a very poor one. The school is in an upper room, and the access to it, narrow and difficult. The number of scholars was about 80. Many were absent on account of the measles. Provision is made in Switzerland for the education of every child, and parents are *obliged* to send their children to school. The teachers are paid by the government, so that the schools are gratis to the parents. We went into one of these schools. It contained about thirty scholars of the poorer families, and appeared to be badly conducted. I suggested to Dr. V. the advantage of uniting several of these schools into one, and adopting the improved plans of tuition, paying more attention at the same time to neatness and respectability of appearance. He said that some measures had already been taken to effect this object, which he considered truly desirable. . . .

[1] Or monitorial school.

30th. Having a letter for Le Pere Girard, whose genius and philanthropy have qualified him to effect the most important improvements, in the education of the children of Fribourg, and to establish a school, which has become famous throughout Switzerland, I hastened this morning to the convent where he resides, and received the unwelcome intelligence, that it was the time of vacation, and that he had gone into the country, to stay some days. I inquired of one of his assistants, who there was, that could give me correct information, relative to the system pursued in the institution, over which the Pere Girard presides, and he referred me to the Chanoine Fontaine, as an enlightened man, and a friend of Pere Girard. Upon waiting for this ecclesiastic, at his house, he came in from the morning service, dressed in his priestly habiliments, and looked at me with some surprise. I apologised for coming to him without an introduction, and explained frankly the object of my visit. He then, very cordially, offered to give me all the information he could, and appointed 10 o'clock, to receive me and my friends. He regretted that Pere Girard was absent, as I should find him, he said, a very interesting man in conversation, and willing to communicate any information, relative to his system.

At the appointed hour, we went to the chanoine's, and were introduced into his picture room, which contained a very neat collection of paintings, one of which, he said, was by Rubens, (the descent from the cross,) and the original design of his great picture at Antwerp. He explained to us, loquaciously, the various pictures of the collection; and then, placing chairs in a circle, invited us to sit down, and commenced an eloquent statement, first of the etymology of the word *Education,* implying to draw out, or develop, and not to increase, or to superadd. He next adverted to the common error, as he called it, of supposing that mathematics can have much tendency to expand and mature the faculties of the mind; and urged the superiority of language, as an instrument or means of effecting this important end. He considered it of high importance, that plans of education should tend to open and perfect the qualities already existing in the mind, as the sun swells and opens the bud, and heightens the colours and fragrance of the rose. He informed us that the Pere Girard's views, and his own, corresponded on this subject; that the latter, being a man of penetration, and acquainted with human nature, and possessing a spirit of great philanthropy, had proceeded, step by step, trusting only to experience, in bringing the school to its present state of improvement. Prior to the commencement of his labours, the schools of Fribourg, were in a state of great depression, without system, and inefficacious, with respect to morals; that Pere Girard's greatest efforts had been, to make the scholars thoroughly acquainted with their religious duties, to render them sober and industrious; in short, to inspire them with a taste and a love for all that belongs to an honourable character, in the respective stations which they are to fill. His success, in this respect, the whole town was ready to attest. The Lancasterian plan of instruction, came opportunely to his aid; but he was rather a *"Belliste,"* than a *"Lancasterien."* The principle which he relies most upon, as an excitement to the energies of the boys, is emulation. This principle, properly directed, he is confident, does not produce envy, or any other injurious feeling. So anxious are the boys, in his school, to improve, they are known often to rise in the night to study; and so lively and interesting to them, has he rendered the exercises of the school, that very young children are fond of attending. A lady of distinction, (the ex-queen of Sweden,) visiting the school, observed a very young child in one of the classes. *"Pourquoi viens tu ici, mon enfant?"* [1] said she, to the tiny scholar. *"Pour m'amuser,"* [2] was the answer. Still more surprised, she asked, *"Comment? est-ce-que l'ecole t'amuse?"* [3] *"Oh, Madame,"* said he, *"nous nous amusons ici tous jours."* [4] But, observed our learned informant, as there is always a struggle between light and darkness, so it was hardly to be expected, that Pere Girard's success, would not meet with opposition. His school has acquired so much celebrity, that not a day passes without visitors. In short, it was to have a little time to write, that he has left the town for a few days. A public examination is held every three months, with a great deal of form, accompanied with music, and a distribution of prizes, to the most meritorious scholars. It is a kind of public spectacle, which gratifies the town. But the religious principles of the Pere, are too liberal for the zealous friends of the Romish Church, and the bell of alarm has been sounded, with notes of danger to the true faith. A division has taken place, and, in the present government of the canton, there is a majority of the disaffected. They accordingly determined, by a decision obtained last month, to reinstate

[1] Why do you come here, my child?
[2] To have a good time.
[3] What! do you enjoy school?
[4] Oh, madam, we always enjoy ourselves here.

the Jesuits in their college, in Fribourg; doubtless with a view to counteract the influence of Pere Girard; and it is probable that they would soon proceed to place his school, "*hors de combat,*" were it not for the very strong popular support, which it receives. The government of this canton is patrician; or, in other words, aristocratical. To retain their power, is a darling object with the patricians; and they are so well aware that the diffusion of learning and morals will work against them, that when the corner stone of a new and commodious house, now erecting for Pere Girard's school, was laid by a committee, the Avoyer, or chief magistrate, happening to pass, he said to one near him, "Voila le tombeau des patricians." [1] The only excitement to emulation, which Girard uses, is an advancement in the classes, medals, and prize books at the examinations. But it is his constant effort to preserve such a tone of moral feeling, as to operate itself as a stimulus to honourable effort, and, at the same time, to prevent the evil consequences of emulation. That a most favourable change has been produced in the moral habits of the children of Fribourg, is generally admitted. . . .

After getting our passports examined, by the Austrian minister, at Berne, and taking our dinners at the table d'hote, we set off in a *voiture* [2] provided by our landlord, for Hofwyl, two leagues from Berne, in order to visit the celebrated establishment, or "*Institut d'education,*" of Emmanuel de Fellenberg. It was a rainy day. We passed through a pretty large wood, and arrived at Hofwyl, about 4 o'clock. I was introduced to Fellenberg, by three letters;

[1] There is the tomb of the patricians.
[2] Conveyance.

38

two from Paris, and one from Geneva. The visiters that resort here are so numerous, and the attention of the principal so much taken up with them, I had been advised to anticipate some difficulty in getting access to him. On presenting myself at the door, I was received by a young man, who appeared to be his clerk, and who, introducing me into the office, requested me to write my name and residence in a book which he gave me. He then announced me to Fellenberg, who politely invited me into the parlour. I produced my letters, which appeared to give him much satisfaction. He is a man of middle age, of a mild and agreeable countenance, and of polite and genteel manners. He seated me on a sofa, and entered upon an explanation of the principles of his establishment, and the particular views of education, which had induced him to engage in it. He considers society as divisible into three distinct parts; the higher, (comprehending the noble and the wealthy,) the middling, and the poor. The greatest defects of education, he supposed to exist in the two extreme classes. That, these distinctions or classes among men, would always prevail, in every civilized country, he believed to be incontrovertible; and, of course, any attempt to break down the distinction, would be fruitless. It is, therefore, of consequence that they should be each educated in a manner conformable to their situations, but both in such a way, as to develope, to the highest extent, the best faculties of their nature; and, while it preserves the proper relation between them, it should, at the same time, encourage the feelings of kindliness and sympathy on the one part, and of respect and love on the other. This, he thought, could be affected upon no plan, so effectually, as by bringing them up side by side, so that they should have each other constantly in view, without any necessity whatever of mixing or associating. The rich, by observing the industry, the skill, and the importance of the labouring classes, would learn to entertain just sentiments respecting them, and the poor, by feeling and experiencing the kindly influence of the rich, would regard them as benefactors.

With respect to the best means of cultivating the faculties, which, in their due operation, are to promote the permanent happiness of men, he considers agriculture, as affording opportunities and advantages of the greatest importance, and next to this, the mechanic arts. Agreeably to these leading views, his establishment consists of two distinct parts; a boarding school of the sons of noblemen and gentlemen, in which no pains are spared, to provide them with teachers in every useful science; and of a house, in which boys, taken from the poorest class, are clothed and fed in a very plain, coarse, and farmer like style, and who work diligently in the fields, at employments adapted to their strength and skill. During two hours in the day, in summer, and more in winter, they are instructed in letters, and in music. They are likewise introduced into the workshops, and taught the business of a blacksmith, a carpenter, a wheelwright, a cabinet maker, a turner, a shoemaker, or a worker in brass, according as a particular talent for any of these, may manifest itself. The produce of the labour of these boys, bears no inconsiderable proportion of the expense of their maintenance and instruction.

After this brief explanation of his principles, Fellenberg introduced my companions and myself, to Count Louis de Villevielle, a gentleman from the south of France, who,

reduced by the revolution, has attached himself to Fellenberg, and appears to live with him, as a sort of companion.
He attends to strangers, and goes with them through the
grounds, shops, &c. of the establishment. He proved to be a
very sensible, well informed man, and altogether disposed
to satisfy our inquiries. He conducted us to the workshops.
In one of them, a new and handsome fire engine, of a
large size, had just been completed in a style which would
do credit to London or New York. In these shops, all the
instruments of agriculture are made, and it is the constant
aim of the principal, to improve upon the form and structure of them, and to invent others which experience may
indicate the use of. As they make more than the farm requires, the surplus is sold to the neighbours.

In the evening the Count conducted us to the farm-
house, where the class of the poor boys are lodged, fed,
and instructed. We found them at supper, on a kind of
hasty-pudding, with whey and boiled potatoes. They breakfast on a piece of bread and an apple, or something as
simple, and dine between eleven and twelve, on vegetable
food alone. Once a week only, (on first day,) they have
meat and wine. They are thus taught a lesson of simplicity,
with respect to their manner of living. The furniture of the
house corresponds with the dress and clothing of the boys.
After supper they went up stairs to the schoolroom, to
take a lesson in music. Their teacher (Vehrly) is a young
man of very extraordinary qualifications. He received
his early education from his father, who filled, in a distinguished manner, the office of schoolmaster for thirty
years. He began at an early age to assist his parent in the
discharge of his office. On coming to reside with Fellen-

berg, his views were further expanded, and he entered with enthusiasm into the concerns of the establishment, and willingly undertook the formation and direction of the class of the poor, in all their exercises, agricultural, literary, scientific, and moral. He lives with them, eats, sleeps, and works with them, dresses as they do, and makes himself their friend and companion, as well as their instructor. He is eminently fitted for such an occupation by his genius, his address, his temper and disposition, and above all by his religious principles. The schoolroom serves also for a shoemakers' shop, and probably accommodates, occasionally, the taylor and harness maker. The boys always take a lesson of one hour, between supper and bed. This lesson is frequently confined to music. They are taught it by principles, but they use no instrument but their vocal organs. Fellenberg lays great stress on music, as a means of bringing the mind and heart into harmony with truth, and of inspiring the mild and benevolent affections. He thinks it has been very beneficial in reclaiming many of these boys, from the vicious habits they had acquired from the low and exposed lives they had been subject to. By teaching them to sing religious songs, together with those that are simply patriotic, he says their attention is diverted from those vile ballads which are common among low bred people; and that they find, in this new entertainment, a happy substitute for the coarse and vulgar expressions to which they were addicted. The boys of this class appeared to be very healthy and contented. They are taught to pay the utmost attention to cleanliness. Their clothing in summer, is of coarse cotton, and in winter, of woollen cloth. They go barefooted, except when they work in the fields, or when the state of the weather requires them to wear shoes and stockings. They are always without any thing on their heads. Many of them, as might naturally be supposed, entered the school with the seeds of scrophulous disorders; but by the effect of a simple and wholesome diet, cleanliness, and labour, they are restored to health with scarcely any medicine. Some of them, on their entrance, were feeble and debilitated, unable to endure cold, heat, or labour; but when once they have become accustomed to the regimen of the school, they willingly encounter rain, storms, and severe cold, whenever their work calls them abroad, without shrinking from, or regarding the exposure. They are taught to mend their own clothes. In summer they rise at five, and in winter at six; and after having dressed themselves and said their prayers, they receive instruction for an hour. They then breakfast, after which they go to work until half past eleven. They have then half an hour for dinner; after which Vehrly gives them a lesson of one hour. They work out till six, and after eating their supper, receive further instruction, which concludes with prayer, and they are generally in bed between eight and nine o'clock. But this distribution of time varies according to the seasons. In winter five or six hours a day are devoted to sedentary instruction. The morning of the first day of the week, is always devoted to exercises of piety, and after dinner some hours are given to instruction in sacred history. But their lessons are by no means confined to the school room. Vehrly takes pleasure in questioning them on subjects of natural history, geography, religion, morals, or any other useful topic, while they are at work in the fields or shops; and it may readily be conceived, that with this devotion to the improvement of his pupils, occasions will perpetually present themselves, of conveying instruction in every kind of knowledge, calculated to expand the minds of children, and to cultivate their best affections.

With regard to the most effective means of eliciting the powers of the mind, and of conducting the literary exercises of young people, great credit is due to Pestalozzi, whose veteran labours, as one of the most enlightened teachers of the age, were well known and acknowledged long before the commencement of the Hofwyl Institution. His plans of communicating knowledge, are in a great measure, practised by Vehrly. Much pains are taken to impress on the minds of the pupils, a deep sense of the importance of time, and of habits of industry; and from the reports that have been published by commissioners appointed to examine the establishments, it is evident that the most favourable results have attended these endeavours. The children are so effectually redeemed from their former vicious habits, that, in their most free and noisy sports, not an expression is heard, offensive to innocence or good manners. After working 10 hours in the day, they give themselves up, when their teacher permits, to the liveliest recreation; but a word from Vehrly, is sufficient to induce them to leave their sport and to engage in some other exercise. The progress which they make in knowledge, is truly surprising, when it is considered how adverse their former habits have been to all intellectual abstraction. In a few years, or even in less time, they learn to read, write and calculate, with and without the use of pencil or pen; the elements of drawing become familiar to them; and they ac-

quire good notions of geometry, especially in its relation
to field surveying, and its application to descriptive drawing. Botany and mineralogy constitute part of their amuse-
ments. They become well acquainted with all the plants of
Hofwyl, and their different qualities, both the salutary and
noxious. Of the minerals also, they acquire the names and
principal uses, and they make collections of all that is valuable and curious in minerals and vegetables. Some of them
are very attentive to the improvement of their little cabinets. The principal, when walking with them in the fields,
is often called upon to decide disputes relative to the nature of stones or vegetables. But the most admirable trait
in the character of this school, is the tone of religious feeling which, it is said, pervades it. This could not be accomplished, were not Fellenberg and Vehrly, both strongly
imbued with a sense of religious obligation, and unremit-
tingly attentive to awaken those sentiments in the minds
of the pupils. They have learned by heart more than 50
hymns, and many portions of sacred history. They are
regularly attentive to one practice, which is a pleasing
source of instruction, and at the same time serves to
demonstrate the progress they have made in useful acquirements. At the close of every week, they write, in a
book provided for the purpose, an account of whatever has
impressed their minds with the greatest force. It may be
either a moral reflection, a description of a plant, or an
instrument, an account of a conversation, or an extract
from some thing they have read. We saw some of these
journals; they were mostly in the German language, and
the greater number were written with remarkable neat-

ness. Some of them contained drawings that evinced no inconsiderable skill, and an eye accustomed to accuracy of observation.

It will readily be conceived that a plan of instruction so admirable, and constantly directed to the best and purest affections of the mind and heart, can scarcely fail to redeem from indolence and vice, those whose habits have been the most degraded. And it has accordingly happened, that notwithstanding the boys under Vehrly's charge have been taken from the very lowest ranks, some of them the children of beggars, but one instance has occurred, of such inveterate vice, as to render it eventually necessary to abandon the culprit to his corrupt propensities, and expel him from the school.

In the religious exercises, which take place on the first day of the week, the boys of the poor school assemble with the superior class, but on no other occasion.

After seeing the evening exercise of these boys, we retired to an inn, at the village of Buchsee, about a quarter of a mile from Hofwyl. This was only a village inn, but we found in it good beds, and good attention.

3d. After breakfast, we repaired again to Hofwyl, and were conducted by the Count, first, to the place where the agricultural instruments are deposited. The drill, or machine for sowing seeds of various kinds, by which one half the seed is said to be saved, has been improved by Fellenberg. The *exterminator*, for destroying weeds, and the *scarificator*, for paring the soil, were among the things in this collection: but I was surprised, when Fellenberg, in reply to my questions, informed me, that no attempts had been made to improve the common plough. That which

appears to be in universal practice in Switzerland, is probably the same used by the great grandfathers of the present
race, and is much more awkward and clumsy than the
English plough. The mould-board is only a flat plank
placed at an angle with the beam. This plank is often
changed to the other side of the plough, at each end of the
field, so as to throw the furrow always in one direction,
but for what reason it is difficult to imagine, except, on the
side of a steep hill, there may be some advantage in casting
the furrows downward. But, as these ploughs are constructed, I am persuaded, it requires nearly or quite double
the team, to perform a given quantity of labour, as in
America. I noticed in the yard, a new sleigh, designed to
hold about eighty persons, and to be drawn by fourteen
horses. This is intended for the amusement of the higher
class of boys. The snow is often very deep in this part of
Switzerland, and continues some months. The stables exhibited a collection of the largest cows I ever saw. They are
kept to the stalls all the year, and are fed with grass in the
summer. The greatest care is taken to economise the ma-
nure. The yard, which receives the litter, is made concave,
and has a well in its centre, whence water is thrown
over it in dry weather. A large reservoir, lined with stone,
receives the wash of the stables, which is from time to
time, thrown over the contents of the yard. The cows
were mostly fat enough for good beef. They seldom give
more than twenty-four bottles in a day, and, upon an average, not more than sixteen bottles, or about twelve quarts.
We were next conducted round part of the farm. It consists, in the whole, of 240 acres, and certainly affords a neat
specimen of agricultural skill. We were shown the garden

and play ground of the upper school, and the fixtures for their gymnastic exercises, &c. Among the latter, throwing the lance is practised. They aim, from a given distance, at a post, the top of which is loosely attached by hinges on the remote side, and the lancers endeavour to strike with sufficient force to overturn it. Each of them has a portion of garden ground assigned to him, which he cultivates as his own; while a more extensive enclosure belongs to them in common, in the labour of which they are governed by rules, adopted by themselves. They have their choice also of the mechanic arts, facilitated by the numerous workshops on the premises.

Although the building, in which Fellenberg accommodates his superior class, is large, he is erecting two others. One of these is for the dwelling house and school-rooms of the students. It is about 100 feet long, and 60 wide, and will contain wine cellars, a chapel, ample dormitories, refectory, &c. for more pupils than his present number. The other building is for a riding-school below, and dancing and exercise rooms above. This building, which is also large, is constructed like many (if not most) of the country houses of Switzerland, by erecting an open and strong frame of wood, and filling the interstices with a mixture of clay and straw. This is moulded by the hand, into oblong portions, which are laid upon sticks, and are forced down in grooves made in the posts of the frame. The mortar is wrapped round the stick, so as to cover it; another is then forced down, &c. This wall is afterwards plaistered and whitewashed.

The Hofwyl establishment, as I have before remarked, consists of two classes, the rich and the poor.

The class of the rich contains at present about 80. Twenty of these, consisting of children under ten years of age, are placed under the care of a respectable gentleman and his wife, in a house belonging to Fellenberg, situated about a mile from his own residence. A teacher or two have the charge of their instruction, both in and out of the house. From this house and ground we had a magnificent view of the eastern Alps. The elevation of some of the summits in this range, is but little less than that of Mount Blanc; and the extent of the chain covered with snow, was much greater than any I had seen. The air was very clear, exhibiting the rich white of this stupendous ridge of mountains, in the finest style imaginable.

The other sixty, constituting the most prominent part of the Hofwyl institution, are provided with more than twenty teachers, or professors. Among the pupils, are several princes, and the sons of ministers of state, &c. The price of board and tuition, varies from 100 to £300 sterling per annum. We were not admitted to the interior of the building occupied by these students. We saw none of their performances, of their schools, or their exercises, except a little riding on horseback, on saddles without stirrups; the horses trotting in a circle, guided by a rope held by a boy in the centre; the professor standing, likewise, in the middle, and directing the rider how to sit. In this exclusion from the interior of his school, we were treated, by Fellenberg, like most, if not all, of his visiters. None are invited to the exercises, and none, of course, would go in without invitation. Either the trouble and distraction, which the general admission of his numerous visiters would occasion, oblige him to adopt this course; or, there is not, in the classification and operations of his school, enough of refinement, talent, and perfection, to support the name, and to correspond with the character of eminence he has succeeded in obtaining. My own impression is, that both these causes operate in producing his decision. The daily, and almost hourly, attendance and interference of company, would certainly be extremely troublesome. He does not profess, either, to have adopted any plan by which his pupils are rapidly brought forward. His system, as he explained it to me, is even opposed to a hasty progress. He wishes to allow his plants to arrive at full and vigorous growth, by a slow, cautious, and well directed training, and by carefully removing from the soil every obstruction; rather than to urge them by a hot-bed culture. He justly thinks, that all he can do, is to lay a solid foundation. That education is, or ought to be, the business of a whole life. Moral and religious principles, he regards as the basis of all that is excellent in man; and accordingly, great pains are taken to inculcate the doctrines of Christianity, agreeably to the profession of the parents and guardians of the pupils. The Catholic scholars have a clergyman or professor of their own sect, and the Emperor Alexander has provided for the instruction of the Russian pupils, in the principles of the Greek Church. Fellenberg's character, as a man of principle and piety, is, I believe, decidedly in his favour. He has the manners of a gentleman, and the whole exterior of his establishment, bears the marks of considerable taste and judgment. Beside the three schools already mentioned, he has another about half a mile from Hofwyl, where young men attend, during the winter, to courses of instruction in those subjects which relate to agriculture. He lectures himself, I believe, on the practical operations of farming. It is here too that the professor of chemistry has his laboratory and lecture room. We were introduced to him (Dr. Strobe,) and judged him to be a good chemist. He is also the physician of the establishment. His laboratory indicates an attachment to his profession and tolerable judgment in its practical details. The philosophical apparatus is, however, very unworthy of the institution, and ought not, I should hope, to be taken as a sample of the whole interior. In taking leave of Fellenberg, he expressed much regret at the shortness of our stay, and the consequent want of more opportunities of conversation. I cannot but regard him as a man of more than mediocrity of talent; a man of penetration and judgment; but rather prone, perhaps, like other German philosophers, to theorise on human nature, and to fancy that new and important discoveries are yet to be made in the principles of human action.

From the information we received from others, as well as from the statements of Fellenberg himself, it is evident that his plans have ever been regarded with jealousy by a great number of his most influential neighbours and fellow countrymen. He was at first condemned as a visionary: but when he had fairly demonstrated the practicability and utility of his schemes for the improvement of education, they accused him of sinister views; and alleged against him, that his motives were mercenary, having an eye chiefly to the profits of the establishment. This narrow-minded spirit has not been content with mere expressions of disapprobation and condemnation. The government of the canton has gone so far as to lay positive obstructions in his way, and to threaten him with the weight of their aristocratical authority. He had a few years ago devised a plan for diffusing some of the benefits of his experience in the government of youth, throughout the canton. He invited the teachers of schools to repair to Hofwyl during the period of their vacation, and there to avail themselves of such information, as the institution would afford, and their time would admit of. This offer was gladly accepted; but the next season the teachers of the canton were most arbitrarily interdicted by the government from resorting to Hofwyl. Fellenberg, thus very ungenerously thwarted in his wishes to do good, opened his establishment for the benefit of other cantons, and has thus had it in his power to extend still more widely the advantages of his system.[1] His great desire is to introduce a taste for agricultural pursuits, connected with an amelioration of the indigent classes. [2] He is himself of a patrician family; and his haughty compeers do not relish what they foolishly consider as a diminution of the dignity of their order, by his resorting to the task of an instructor. But though the Bernese government is thus actuated by ignoble sentiments towards the Hofwyl establishment, the most distinguished and enlightened characters in other parts of Switzerland, are decidedly in its favour. At Geneva it is considered as an honour to Switzerland; and if we may judge from the patronage that its founder has received from other countries; from England, Scotland, Germany,

[1] This part of the institution, which he called the *Normal School,* has been entirely prohibited by the cantonal government.

[2] His farm is intended to serve as a *model* of the best course of cultivation and management. About one twentieth of it is devoted to experimental inquiries, and the results are gradually adopted in his practice.

## JOHN GRISCOM

Russia, &c. it may be inferred that the Fellenberg system of instruction, is highly approved by the most competent judges of real merit in Europe.[1]

Without attempting to justify ALL the views which have influenced the founder of the Hofwyl institution, either as it regards its general arrangement of distinct and independent classes, or its minute practical details. I have no hesita-

[1] By the latest information in my possession, the superior class consisted of nearly 100 pupils, taught by upwards of thirty professors! The course of instruction embraces the Greek, Latin, German and French languages and literature; History, civil and sacred; Geography; Mathematics, pure and mixed; natural and mental philosophy; chemistry; music; drawing; gymnastics, including riding, swimming, dancing, &c.; natural history in all its branches; and religious instruction.

The pupils rise at six in winter and five in summer; they breakfast at seven, eat a little at ten, dine at noon, take a luncheon at five, and sup at eight. Five hours are appropriated to study in the forenoon and four hours in the afternoon; the rest of the day being devoted to their gymnastic, agricultural, and mechanical exercises. This arrangement however is not absolutely restrictive, but is made to conform to the varying circumstances of the establishment, the health and genius of the pupils, &c. The greatest pains are taken to cultivate their moral and religious sensibilities. The language chiefly spoken is the German. The internal or civil government, (if it may be so called,) of the school, is regulated by a constitution and by-laws, administered by the pupils themselves, and for which object they have their legislative and executive officers, under the supervision of the principal. The motives of emulation, as they are ordinarily excited by rewards, medals, honours, &c. or by a division into classes in the numerical order of first, second, third, &c. form no part of the Fellenberg system. His aim is to address his instruc-

53

tion in saying, that from all that I have read, and all that I have seen of this establishment, it does appear to me to be conducted upon principles which are calculated to afford the very best kind of education which it is possible to confer upon a young man, whatever may be the situation which he is to fill in active life. As it regards the poor, it is difficult to conceive how they could be brought up in a way which would better prepare them for filling the station of industrious, skilful and intelligent labourers. With respect to the

tions to the more reasonable and noble principles of their nature, and by the number of his professors, (for he has had as many as thirty-five with less than 100 pupils,) to unite all the advantages of private, with those of public instruction.

It appears from a recent and very interesting exposition of the Hofwyl institution, by the Count de Villeveille, that the principal of that establishment began his enterprise with a fortune of 400,000 francs, (nearly $80,000,) and that by a prudent economy in his expenditures and management, he has, in the course of twenty-two years, more than doubled his original capital, notwithstanding the constant maintenance of 40 poor boys, and his liberal provision for those of the higher class.

Such is the attraction which Hofwyl now presents, to the enlightened curiosity of travellers in Switzerland, the number which daily visit the institution during the travelling season, cannot be estimated at less than 12 or 15. Of this number, it is scarcely possible that De Fellenberg, intensely occupied as he must be with his extensive concerns, can have time to see and converse with more than one. It is in consequence of the concourse of visiters, that so few are admitted to the interior of the school; for it would be an injustice to the parents, if, instead of devoting himself to the interests of their children, he should offer them as a daily and almost hourly spectacle to visiters.

54

rich, while they are cheerfully pursuing an excellent course of literary and scientific instruction, they are effectually preserved, by the principles of this institution, from those idle and vicious habits which so commonly result from the vacant time of colleges and universities. By turning their attention to agriculture and the mechanic arts; by inspiring them with a love of labour, or at least of a useful application of their strength and muscular activities; by exercising their ingenuity in the use of tools and instruments; by familiarizing them to an attentive observance of nature in her different kingdoms, and in the revolution of seasons,—a foundation is laid for those more expanded feelings and generous sympathies, which bind the upper to the lower classes of the community, and eventually tend to exalt the condition of humanity.

But the greatest recommendation of the Pestalozzian and Fellenberg plan of education, is the moral charm which is diffused throughout all its operations. It cannot but happen, (all other things being equal,) that pupils thus educated, will become not only more intelligent men and better philosophers, but also more moral and dignified members of society. I cannot but cherish the hope, that this scheme of education, of combining agricultural and mechanical, with literary and scientific instruction, will be speedily and extensively adopted in the United States. I am aware that it would have to contend with serious difficulties. The prejudices and habits of the people would be against it. The high notions of independence, so early imbibed and strongly cherished among us, would submit, in all probability, with an ill grace to the alternation of labour with the exercises of a school. The pulse of the nation has already been felt on this subject by a benevolent individual, (our friend M******,) who, having visited the institutions of Pestalozzi and Fellenberg, was resolved, if possible, to establish one or more schools in the United States, on a similar plan. But after travelling from New-York to lake Erie, he could find no one who would agree to second his views; none who did not consider the plan, as either unnecessary or impracticable. Thus discouraged he relinquished the project, though few persons in the world would have supported it by greater pecuniary sacrifices. Still I cannot but believe, that, if it were once introduced and brought fairly into operation, its superiority would be immediately manifest, and that the first successful example would be rapidly followed in different parts of the country. I have but little doubt, that on a good productive farm, of 250 or 300 acres, provided with suitable buildings, (which need not be very costly,) and well stocked, a school of twenty-five or thirty boys, conducted on the plan of Fellenberg's poor school, would maintain itself, and leave a gain in favour of the proprietor. A few such schools would soon impart, to a large and populous district of country, a moral tone, of incalculable importance to its highest interests and welfare. I know of no means by which a benevolent and wealthy individual could do so much good, at the same expense, as by erecting one or more such institutions, in any of our middle states. If white children could not at once be obtained to begin with, I would take the children of blacks. These could be procured of a suitable age, and taken on indentures to remain a certain number of years, or until they were of age, if it should be found requisite, as in some cases it might be. Such an experiment, with persons of this description, would be highly interesting. It would put to flight the ridiculous theory of those who contend for an organic inferiority on the part of the blacks. It would in time produce examples very beneficial to our black population; and in reference to the scheme of colonization, now becoming popular, it might prove extremely important, by furnishing individuals admirably qualified by education, habits, and morals to aid in the management of an infant colony. The great difficulty would be, either in America, or anywhere else, in finding persons qualified to conduct such schools. Such characters as Vehrly are rare. Without a deep sense of religion, united with the proper intellectual endowments, on the part of the teacher, the scheme could not prosper. Its basis is the mild, but fervent spirit of Christian love. It is, however, the happy nature of such a temper, to beget its own likeness in the hearts of others; and it might reasonably be presumed, that one successful example, would readily prepare the way for others.

We could not part with the Count de Villevielle, without feeling and acknowledging his indefatigable attention. He is strongly impressed with the superiority of the Hofwyl system. In other places, he observes, *instruction* is the end, and *education* is only secondary. At Howfyl, *education* is the end, and *instruction* is regarded only as the means of attaining it. . . .

In our descent from Locle, we passed through or near Colombier, St. Aubin, Grandson, and other villages, and arrived at Yverdun about nine in the evening. We put up at the Hotel de la ville de Londres, where we found the accommodations rather of a superior kind.

8th. Breakfast finished, our first and chief concern here was to visit the celebrated institute of Pestalozzi. This establishment occupies a large castle, the use of which was granted to Pestalozzi by the canton of Berne, when the town of Yverdun was included in that canton. The government of the Pays de Vaud, to which it now belongs, continues the grant. On entering the castle, we were invited into a private room. I gave my letters to the person in attendance, who took them immediately to the chief. The good old man soon came in, and seized me warmly by the hand, and seeing my hat on my head, he pointed to it in a sort of ecstasy, with his eyes almost filled with tears. I hardly knew how to interpret this emotion, and asked him if he wished me to take it off. He answered very earnestly, "no, no, no, keep it on, you are right." He seemed very glad to see us, and as he speaks French very imperfectly, and with an indistinct accent, he said he would call Monsieur G****** to talk with us. This gentleman soon came and entered immediately into a detail of the institution, its principles, its spirit, its arrangement, &c. He is an Englishman, and, as I found upon enquiry, brother to the lady whom I had seen at Lausanne. He has been some weeks with Pestalozzi, for the purpose of understanding his system thoroughly, in order to aid a sister in England in the education of her children. He enters warmly into its concerns, and will be useful in making it better known. He explained to us very clearly the leading ideas and views of human nature, which induced Pestalozzi to become an instructor of youth. The two great instruments with which he works are faith and love. He discards the motives of ambition and emulation, as unnecessary, and as tending to counteract the sentiment of good will toward others. He thinks there is enough in the intuitive understanding of every child to accomplish the complete growth and maturity of its faculties, if its reason be properly trained and nourished, and not warped by injudicious treatment. The common plans of education he regards as too artificial, too wide a departure from nature. Too much stress is laid upon the memory, while the imagination is too much neglected. If the native feelings of the heart, are allowed to operate, under the dominion of the native powers of the mind, drawn out and expanded by faith and love, the child is competent of itself to arrive gradually at the most correct and important conclusions in religion and science. There is a native and inherent life, which only requires to be cherished by genial treatment, to bring it into the full attainment of truth, and to the utmost perfection of its being. He therefore insists upon the greatest pains being taken to draw out this native life and to preserve it in full vigour. There is a constant danger of urging the child forward beyond its natural strength, of anticipating its conclusions and thus weakening its confidence in its own powers. In the plans he adopts nothing is to be got by heart. The understanding is to be thoroughly reached, and then the memory will take care of itself.

The school consists at present of about 90 boys, German, Prussian, French, Swiss, Italian, Spanish and English. It is divided into four principal classes, according to the attainments of the pupils. These classes are subdivided into others. There are seven school rooms in the castle, and twelve teachers or professors. His head professor, Joseph Schmidt, has been brought up in the institution, and is a very efficient and worthy man. He is a native of one of the German cantons, and speaks and writes perfectly the German and French. He is a man of modest demeanor, and entirely devoted to the institution. He has written treatises on several of the subjects taught in the school, and adapted to its methods.

We spent most of the day in the different schoolrooms, witnessing the exercises of the scholars. Very few books are used, as it is expected the children can read well before they come there. But to describe the modes of teaching, so as to render them clearly intelligible, would require much more time and space than I can possibly allot to it, were I ever so competent to make it known. We saw the exercises of arithmetic, writing, drawing, mathematics, lessons in music and gymnastics, something of geography, French, Latin, and German. To teach a school, in the way practised here, without book, and almost entirely by verbal instruction, is extremely laborious. The teacher must be constantly with the child, always talking, questioning, explaining, and repeating. The pupils, however, by this process, are brought into very close intimacy with the instructor. Their capacities, all their faculties and propensities become laid open to his observation. This gives him an advantage, which cannot possibly be gained, in the ordinary way in which schools are generally taught. The children look well, appear very contented, and apparently, live in great harmony one with another; which, considering the diversity of national character and temper here collected, can be attributed only to the spirit of love and affection which sways the breast of the principal of the institution, and extends its benign influence throughout all the departments. In the afternoon we went, with Pestalozzi, G\*\*\*\*\*\*, and B\*\*\*\*\*\*, a German clergyman, (who is here on a visit to the institution,) and one or two others, to visit a free school of twelve or fourteen children, which Pestalozzi has established in the village of Clendy, at a short distance from the castle. These are children taken from the families of poor people, selected on account of their character and talents, in order to be educated as teachers, with a view to extend and perpetuate the principles and operation of the system. One half of them are boys and the other half girls. Their principal instructer is a sister of Schmidt, the chief master, an exceedingly clever and interesting young woman. She has another sister also with her, younger than herself, who will soon become qualified to act as an instructer. These pupils were exercised before us, in drawing, in arithmetic, and in music. The girls, seated round a table, and busy with their needles, had questions in arithmetic given them by the mistress, which they were to solve by their heads. They are thus led on, from the most simple beginnings, to comprehend the principles of arithmetic, and to work questions with great expertness, solely by a mental process. A male teacher is provided for the boys, though the mistress often assists in their instruction. This little school promises to be well cared for, and of service to the Pestalozzian cause. We were much pleased with its appearance, and with the assurance it affords, that whatever there is of value and importance in this system, will not be lost.

The success of this mode of instruction, greatly depends on the personal qualifications of those who undertake to conduct it. There is nothing of mechanism in it, as in the Lancasterian plan; no laying down of precise rules for managing classes, &c. It is all mind and feeling. Its arrangements must always depend on the ages, talents, and tempers of the scholars, and requires, on the part of the teachers, the most diligent and faithful attention. Above all, it requires that the teacher should consider himself as the father and bosom friend of his pupils, and to be animated with the most affectionate desires for their good. Pestalozzi himself is all this. His heart glows with such a spirit, that the good old man can hardly refrain from bestowing kisses on all with whom he is concerned. He holds out his hand to his pupils on every occasion, and they love him as a child loves its mother. His plan of teaching is just fit for the domestic fireside, with a father or mother in the centre, and a circle of happy children around them. He is aware of this, and wishes to extend the knowledge of his plan to every parent. Pestalozzi is seventy-two years of age. It has been quite unfortunate for the progress of his system on the continent, that he pays so little attention to exteriors, regarding dress, furniture, &c. as of no moment whatever, provided the mind and heart be right.

9th. The weather continuing wet, we resolved to wait till to-morrow, and take the diligence to Lausanne and Geneva. Much of the day was spent at the castle, in the school-rooms, and in conversation with G******. I omitted to mention, that we attended last evening, to the religious exercise which terminates the business of the day. The scholars assembled in a room called the chapel, but very simply furnished, with benches, and a table. When all were collected, Pestalozzi, directing his face chiefly to the boys, began to speak in German, moving about, from side to side, directing his attention, for some time, to the boys on his right, and then advancing towards those on his left. This motion, backwards and forwards, continued about twenty minutes; he was constantly speaking, and sometimes with considerable earnestness. It was altogether unintelligible to me, but I afterwards learned, that it consisted of a recapitulation of the occurrences of the day, noticing particularly everything of moment, and intermingling the whole with short prayers, adapted to the circumstances mentioned in the discourse. If, for example, any of the boys had quarrelled, or behaved unseemly to each other, or to their teacher, he would speak to the case, and accompany his remarks with a pious ejaculation. It is probable, that he sometimes engages more formally in this exercise. As it was, it appeared to gain the whole attention of his audience. It was concluded by reading, from a small book, what appeared to be a hymn or psalm.

A company of English visiters attended at the castle to-day, consisting of men and women. The boys performed some of their gymnastic exercises before them, consisting chiefly of simple, but simultaneous movements of the arms, legs, feet, head, &c., stepping, marching, turning, and jumping, all intended to exercise the various muscles, which give motion to the limbs and head, and to make the boys acquainted with the elements of all those movements. This exercise took place in one of the large bed-rooms. We attended, by invitation, last evening, a lecture given by Schmidt, the head teacher, to a number of young men, among whom were four Russians, sent by the Emperor to gain information, in England, and other countries, relative to the best modes of teaching. They had been in England, and spoke our language tolerably well. The lectures are to illustrate more fully, the principles and processes adopted in the Pestalozzian institution.

We had the company, this evening, at our lodgings, of

Frederick Bucholz, who was late a chaplain to the king's German legion in England. He had been some time with Pestalozzi, and was able to inform us, more fully, with respect to some parts of the system, than we could obtain by a short visit to the school itself.

10th. The town of Yverdun is pleasantly situated, at the head of the lake of Neuchâtel, and contains, probably, 2500 inhabitants. It is pretty well built; the streets, in common with most of the towns in Switzerland, are paved with round stones. We have been surprised, in observing the large droves of cows, which have passed through the streets, to-day, most of them with huge bells round their necks. The noise they make is almost deafening. These cows are taken to the mountains to pasture, during the summer, in great numbers; the shepherds, or rather cowherds, allowing a certain sum for the produce of the milk and butter. On the day of St. Denis, they are returned again to the valley.

We have had at our table d'hote, the last two days, ten or twelve boys, with their three preceptors, constituting a boarding school at Geneva. They are on an excursion, round the lake of Geneva, taking Yverdun in the way. They came to this place on foot, through the rain, and intended to perform the whole journey on foot; but the weather continuing very wet, they went off this morning in carriages. One of them is a young prince of Wirtemberg, about twelve years of age, of plain juvenile manners, exhibiting no extraordinary talent, but apparently of an amiable temper.

We left Yverdun in the diligence, after going again to the castle, and taking leave of some of the professors. Pestalozzi was not in; he had been to see us at the inn, but missed of us. Before we set off, however, the good old man came down again, and parted with us very affectionately. In the course of the two days which we have spent at the castle, he several times pressed my hand to his lips, and seemed to possess all the love and fervency of a true disciple in the cause in which he is engaged. If his personal talents, address, and management, were equal either to his genius, or his zeal, his influence would have been much greater even than it has been. Nevertheless, his life and labours will, I fully believe, be hereafter regarded as a most important epoch, in the history of education. When his principles come to be more generally understood, they will be found to contain much that is extremely valuable. It is to be feared, however, that many years will still elapse, before the world is put in possession of a complete explanatory view of his whole system. He does not himself possess the faculty, (as Bucholz informed me,) of explaining, in familiar and intelligible terms, his own principles. He conceives with wonderful acuteness, and expresses himself in language of extraordinary force and energy, but it requires a deep and steady attention, to be able to embrace his whole meaning. He has published largely in explanation, and in support of his plans of instruction; but there is so much of vernacular pith—of idiomatic force and peculiarity, in his style and manner, as to render it rather difficult to read him, and still more so, to translate his writings. He is now, however, anxious to have all his works translated into English, fully believing, that the merit of his plans will be better understood, and his principles more industriously supported by the English nation, than by his own people. His career has been marked with perplexities. He has had to struggle intensely against poverty, neglect, prejudice, and gross misrepresentation; but his patience, his meekness, his perseverance, his ardent love of his fellow creatures, have borne him through all of his trials; and not-withstanding his advanced age, the reputation of his school, is now as high, if not higher, than it ever has been. Towards those who have generously contributed to aid him in his pecu-niary difficulties, his heart glows with the liveliest gratitude. Of two of my acquaintance, one of London, and the other of Philadelphia, who had thus befriended him, he could not speak without evident emotion. . . .

T. Clarkson, having obligingly furnished me with letters for Cambridge, I left Bury early in the afternoon, with one of my female companions from Ipswich, whom I had the pleasure of escorting to London, whither she was return-ing from a visit to her sister. The road from Bury to Cam-bridge, is uninteresting, from the great extent of dreary waste. It leads through Newmarket, so notorious in the an-nals of jockeyism, racing, and gambling. This town consists of one street, and, as might be expected, it abounds in inns. It is surrounded by a large plain. The house built by Charles II. in which he resided during the season of frolic, is still shown.

We reached Cambridge at six, and obtained, at the Hoop inn, comfortable quarters, with the important addition, so creditable to the inns of this country, of good attendance. The entrance to Cambridge is not imposing, nor does its general appearance bear any comparison with Oxford, in the venerable richness of its edifices, combined with the width and beauty of its streets.

My letters of introduction were to two of the tutors, both

of whom were fellows; one of St. Peter's, and the other of Jesus College. The latter is the Registrary of the university. As it was dark before we were settled in our quarters at the inn, and wishing to avail myself, as fully as possible, of the short stay I should make, I sent my letters by a servant of the inn, to the persons to whom they were addressed. He returned with information that one of them would call upon us in the course of the evening, and a note or message from the other, assured us that he would call in the morning. The former, *. ********, a clerical gentleman, soon came, and by the most easy and affable deportment, opened the way for an immediate friendly acquaintance. We were thus assured, in the most obliging manner, of their readiness to procure for us every practicable facility in visiting the colleges.

9th. The registrary,*.*******, called at half past ten, and conducted us to St. John's and Trinity colleges, and through the ornamented grounds, along the margin of the Cam. We found him as open and affable as his friend had been, the preceding evening.

Trinity college makes a noble appearance. It is the most magnificent member of the university. Its buildings enclose two spacious quadrangular courts, the largest of which is nearly a quarter of a mile in circuit. Its entrance is through a tower gateway, which is surmounted with a statue of Henry VIII. the founder of this college. In passing through the kitchen, the vast extent of the fireplace, and the size of the roasting jack, naturally excited our astonishment; and it appeared very evident, from the structure of the grate, and other apparatus, that the learned members of this university, prefer roast to boiled. The walks along the river, and through the grounds, are beautiful even in winter; but less various and attractive than those of Oxford. The trees are planted so as to form agreeable vistas, opening to the principal buildings. Many of them are chestnut and linden, of great size, and towering height. The Cam is a trifling stream,—not larger than a common canal.

Our agreeable guide next conducted us to the Fitz Williams museum, where we were introduced to Professor Cumming, who holds the department of chemistry in the university. This museum is a recent and important acquisition. It is a bequest to the university, by Viscount Fitzwilliams, who died in 1816, leaving to his alma mater his splendid collection of books, paintings, drawings, engravings, &c. together with £100,000 in South Sea annuities, for the erection of a museum for their reception. The building is not yet commenced, but the museum is temporarily accommodated in a place obtained for that purpose. Among the paintings are some valuable productions from the pencils of Reubens [sic], Rembrandt, and Titian, and two from Gerard Douw. The library contains a fine selection of important works.

Professor Cumming conducted me to his lecture room and laboratory, and showed me his apparatus. The collection appeared to be extensive and interesting, but, as might be expected during the time of vacation, it was in some confusion. In the same building Dr. E. D. Clarke, the celebrated traveller, who is professor of mineralogy in this university, has his collection, and delivers his lectures. Being informed of our intended visit at the laboratory, he agreed to meet us, though suffering from a recent indisposition. Having previously ordered a fire in his lecture room, he joined us at the appointed time, and exhibited to our particular notice all that was most interesting in his curious and valuable cabinet of minerals; and also his mode of experimenting with the compound blow-pipe, the results of which have gained for him a considerable share of popular, scientific reputation. He was anxious to clear himself from the imputation of unfairness in neglecting to attribute the original invention of this instrument to its rightful claimant Professor Hare of Philadelphia; and took pains to convince me that he had never deviated from candour and justice in what he had published respecting it. My impression is, that he has not been fully aware of Professor Hare's claims, nor of the results that have been obtained in America. Dr. Clarke's style of conversation and action is unusually vivid and energetic. He appears to be by nature an enthusiast; but the ardour of his fancy is tempered by learning, extensive knowledge, and the love of order. At his own house, whither he kindly pressed us to accompany him, he showed us a variety of curious things, arranged and preserved in the greatest neatness. His person is not particularly prepossessing; but three of his children whom we had met walking with their nurse in the public grounds, were, we thought, uncommonly beautiful. Dr. C. showed us, in his private cabinet, a volume of original letters of Linnæus and other distinguished men. His character, from the peculiar cast of his mind, and the store of information he has acquired from his travels, excites, even upon a hasty interview, far more than common interest; and I could but regret that the shortness of my stay in Cambridge forbade a more extended acquaintance.[1]

In the same building in which Dr. Clarke and Professor Cumming give their instructions, Professor Farish delivers his lectures on practical mechanics. We were shown a considerable portion of his apparatus, but, as he was not in town, I had not the pleasure of entering, as I should have been glad to do, more minutely into the subjects of his important and very useful department.

At five we accepted an invitation to dine with our friend H******, the Registrary, in Jesus College. Professor Cumming, who is a fellow of Trinity College, was also a guest. The apartments occupied by the Fellows, are large and well furnished; and, in every respect, a fit residence for private gentlemen. The suite of rooms into which we were introduced, was sufficient for a common family; but the Fellows are not allowed to marry, except at the expense of their collegiate living. The manners of these gentlemen were perfectly easy and agreeable, without any mixture of the pride of learning, or affectation of superiority. The evening passed pleasantly in their society till nine o'clock, enlivened by a current of agreeable and polished conversation. Our dinner, though not luxurious, was excellent in its kind, and in ample variety for the occasion.

Jesus College is at a considerable distance from all the

[1] Lamented by the scientific world, this eminent man breathed his last on the 9th of March, 1822, aged about 53 years. His health had been long declining. The degree of LL.D. was conferred upon him in a full senate of the University, as some return for the lustre which his name had reflected upon it, and in gratitude for his numerous contributions to its library and museum.

others, and, indeed, from the town itself. It has accordingly, more extensive grounds and meadows, than either of the sister institutions. Its front is 180 feet. It was formerly a convent of Benedictine nuns. It has a Master, and sixteen fellows, each of whom has a large and separate garden. The number of its members, including students of every description, is about 130.

The whole university consists of twelve colleges and four halls. Peter House, the oldest, was founded in 1247; and Sidney Sussex, the latest, in 1598. A new institution, called Downing College, from the name of the founder, was commenced in 1807, but is not yet completed. The sole founder was Sir George Downing, a wealthy gentleman of Cambridgeshire, who died in 1749.

10th. At an early hour we renewed our rambles through the courts and grounds of some of the principal colleges. They all have an antiquated, and some of them a gloomy exterior. The chapels of Kings and Trinity, are splendid monuments of the wealth, the pride, the skill, and, I would fain add, the piety of former ages. The interior of Kings' Chapel, more than realized the expectations I had formed from the animated description of it, given me by Thomas Clarkson. Walpole styled it, and with great reason, "a work, alone, sufficient to ennoble any age." The chapel is 316 feet long and 84 in breadth. It has a tower at each corner 114 feet high. The ceiling or internal roof is of white marble, and is, by far, the most elegant specimen of this kind of architectural beauty I have ever beheld. It is composed of Gothic arches, filled up with beautiful groins; and in the centre, between the groins, are suspended twelve massive stones, of at least a ton weight each. The under surface of these stones, is beautifully carved into a rose and portcullis alternately. The windows are Gothic, and each of them nearly 50 feet high. On these windows there are about one hundred paintings, done in the most exquisite style. The subjects are all taken from the Old and New Testament. This superb structure was founded by Henry VI., but not completed before his death. The chapel of Trinity College, was erected by Mary and Elizabeth. It is also an elegant Gothic structure, but more simple than the other. Its interior is 204 feet by 34, but divided by a transverse gallery which contains, it is said, one of the largest organs in England. The altar piece is a fine painting by B. West, of St. Michael binding Satan. In the anti-chapel, is an admirable full length statue of Sir Isaac Newton, who was a member of this college. He is standing on a pedestal, in full dress, with a gown over his other garments, the folds of which, appeared to me to be too complicated and clumsy. His features are thinner and sharper than I had imagined to be those of Newton. In his hand is a prism, and his benignant countenance is directed upwards with a look of profound and abstracted meditation.

> "Such was his brow and look serene,
>     His serious gait and musing mein,
>     When taught on eagle's wings to fly,
>     He trac'd the wonders of the sky."

On the pedestal is an inscription from Lucretius,

> "Qui genus humanum ingenio superavit."

Porson, the great critic and scholar, lies buried on the left of Newton; and behind the statue of the philosopher is a large and handsome tablet, in honor of the memory of his friend Roger Cotes, a man of kindred genius, and fellow of the same college. He died at the early age of 34; and in reference to the loss which the university had sustained by his death, Newton is said to have remarked, "If he had lived, we should have known something." The inscription on the tablet states him to have been,

"Inferior only to the great Newton,"

and

"The second hope and contemporary ornament of this society,"

and

"Possessed, in addition to the highest reputation for learning,
Of all the advantages of morals and virtue."

He died in 1716.

We had the pleasure of breakfasting with our clerical friend, T*******, of Peter's College, in the identical room, as he informed us, which had been occupied by the poet Grey, who was a member of this college. The apartments are very genteel and comfortable, and we were served with a good English breakfast. At 12, we called by previous invitation, on Professor Cumming, at his rooms in Trinity College. His accommodations are also spacious and well furnished with books, and various other scientific ornaments. He politely accompanied us to the library of Trinity College, a truly superb structure, forming the west end of one of the great courts. It is 200 feet in length and 40 in breadth. The steps of the great staircase, which leads to this grand apartment, are of black marble, and the wainscotting of cedar. The south end is terminated by a window of painted glass. The subject is the presentation of Sir Isaac Newton, to his present majesty, George III. who is seated under a canopy, with a laurel chaplet in his hand. Below the throne is Lord Bacon in his robes, with a pen and book, as if preparing to register the reward to be bestowed on Sir Isaac. The original drawing, executed by Cipriani, cost 100 guineas, and is here preserved. The library is floored with marble, and is ornamented, at each end, with busts, of Ray, Willoughby, Bacon, and Newton, by Roubiliac. The books are divided into thirty classes, and disposed in cases of oak. On the top of each case is a marble bust of some distinguished literary character. A number of interesting manuscripts are also preserved in this library, among which is a folio of Milton's papers, containing, with other things, the original copy of the Masque of Comus. We saw, also, a collection of Newton's letters. They are written in a plain, but good, legible hand. A number of curious antiques, natural and artificial, are also arranged in this spacious building.

We visited to-day, the senate house and university library. The former is an elegant building of Portland stone, consisting of one principal room, more than 100 feet in length. The galleries are capable, it is said, of containing nearly 1000 persons. In this room degrees are conferred, officers and magistrates are elected, and other public business transacted. The heads of the university, i. e. all the doctors and masters of arts, are a corporate body, endowed with legislative powers, and called the *senate*. No language but Latin is permitted to be spoken at any official meeting in the senate house. The statutes require three years study in the university, before the student can be capable of taking the degree of bachelor of arts, and four years more for a master of arts; seven years after that he may commence bachelor of divinity, and then five years more are required to take the degree of doctor in divinity. The nobility are entitled to degrees without waiting the statutable time.

The vice chancellor's chair is at the upper end of the senate house. This apartment contains four marble statues, viz. of George I., George II., Duke of Somerset, and the Right Honourable W. Pitt. The latter is one of the most admirable specimens of statuary I have ever seen. It was executed by Nollekins, and is considered as his *chef-d'œuvre*. Upwards of £7000 was subscribed by different members of the university, to pay for it.

The university library consists of four rooms, and contains more than 90,000 volumes. The famous statue of the goddess Ceres, brought from the temple at Eleusis, by Dr. Clarke, is placed in the vestibule of this building. It weighs a ton and a half. This library is rich in ancient and illuminated manuscripts. A copy of the Koran, an eastern manuscript, remarkable for the beauty of its writing,—a finely illuminated Persian manuscript, written in 1388, being a treatise on astronomy and natural history, and embellished with drawings of beasts, birds, and reptiles, some of them as fresh as if lately finished,—are among the most remarkable in the collection. The latter volume is superbly bound. It cost in Persia £100. In another part of the library is a manuscript of the Gospels and Acts of the Apostles, given to the university by Theodore Beza, and believed to be as old as any manuscript extant. The library contains also an Egyptian mummy; and a cast from the face of Charles XII. of

Sweden, taken a few hours after his death. It shows the nature of the wound by which he fell, and from which it appears probable that he was shot by the officer who conducted him in his survey of the enemy's works; and thus, after a meteoric career of fury and devastation,

> "He left a name at which the world grew pale,
> To point a moral or adorn a tale."

There are also in the same collection, casts of Pitt, Fox, and Percival, taken by Nollekins immediately after death.

The botanic garden of the university contains between three and four acres of ground. Among the plants are many rare species from the east.

In the evening we heard the religious exercises in the chapel of Trinity College. As this is not term time, the number of students is probably much less than it is during the term. They all wore, on this occasion, a white mantle over their other dress. The music of this chapel is admitted to be of the most exquisite and sublime style of performance. It consisted this evening of the psalms of David, chaunted in prose, with other usual church exercises. But fine as the tones were, I was scarcely able to realize from the service, any feelings of religious solemnity, nor can I suppose that the students were, generally, in a disposition much better adapted to the performance of pious worship. I remarked that several of them, while on their knees, were whispering and smiling with each other.

11th. We were amused this morning with a company of country people, who came into the court of the inn, fantastically decorated with ribbands, and dancing to the sound of a musical instrument. Among them were two women, who capered before our windows along with the others. This it appears, is an anniversary called Plough Monday, on which the boys and girls from the neighbouring farms, have the privilege of coming into Cambridge for the purpose of amusing the citizens by their drolleries, and of reminding the collegians, that they are indebted to the plough for all their solid comforts. They calculate, of course, to be paid for their trouble, and most of the citizens make it a point to give them something. One or more of the companies drew a large plough through the streets. Some of them were dressed in coats made of straw, with a crown of the same material on their heads; in short, the town has been kept in a bustle most of the day, by these merry-makers, who, though they levy an annual tax on the good natured inhabitants, doubtless contrive to leave much of their money behind them, for articles of holiday purchase.

In waiting for the coach to convey us to London, we received a visit from two of the Fellows of Peter House, whose friendly and social manners could not but inspire me with favourable impressions of the temper which prevails in the society of this distinguished community of learning. To the Fellows and Professors to whom we have been introduced, my acknowledgments are especially due, for their kind and obliging attentions.

The whole number of members on the boards of the university, for the present year, is 3444; of these 955 are in Trinity college, and 819 in St. John's. But so insufficient are the colleges and halls, to accommodate all those who resort to Cambridge for instruction, that there are in the town, as the tutor of Peter House informed me, three hundred boarding houses. Hence it would appear that another university is wanting; which, should it ever be undertaken, will probably receive its location in one of the northern counties. The two universities are powerful instruments in the hands of government, and are, doubtless, very influential in wielding the political destinies of the nation. The gifts and emoluments of the church are distributed principally to those who have received their education in these schools; and these tangible and material benefits are, as one of the clerical gentlemen acknowledged, among the chief inducements for taking orders, at least with a majority of those who enter upon the ministerial office. Since the late peace, a great number of persons from the army and navy, have entered as students of divinity, relying on family influence for promotion; and, in consequence of such influence, no inconsiderable number have been promoted, and over the heads, too, of others who have devoted many years to the duties of the university. Surely no wound can be inflicted upon religion, more deep and deadly, than to place a man, by the mere dictum of hierarchical authority, in the station of a Christian minister, who is just reeking from the camp, and who has no qualifications, either of head or heart, for the solemn office which he thus presumes to fill; and probably no taste for any of its accompaniments, except for the loaves and fishes.

The annual income of the university is about £16,000, arising from stock, manors, lands, fees for degrees, government annuity for surrendering the privilege of printing almanacs, &c. Its annual expenditure is about £12,000 disbursed to the various officers, professors, library, taxes, donations, &c.

The examination for degrees [sic] in this university are

almost altogether in mathematics and natural philosophy. Within the colleges there are some examinations in the easy classics. About three medical degrees are conferred here every year. At Oxford the examinations are chiefly in the classics.[1]

The town of Cambridge has a population of about 12,000. It is supplied with water by a conduit erected at the expense of Thomas Hobson, one of the inhabitants, who is famous for having given rise to the common or vulgar saying of "Hobson's choice:—*this,* or none." He was a carrier between London and Cambridge, and the principal person who furnished the students with horses. He made it an unalterable rule that every horse should have an equal share of rest and fatigue, and would never let an animal go out of his regular turn. A member of the university has eulogised this benevolent man, as Pope did the man of Ross, and in numbers equally harmonious. In reference to his horses, the following is an extract:—

"Nor let the learn'd disdain the poet's voice,
  Who fain would sing in verse old *Hobson's choice;*
He let out horses for the public hire,
  But not at each capricious youth's desire:
Each horse in turn partook of work and rest,
  As mercy prompted in his feeling breast;
And when a customer would take his ride,
  And wishing for his favourite horse, applied,
Fill'd with humanity, in friendly tone
  Old Hobson cried, "You must take *this, or none.*"

[1] In 1822, both Divinity and Classical Literature were, by a vote of the Senate, added to the list of subjects for examination in the University of Cambridge.

From an artificial hill on the border of the town, we had a charming view of Cambridge, with the various buildings of the university. The town of Ely, with its famous cathedral, was also distinctly seen. Near this hill is a new prison, erected on the same plan as the prison at Bury St. Edmunds. We were readily admitted to the interior, and found in it the same style of neatness, and the same excellent discipline as in the last named prison. The two keepers are brothers. In this prison are fifty-five convicts, five of whom are females. Water is forced from a well to a reservoir under the roof, and is thence distributed by pipes over the house. The well which supplies the reservoir is 140 feet deep, but when the water was once attained, it rose nearly to the surface, where it still remains.

Nothing occurred to my notice, which would induce the belief, that there is a greater degree of licentiousness among the students in this university, than in other places, where young men are collected in large numbers, in collegiate institutions. In this respect, one of the tutors assured me, that there had been recently a very decided improvement, and that the discipline of the place is now such as to ensure the preservation of order, without embarrassment or difficulty. That breaches of morality do [1] sometimes occur, disgraceful to the perpetrators, is hardly to be expected, when the propensities of human nature, and the almost unbounded wealth which many of the students have at their command, are taken into the account. Upon such, however, whatever occasional disorders they may be guilty of, it is scarcely to be doubted, that the restrictions of the university, and the obligations they are under to comply with its laws, have a salu-

[1] Evidently "not" is omitted after "do."

tary influence upon their future lives; and that the effect of these great schools is, upon the whole, favourable to the progress of morality in the nation. It would be a curious and interesting subject of inquiry, to ascertain, with as much accuracy as possible, the relative morality of Oxford and Cambridge; as it is well known, that in the former university, the collegiate studies are directed with paramount assiduity to moral philosophy, and the higher range of classical learning; while in Cambridge, mathematics and natural philosophy have a transcendant influence. As far as my own very slight opportunities have extended, of forming an opinion on this subject, I should assign to this university, the higher degree of moral respectability. But I state this rather as a surmise than an opinion, and should it be correct, I know not how far the preference may be due to the superior discipline and government enforced at Cambridge.

It would be unnatural, and perhaps impossible, for a stranger, educated in the English language, to leave Cambridge, after passing through its venerable halls and colleges, and traversing its shades and gardens, without feeling a degree of reverence for a place which has fostered and matured the genius of Bacon, Newton, and Milton, of Cranmer, Porteus and Paley, of Pitt, Coke, Porson, and a host of other great men, whose attainments have shed so much lustre upon the human mind, and whose writings have done so much to extend the sphere of moral and physical truth. . . .

At Cromford, a village one mile from Matlock bath, we passed the cotton mill erected by that prince of mechanics, Sir Richard Arkwright. It was the first that was ever worked by the power of water. How deeply is the present prosperity

of England indebted to the talents of this extraordinary man!
It would be difficult, I think, to name an individual, with
the whole civilized world before us, whose inventive powers
are better entitled to the grateful applause of his country.
This, I am aware, will be contested by those who entertain
the belief, that the introduction of labour-saving machinery
has, upon the whole, been attended with more harm than
good, to the morals and happiness of the working classes.
There are, indeed, few of the blessings of Providence, which
are not liable to perversion and abuse. That no evils have
attended the erection and multiplication of large cotton
factories, in this and in other nations, it would be folly to
deny; but these evils are doubtless of a nature that do not
forbid the application of remedies adequate to their removal. The progress of a humane and enlightened policy,
with respect to education, and the gradual amelioration of
the system of management, in these extensive manufactories,
seem to afford the promise of an eventual triumph over the
principal evils with which they have been attended; and
whoever takes a rational survey of the immense benefits
which man derives from every important extension of his
dominion over matter,—the vast accession to his comforts,
which the arts afford, and the innumerable friendly ties
which are thus made to bind the various parts of a nation
into one united brotherhood, and even to form a cementing
charm between distant and remote nations, will not hesitate
a moment, to admit the vast amount of obligation, which
England and the world are under, to such a genius as Sir
Richard Arkwright. It is creditable to his country, that his
talents were so well fostered by its beneficent patronage, as
to raise him from obscurity and poverty, to distinction and

wealth. He died in 1792, and his remains were deposited in the chapel of Cromford, which was built and endowed by himself. But where is his monument? It is not to be found in the hamlet which protects his ashes; nor need it: it will long live in the memories of thousands, in England and America,—it will live in the page of history. . . .

We visited a private boarding school[1] kept by a friend, (F. H. S.) and conducted, apparently, with much efficiency, in relation both to the intellectual and moral progress of the pupils. The number of the latter, is now about twenty, and yet there are two distinct classes, separated chiefly by price and the nature of the studies which they pursue. Private boarding schools of a superior order, are much more common among the society of Friends in this country, than in the United States; though the society here is less numerous, and in the aggregate, perhaps, not more wealthy. But notwithstanding all the advantages, which the best private boarding schools can afford, I cannot but believe, that if the united wisdom and prudence of the society were directed to the establishment, both here and at home, of a large and well endowed public school or college, for the higher branches of learning and science, very essential benefits would result to our youth; and the soundest principles of our profession, receive a confirmation, that would go further toward their preservation, than by any other step or procedure, which it is in the power of the society to adopt. I am persuaded, that the friends of humanity and virtue among other sects, would be glad to see such an evidence of liberality and good taste, as this would demonstrate; for there is as little of the spirit of proselytism among us, prob-

[1] In Darlington, in the County of Durham.

ably, as in any other body of professing Christians. The general habits of this society are, moreover, deemed to be, in a particular manner, favourable to the cultivation of useful knowledge. The day, we may hope, is nearly passed, in which it has been supposed that ignorance is necessary to the propagation of truth, or that the purest principles of morality and of Christianity, will not receive strength, power, and influence, by the increasing cultivation of the higher faculties of our nature. Truth, indeed, is a unit; and whether it be sought after by the metaphysician, the mathematician, the astronomer, the chemist, or the Christian, it will be found, that there is nothing discordant in its doctrines, but that it conspires, in all its parts, if rightly pursued, to the production of a harmonious result—the dignity and happiness of its votary. . . .

The charity schools of this town [Newcastle] are well supported. The largest, called the Royal Jubilee School, was erected in commemoration of the king's entrance into the fiftieth year of his reign. It contains 450 boys. Another for girls, contains 300. In hearing one of the classes read, I was surprised at the singular and disagreeable twang of the voice, in which even the monitors indulged themselves. It arises from the provincial habits of this county, and is certainly more unpleasant to the ear, than any of the provincialisms I have yet heard. It rendered the reading, to me, almost unintelligible. The ordinary conversation of the uneducated classes, I found, on this account, scarcely more easy of comprehension than an unknown, foreign tongue. . . .

With an American acquaintance, I went to the high school of Edinburgh, and was introduced to the rector, J. Pillans. This grammar school is of ancient standing, and like the university, it is under the direction of the magistrates of the city. It dates an existence of nearly 300 years, but the present building was erected in 1777. It is 120 feet long. The number of scholars is at present between 8 and 900. Four teachers are employed, in addition to the rector. This gentleman, by the effort of a particular genius, and indefatigable activity, has completely succeeded in introducing into this large school, the system of monitorial instruction, and applying it to classical learning. He has under his exclusive charge, twenty-three classes, each containing nine boys. Every class has its monitor, who hears the rest recite. They occupy three rooms, and are all engaged at the same time. The rector superintends the whole, and decides all questions of dispute, when appeals are made to him against the decision of the monitors. In each room is a *custos morum,* who watches the behaviour of the scholars and notes every instance of remissness. Almost the only punishment resorted to, is the imposing of additional tasks on offenders, and obliging them to attend the school, during the hours and half days of ordinary vacation. The twenty-three classes all recite the same lesson at the same time. The noise they make is unavoidably great, but it is the sound of useful activity. We were highly gratified with the evidences of intelligence and attainment which the boys displayed when collected into one room, and examined before us by the rector. The superiority of their instruction appeared not only in the facility of their translations, but in the readiness with which they recited parallel passages, and referred to the illustrations of different classical authors, and in their acquaintance with the geography, chronology, &c. of the historical passages, which were given them as extemporaneous exercises. Great merit is obviously due to the rector, for bringing this method of teaching so perfectly to bear upon the higher parts of education, and showing its adaptation to subjects which have generally been thought beyond its reach. The high school contains a good library for the benefit of the teachers and boys of the upper class. The whole cost of tuition in this excellent school, is but three pounds per annum, including the use of the library. There are few boys in the school above sixteen years of age, a period which leaves them sufficient time for apprenticeship to almost any kind of business. With such advantages of intellectual and moral instruction, is it surprising that Scotland should have taken such an elevated stand among the nations, for the intelligence, industry and sobriety of her people? [1] . . .

[1] The very flourishing condition of the High School of Edinburgh, in which about 900 boys are taught by four masters and a rector, afforded, to my mind, a very satisfactory demonstration, not only of the practicability, but the excellence of the monitorial system, when applied to any or all of the exercises of a superior grammar school. The public, in all the large cities of England, Scotland, and the United States, have long since been convinced, that this system is of inestimable importance in the education of the lower classes; and because it has been adopted chiefly in the *Free Schools,* many persons seem to have drawn the illogical conclusion, that it is not adapted to higher seminaries, or to the instruction of boys in the more elevated parts of learning. The example of the High School has clearly shown the error of this opinion. By the partial employment of this easy and pleasant mode of instruction, the rector of the High School, (since chosen professor of humanity in the university,) was able, as he informed me, to manage his 207 boys with more facility, than he

We had an agreeable dinner party to-day at J. P******s, the Rector of the High School [Edinburgh]. I have seldom seen a table more variously spread, especially at this season of the year.

Although the system of instruction adopted in the High School, is professedly intended to be chiefly classical; P— remarked, that he should think himself very deficient in his duty, in teaching the boys only Latin and Greek, and omitting to avail himself of every suitable occasion to inculcate moral truth, and to excite them to intellectual exertion. This he regards as one of the most important advantages of classical instruction. He thinks it might be practicable to frame a course of English study, that would be equally efficacious in training the mind to the pursuit of knowledge, and in disciplining its powers to a close and vigorous application; but such a course of study would be exceedingly unpopular in Scotland. The government of the High School, was

could have taught 100 upon the old plan, and with greater efficiency. It is not to be supposed, that the whole instruction is to be communicated through the monitors. Such parts only of the recitations are confided to them, as it is ascertained, that they are fully competent to attend to; much of the time, (probably one half,) is spent by the rector in explanations and examinations before the whole school. By this judicious course of proceeding, a high degree of emulation is excited, habits of great industry and activity are maintained, and an education of the best kind is afforded at about one third of the cost of the ordinary grammar schools of our cities. So well convinced are the citizens of Edinburgh of the advantages of this plan of instruction, they have under consideration the establishment of a High School in the new town, in which provision is to be made for the more complete introduction of the monitorial system.

formerly dependent on the authority of the ferula; but at present, the system is happily changed. The emulation produced by the present mode of instruction, and the punishment of additional tasks, joined to the paternal treatment of the rector, are found entirely sufficient, without recourse to the *"argumentum baculinum."*

23d. A fondness for strong liquor appears to be still a national appetency in Scotland, and the more fashionable English beverage of port wine, has not been able to inhibit, even in the most intellectual circles, an occasional resort to the keener stimulus of punch and toddy. Highland whisky is in great repute; but the common kind, obtained by the usual process from fermented grain, finds a copious and ready sale. In walking this morning with several acquaintance, we stopped at a distillery on the borders of the town, merely to observe its prodigious extent. The engine employed in grinding the grain, is a machine of fifty-seven horse power, and moves five pairs of stones. The fermented liquor is distilled by the old fashioned boiler and condenser; but these are of so large a size, that the spirit ran from the worm in a large stream. The grain which is thus sacrificed— I would say, to the turbulent and mischief making, rather than to the jolly god, is chiefly barley. Our next object of curiosity was a very different place. It is a foundation for the education of poor boys, called after the name of the founder, Heriot's Hospital. The building is large and accommodates 175 pupils, who are gratuitously maintained and educated. None are admitted under seven, nor retained over fourteen years of age. There are four masters,—one for Greek, Latin and French,—one for English,—one for mathematics,—and one for writing and book keeping. The pronunciation of the reading master was strongly Scottish. One of the boys, in reading his lesson, pronounced the word *conclude* as it is done in England, sounding the u like oo. "There is no *concloode* there," said the master. The boy was much puzzled, for the word was under his eye. "It is *conclyude*," vociferated the teacher, and the child had to conform. This institution was founded by George Heriot, in 1650. He was a jeweller and goldsmith to James VI. The building makes a handsome appearance, though erected in the antiquated style of turrets at the corners, and a square court within. It is said to have cost £30,000. The revenue left it by the benevolent founder, goes to the maintenance and education of poor and fatherless boys, the sons of free-men, belonging to the city of Edinburgh. Their living and tuition, are said to cost at least thirty pounds each per annum. . . .

25th. Furnished with various letters to Glasgow and Ireland, by my Edinburgh friends, among whom I am happy to rank some, who, by those that go no further than the surface of mind, might be denominated *blue stockings;* but whose actual strength of intellect, would justify them in retorting the epithet:—and last of all, taking a kind leave of those "friends," to whom I was indebted for the first offers of hospitality. I left Edinburgh in the coach for Lanark, where I arrived about five, P. M. The weather was cold and windy, and the road, during much of the distance, lay through a black moor. As my visit here was to the noted establishment of Robert Owen, I repaired to Braksfield House, his residence, and being informed he was at the mills, I immediately took the direction, and met him at New Lanark, in the centre of its busy population.

I know no man of equal celebrity, whose manners are less imposing, and who has more of the candour and openness of a child.

This manufacturing village, of which R. Owen is almost the sole director, has become famous throughout Great Britain. A brief description of it will, I am confident, be agreeable to you; and I shall proceed in it, in the same regular order of occurrences, which I have hitherto observed.

The village presented, upon my entering it, a very neat and interesting appearance, affording, in this respect, a remarkable contrast with old Lanark, about two miles distant, where the coach stopped. It is beautifully situated, on the right bank of the Clyde, which is here a small but romantic stream. It has grown entirely, and recently, out of the manufactory, which is exclusively that of spinning cotton. The whole population is about 2500, 1600 of whom are employed in and about the mills; the rest being mothers, engaged in their domestic affairs, or children too young for labour. The houses are mostly uniform in their structure, built of stone, with a roof of slate, and kept, to all appearance, in great decency, attention being evidently paid to cleanliness throughout the whole establishment. The people were returning from their work, as we approached the mills; and in passing us, they showed a cheerfulness and courtesy of demeanour, which evinced their content; and indeed, their general appearance bespoke health and satisfaction. Two of the boys fell into a dispute as they moved along, and one of them struck the other. Owen reproved them for this misconduct, and told me it was the first blow he had seen struck for years. The avowed principle upon which this large concern is regulated and conducted, is that of humanity to the labourers, in the most extensive and philosophical application of the term. It includes of course the consideration of their welfare, physical, intellectual, and moral. The whole is subjected to a strict discipline; but this discipline is studiously adapted to their wants, and is intended to produce the greatest possible share of cheerfulness and contentment, which their situation will admit of.

No one can converse with Robert Owen half an hour on this subject, without perceiving that his views are, in some respects, original; and without hearing him announce principles, which appear to be at variance with all established notions of the fundamental doctrines of genuine philanthropy. His theory, judging from his writings, as well as his conversation, appears to be that of a visionary schemer; destitute of the principles which we are accustomed to consider as lying at the root of all true benevolence. His practice, however, is obviously the reverse of all this. No man, perhaps, ever took more pains, or exerted himself more successfully, to promote the happiness of his own family, than Owen has done to render his 2500 villagers, harmonious, contented, and happy. The materials he had to work with were very discordant. When he first introduced his particular schemes of reformation, he was regarded by almost everybody with distrust; and so strong was the prejudice against his measures, that he found it difficult to procure, even among the half starving population of the district, labourers, who would consent to fall in with his regulations. At present, he has applications from far and near, to a

greater amount than he can possibly furnish with employment. But to proceed with the description.

After taking coffee in the house of one of his clerks, we
awaited the hour of school. A neat and commodious building has been erected for the purpose of instruction, in a
pleasant spot near the centre of the village. The manufactories close uniformly at half past six; hence none of that
overstraining by which the health of children and young
people are so much injured in other manufacturing towns,
is here permitted. The evenings of the youth are devoted to
the schools, and as many of the adults as choose, may also
avail themselves of the instruction of the teachers. The first
room we entered was a singing school, in which were both
boys and girls, arranged on benches, and singing in chorus,
under the direction of an instructer. On listening to the
words of the song, judge my surprise on finding, that, instead of a hymn, it was a love song, beginning with,

"And will you love me, deary."

Passing into the next room, I found there a music-school.
Half a dozen or more little fellows had each a flute, and
were piping it away in notes that did not preserve the
strictest accordance. The next apartment we entered, was a
large room for reading, writing, and arithmetic. Some of
the pupils in this room were pretty well advanced in age.
From this we went into a large room above-stairs, where
were fifty or sixty young people, both boys and girls, attending to the lessons of a dancing-master. These young
students of the "merry mood," were not equipped in all the
gaiety of a fashionable ball-room; though there was, probably, as great a diversity of costume as would be seen in a

"belle assemblée" of Paris or Edinburgh. In fact, they were in much the same style as that in which they had left the manufactory,—some with shoes, and others barefoot. The dancing-master, too, was the painter and glazier of the village; who, after handling the brush all day, took up the fiddle in the evening, and instructed his motley group in the profound mysteries of the highland reel.

Owen's aim in all this is to make his villagers a *moral* and happy people. He wishes to relieve their minds and bodies as much as possible from the fatigues of labour, and he goes to work in his own way. He does not, I believe, compel any of his subjects to dance; but, if they choose it, he gives them the opportunity of learning how. Human nature, he says, is not understood by any class of society, and he has discovered that dancing is one of the means of reforming vicious habits. This he thinks it effects by promoting cheerfulness and contentment, and thus diverting the attention from things that are vile and degrading. Before the evening school closes, the pupils all collect into one room, and sing a hymn.

After leaving this singular school of moral reformation, he took me home with him, and gave me a kind introduction to his wife and family. He is so zealous in his wishes to benefit society, and so confident of the soundness of his views, and the importance of his plans of improvement, that if his visiters are inclined to hear, he will entertain them as long as they please, with the details of his system. His manners, as I have already remarked, are altogether unobtrusive. He wishes to gain his point by illustration and persuasion; but as it is impossible to listen to him without objecting to some of his fundamental positions, argument becomes unavoidable. We sat up till twelve, engaged in a wordy warfare upon the best means of correcting the abuses of society, and making the whole world a band of brothers. He is confident that this would be the happy result, were his measures universally adopted. Pauperism would become unknown; for every individual would be at liberty to exert his faculties of body and mind, in such a way, as to provide most efficaciously for all his natural wants. Wars would cease, because no one would have the inclination to invade the rights of another. Idleness would vanish, because every man would find more pleasure in useful activity. The turbulent and angry passions would subside, for every one would find it his interest to treat others rationally and kindly. The pursuit of gain and the thirst for riches would disappear, because every man, finding himself perfectly comfortable, would have no wish to be richer than his neighbour. Ambition, as a passion of the human breast, would die a natural death; for, in this happy state of things, it would find no aliment to subsist upon. In short, such would be the just and equal balance between the wants of mankind, and the means of supply—between rational desire, and the power of gratification, that discontent and distress would become unknown.

This, you will conclude, is to be the millenium of *Christianity,* and brought about by the mild and powerful influence of the *Gospel.* But here you are mistaken. Christianity is to have nothing to do with it. The world has always been in an error, and human nature has never been understood. In point of merit, there is no great difference in the various systems of religion. Christianity, Judaism, Mahommedanism, Hindooism, and all other

94

creeds, are founded in prejudice and delusion. All you have to do, is to place men exactly in that situation in which every one will find it most conducive to his pleasure and comfort to act justly, and to study the welfare of others as well as his own.

As it might be imagined, there is very little logic in Owen's reasoning. You may encircle him with the cords of reason and argument, but instead of labouring to untie the knots, he snaps the string, and takes his stand in another position. He neither interrupts nor contradicts one. His good nature suffers no perturbation, either from argument, wit, or ridicule. Though he has no religion of his own, holding to no system that has ever been promulgated, and even believing that they have all done much more harm than good; he is willing others should enjoy theirs, provided they fulfil its duties without molesting their neighbours.[1] His favourite maxim is that "man is the creature of circumstance." His character is always formed by others, and not by himself; surround him therefore with circumstances, favourable to the development of his best dispositions, and he will become exactly the being which he ought. But, instead of connecting this sentiment, as the Christian religion teaches us to do, with the motives which spring from our immortal prospects, and with our dependence on the promises and the providence of God, he rejects this as unnecessary, or even regards it as a prejudice that may do more

---

[1] That it may not be supposed that I have misunderstood, or willingly misrepresented Robert Owen's views of religion, I avail myself of an address of his to the editor of the Limerick Chronicle, on this particular topic. The following is the letter:—

# REPORTS ON EUROPEAN EDUCATION

*Limerick, Jan. 27, 1823.*

SIR—In your paper of Saturday last, I am requested by a gentleman who signed himself "A Citizen," to explain what my views are respecting religion, with the arrangements for its support in the intended colonies—and, as I feel the time is arrived for this development, I meet his wishes with pleasure.

I have often been urged to declare myself in favour of some one sect of religion, and it is, perhaps, due to the public, that I should now explain my sentiments on this important subject.

For nearly forty years I have studied the religious systems of the world, with the most sincere desire to discover one that was devoid of error—one to which my mind and soul could consent; but the more I have examined the faiths, and practices which they have produced, the more error in each has been made manifest to me; and I am now prepared to say, that all, without a single exception, contain too much error to be of any utility in the present advanced state of the human mind. There are truths in each religion, as well as errors in all; but, if I have not been too much prejudiced by early education, and surrounding circumstances, to judge impartially between them, there are more valuable truths in the Christian Scriptures than in others,—but a religion to be pure and undefiled, and to produce the proper effect upon the life and conduct of every human being, and to become universal, must be so true, that all who run may read, and so reading, may fully comprehend. A religion of this character, must be devoid of forms, ceremonies, and mysteries, for those constitute the errors of all the existing systems, and of all those which have hitherto created anger, and produced violence and bloodshed throughout society. A religion devoid of error will not depend for its support upon any name whatever. No name, not even Deity itself, can make falsehood true—no name, not even Deity itself, can make truth into falsehood. A pure and genuine religion, therefore, will not require for its support, or for its universal promulgation and acceptance by the human race, any name whatever, nor ought, except the irresistible truths which it shall contain. Such religion will possess whatever is valuable in each, and exclude whatever is erroneous in all, and, in due time, a religion of this character, freed from every inconsistency, shall be promulgated. Then will the world be in possession of principles which, without any exception, will produce corresponding practices, and then all shall see, face to face, clearly and distinctly, and no longer through a glass, darkly. In the mean time, however, while the change shall be gradually working in the minds of those who have been compelled to receive error, mixed with truth, it is intended, that no violence shall be offered to the conscience of any one, and that, in the proposed new villages, full provision shall be made for the performance of religious worship, according to the practices of the country in which the villages shall be situated. That to the extent which the present form of society admits, there shall be full liberty of conscience for every individual, and all will be recommended to have real charity for their brethren of the human race, who have been made to differ from them in opinions, which all must now perceive have been formed by the geographical circumstances of their birth.

Ample provision will also be made by the inhabitants of each village for the support, in the highest comfort, of the ministers of the respective persuasions, and, in consequence, all of them will be held in estimation, according to their real usefulness in the community.

To me it appears, that this mode of proceeding can alone calm the present irritations of society, and prepare the human mind for the reception of that divine charity, which, when received, will insure peace to every bosom, and extend its beneficial influence over the whole earth.

ROBERT OWEN.

harm than good. He even maintains the opinion, that the doctrine of future accountability, has been the occasion of most of the evils with which the world has been afflicted! That such sentiments should be found in union with a practical philanthropy, apparently as disinterested as it is beneficent and effective, is a circumstance which has seldom occurred in the history of civilization.

His wife appears to be a religious and pious person, educating her children in the belief in which she was brought up. To this her husband makes no opposition; nor does he object at all to the religious exercises of the different sects, which prevail among the labourers at New Lanark.

26th. The servant, on entering my chamber this morning, with a dressing apparatus, brought with him also a Bible. Whether this was by the particular direction of his master, or whether my host usually takes this method with his guests, to denote his liberality, I do not know. It was the first instance of the kind which has occurred to me, since my arrival in Europe, though I have not unfrequently found a Bible on the table of my lodging room.

After breakfast we went to the mills, and spent the interval till a late dinner hour, in viewing the improvements and in walking to the falls of the Clyde, about a mile above the village, and surveying the delightful scenery of that region. The buildings of the factory are very large, and the machinery is in excellent style. The whole of it is made on the premises, by workmen skilled in all the complicated operations of metal and wood, connected with the fabrication and erection of the extensive apparatus of such an establishment. The hours of labour are from six till nine, when they breakfast; from ten to two, when they dine; and from three to half past six; making in the whole ten and a half hours. The wages of the spinners vary from 10s. to 1s. 6d. per week, according to age and ability. The education of their children is given to them without cost, or at least upon very moderate terms, though its expense to the establishment is not less than £700 per annum. At present, every family cooks its own provision, but a building is nearly completed which is designed as a kitchen for the whole village; and a refectory in which about one-fourth of them may take their meals at a time. Owen believes, that from four to five thousand pounds a year will be saved by this arrangement, besides the superior training and improved habits it will produce. The second story of this large building will contain a reading and lecture room, and a ball room for all the adult fashionables of the village; for I am told, that were I to see these people in their "Sunday decorations," I should be astonished at the contrast. A library is also nearly in readiness for the use of the villagers. All the principal buildings are warmed by steam, and a plan is on foot to extend this mode of warming to the dwelling houses, after the necessity of cooking in these shall be superseded by the general kitchen. There are four distinct religious societies among the labourers; viz. the National Kirk, the Gaelic, Methodists, and Independents.

Inglesby, a famous conjuror, has been exhibiting at Lanark his thousand tricks, and has obtained leave to show his feats in the new town to-morrow evening. But this, I believe, is to be at the expense of the work people themselves. This man travels with his daughter, in a handsome equipage; having, it is said, realized a fortune by his dexterous exploits.

Such assiduous and expensive efforts to ameliorate the condition of labourers, as have been made at New Lanark, have occasioned manufacturers in other places, to prophesy its dissolution, from a belief that such heavy expenses could not be supported by the profits. The whole concern belongs to a few proprietors, (in addition to Robert Owen,) who joined in the enterprize, from a wish to give a fair trial to a lenient and benevolent system of management; and so far from its having proved a loss to the company, it has yielded them an interest of twelve and a half per cent on the original stock.

Large manufactories, in which young people, of various ages, and of both sexes, are indiscriminately employed, are considered as unfriendly to morals; but it would appear from the results of New Lanark, that the superior instruction here bestowed and the more elevated tone of social intercourse which arises from it, tend to counteract the vulgar propensities and to prevent the evils which so commonly prevail in those crowded establishments.

We visited the schools again to-day. The children are not allowed to go into the factories, till they are about ten years of age, but are kept till that time steadily at the day schools. One apartment of the school afforded a novel and pleasing spectacle. It consisted of a great number of children, from one to three or four years of age. They are assembled in a large room, under the care of a judicious female, who allows them to amuse themselves with various selected toys, and occasionally collects the oldest into a class, and teaches them their letters. They appeared perfectly happy, and as we entered, the little creatures ran in groups, to seize their benefactor by the hand, or to pull him by the coat, with the most artless simplicity. This baby school is of great consequence to the establishment, for it enables mothers to shut up their houses in security, and to attend to their duties in the factory, without concern for their families.[1]

The scenery at the falls of the Clyde, is picturesque and beautiful. It reminded me of Passaic in New Jersey, though there is more wildness and sublimity at the latter place, and the perpendicular height of the fall is greater.

In the course of our rambles to-day, my attentive friend manifested the same zeal for the welfare of the indigent

[1] Schools upon a similar plan, have been since established in several other places, particularly in Westminster, London, and in the city of Bristol. If rightly planned and conducted, the tendency of such infant seminaries cannot but be propitious to the best interests of the poor, to morals and to humanity. Children are admitted in them, from two to five years of age; and by various contrivances, attended with little expense, they are so amused as to remain all the day long contented and happy; while, at the same time, the waywardness of their tempers is overcome by the most rational and gentle means, and they are gradually initiated into the rudiments of knowledge, by methods which excite neither pain nor aversion. Mothers, by being thus relieved from the charge of their younger children during the day, are at liberty to go out to work, or to attend more uninterruptedly to their concerns at home; and children, thus early introduced to habits of order and decency of behaviour, must become more docile and fit subjects for the Lancasterian schools.

An interesting exposition of the rise, progress, plan, and utility of these infant schools, has recently been published by Dr. Pole of Bristol, which deserve to be read by every person interested in the welfare and education of the poor in large cities, and other populous places.

classes throughout the kingdom, that he has shown in his writings and on various public occasions, and the same confidence in the issue of his plans of reform. It is in vain that his friends have urged to him, that the total destitution of religious faith and principle which marks his scheme, must inevitably, in such a community as this, prevent its adoption; or if adopted as the means of national relief, prevent its success. No argument can dislodge him from his strong hold. It is not, perhaps, wonderful that the extraordinary success of his plans in this now interesting village, should have given a confidence to his opinions, which, under other and very different circumstances, would not be justified.

There is not, I apprehend, to be found in any part of the world, a manufacturing village, or a community of equal extent, composed of persons indiscriminately brought together, without any peculiar bond of fraternity, in which so much order, good government, tranquillity and rational happiness prevail. It affords an eminent and instructive example of the good that may be effected by well directed efforts to promote the real comforts, and I may add, the morality of the indigent and labouring classes. No person, I am persuaded, can retire from this charming village, without a renewed conviction of the vast influence which an enlightened philanthropy may exert over the destinies and happiness of mankind. But still, it is evident that any inference drawn from the results of New Lanark, would be very unfairly applied to colonies or communities, in which the precepts of Christianity were totally neglected, and all the sanctions of religion entirely withheld. Here, the moral influence of the Gospel is in active operation. The inhabitants of the village are attentive to their religious observances. The founder of the establishment, David Dale, the father in law of Robert Owen, under whose superintendence the village acquired considerable reputation, was a religious man.[1] The other proprietors also, (the principal of whom are our friends*.*****, and ****** ******, of London,) are solicitous to preserve undiminished among these people, the force of religious obligation, and they add the weight of their names, their injunctions and example, to that effect.

But Owen, as I have before hinted, goes far beyond this. He considers New Lanark as affording a very imperfect specimen indeed of the happiness and dignity of a community, governed solely by the principles of an enlightened reason, and freed entirely from that mass of prejudice and superstition, which the various religious systems of the world, one and all, have saddled upon the human mind. Nothing can be more simple too, than his plan of reform. Man is the creature of circumstance. He has nothing to do

---

[1] In the reports of the "Society for bettering the condition of the Poor," vol. 2, the village is stated to contain 1500 inhabitants, "of whom all capable of work, are employed about the mills—of these, there are 500 children fed, clothed and educated by Mr. Dale. Out of 3000 employed during a period of twelve years from 1785 to 1797, only 14 have died, and not one has been the subject of judicial punishment. Mr. Dale has engaged three regular masters, who instruct the lesser children during the day; in the evening they are assisted by seven others, one of whom teaches writing. *On Sundays, they conduct them to the place of Divine Worship, and in the evening of Sunday, attend to assist them, by religious and moral instruction."* Such was New Lanark, under its pious founder, David Dale, in 1800.

with the formation of his own character, his own faith, or his own opinions. Born and educated in China, he would follow Confucius; in India, he would worship Juggernaut: in Turkey, he would be a Mussulman, and in Rome, a Papist. He is ferocious, placable, avaricious, or generous, merely as circumstances impel him. All you have to do, therefore, is to surround him with circumstances exactly adapted to the dispositions and habits he ought to possess, and he would become just what he should be. His evil propensities would be either entirely suppressed, or they would be rendered harmless, by the irresistible weight of the good example around him. Such is the philosophy of a man, who maintains that human nature is not understood by any class of society; that there must be an entire change in all existing institutions; that the world has ever been in an error; and that all the governments and religions that have ever existed, have done little more than heap one prejudice and delusion upon another. A new light, however, is now dawning upon the world, and the germ of a glorious revolution has at length sprung forth at New Lanark, and will unquestionably spread throughout the earth!! There is no want of candour in Robert Owen. He makes no false claims to originality in his principles, though he maintains, I believe, that he is new, in his views of the best mode of promoting general reformation. It delights him to find that other persons have held the same doctrines that he does. He has written and published much, in illustration of his plans, and he has enforced them by public discourses in various parts of the kingdom. Very few indeed, are yet convinced; but he still fully believes that his principles are gaining ground, and will eventually triumph over all opposition, as certainly as the light of the sun overpowers all the minor luminaries.

That his views are extravagant, and, considered in relation to the extent to which he proposes to carry his plans, quite absurd, I think it can require but very little reasoning to prove. If he could point out a single instance in the history of the whole world, in which communities of men have remained united for any considerable length of time, studious of each other's welfare, and pursuing a course of justice and moderation with all around them, independently of the powerful influence of religion, or of the stimulus of some common danger, or common ambition excited by some peculiarity of personal or local condition, we might admit that his theory is not without some basis to rest upon.

But although we have multiplied instances, in which the selfish passions are effectively controlled by surrounding circumstances, yet in every case within my recollection, there is an operative principle far different from, and far superior to, that of considerations of mere temporary advantage. In all military communities, to which Owen sometimes refers as an example of unity of action, the primary motive is either pay, patriotism, or ambition; and when these bodies are once formed, the controling principle is despotic force, or military law. In all civil associations, in which property is held in common, as in the instance of the Shakers and Harmonists of America, the fraternizing principle is evidently the force of religious persuasion, founded upon some peculiar views of Christianity. And so in all other cases, the connective bond is either a common sentiment of religious duty, or a common feeling of external danger. Now, there can be no doubt, that an individual or a family, depressed by poverty, and distressed by actual or anticipated suffering, would willingly become an obedient member of a community, which would afford them an adequate protection from the evils they have endured. And if, on such a change, they experience a greater share of comfort and happiness, than they have before enjoyed, their wants easily satisfied, and their children well educated and taught to labour, they may, doubtless, resign all views of further change, and willingly conform to the duties of their new allotment.

As a means therefore, of promoting the welfare of the poor, far more effectual as it regards both their morals and their happiness, and infinitely less expensive and oppressive, than the existing system of workhouses and poor laws, and forced maintenance, such manufacturing and agricultural communities as New Lanark, and that before alluded to in Holland, I have no doubt, may become eminently beneficial: but to suppose, as Robert Owen does, that all human enterprise can be circumscribed within his quadrangular villages, and his agricultural colonies; that the vast policy of cities, the energies of commerce, and the powerful rivalship of nations, can be reduced to such mathematical dimensions; or that it would be eventually profitable to the human mind, to have them so reduced, is, I cannot but believe, to betray a wonderful deficiency in the knowledge of human nature.

But independently of the utter insufficiency and emptiness, of any extensive scheme of human improvement, which does not embrace the inherent force of moral power, —and of all attempts at moral power, which do not recognise its foundation upon religious faith and the sanctions of futurity—Robert Owen's views of what he calls the "influence of circumstances," carry him, I think, to an extravagant length. I have no belief that the human mind, when its powers are perfectly expanded by education, can be subjected to the mere machinery of circumstances, to the extent which his system supposes. How often do we discover, in particular individuals, an inherent vigour, which, bursting the shackles of education, and disdaining the control of surrounding examples, soars into a new sphere, and exhibits the human character in a new and peculiar light. And may we not suppose, that in proportion to the extension of education, and the advancement of science and the arts, will be the frequency of such instances of aberration from the ordinary track of circumstances?

Such powers and propensities have not been planted in our mental soil for unimportant purposes; and it cannot be the part of a sound and discriminating philanthropy, so to pare down their exuberances, and to give them such an artificial direction, as to injure their native strength, or prevent their natural uses.

There is something in the great mixture of human things, which is beyond our comprehension; and certainly beyond our control. That a vast amount of good can be done by benevolent effort, and that no age was ever more distinguished for a wise and extended beneficence than the present, I fully believe. Nevertheless, it will be dangerous to attempt too much,—to make an effort to accomplish what the moral power of society is unable to execute.

That every attempt to produce a material change in the exterior relations of mankind, upon a system which even admits that the bonds of religious union are useless and unnecessary, must inevitably fail, is my firm persuasion; and no person, I think, can spend a day at this village, as I have done, in company with its intelligent director, without re-

gretting that so much practical talent and such unaffected
benevolence, should be found united with the cold specu-
lations of a stubborn scepticism, which finds no motives for
the cultivation of its highest powers of mind and heart, but
such as are limited to this momentary stage of existence.
Such a union presents, as it appears to me, quite an anomaly
in the human character.

In our return from New Lanark to dinner, we were met
by a woman, who earnestly solicited a place in the manufactory, she said she had eleven *bairns,* and had come a
considerable distance to obtain the situation. But as there
was no immediate opening for such a family, her petition
could not be granted.[1] . . . :—

The Lancasterian school of Manchester is admitted to be
the largest, and one of the best organized free schools in
England.

The house is a plain edifice of brick, and is capable of
seating in one room, nearly 1100 children. It was built by

[1] If I have in any respect mistaken, or in any degree misrepresented, the views of Robert Owen, I am persuaded that *he* would
be one of the last to regard it as an intentional error. No man
more openly courts investigation, or, with more candour, calls
upon those who have seen his village, and heard him explain his
views, to state their objections. His plans for improving the condition of the labouring classes, and for the relief of the indigent,
are now pretty well known, both in Europe and America; and
could they be deprived of their most objectionable feature, (the
exclusion of their extensive generalities, I cannot but believe that
his scheme of establishing agricultural and manufacturing villages, if placed under the management of a mild and generous
enthusiasm, like his own, would have a most beneficial influence
in many parts of the world.

subscription and donation, and is supported by public bounty. Both sexes are accommodated in one general apartment. It was opened in 1813, and the principal teacher, J. H. P\*\*\*\*\*\*, who relinquished his charge not long since, has been uncommonly successful in organizing and training the pupils. A book is kept in which every visiter is requested to record his observations relative to the order of the school, the progress and behaviour of the pupils, &c. These testimonials are almost universally flattering to the teacher. Among them I noticed that of Dr. M\*\*\*\*, of our city, who was very favourably impressed with the plan and improvement of the school. The arithmetical performances of some of the boys really surprised me; and they served to show how rapidly and dextrously the mind, as well as the body, may be made to move by diligent and judicious instruction. About half a dozen boys were called up before me, and such questions as the following were put to them, which they were to solve altogether by a mental exercise, without slate, or paper, or making any use whatever of their hands.

If a grain of gold is worth $7\frac{1}{2}d$. what will be the value of a pound? Ans. £180.

If an ounce of silver is worth £4 16s. 2d. what will be the value of a grain? Ans. 2d 1 gr.$^{37}\!/_{60}$.

If a lb. of sugar is worth $7\frac{3}{4}d$. what will be the value of 1 cwt.? Ans. £3 12s. 4d.

If 1 cwt. of sugar is worth £5 16s. 4d. what is that per lb.? Ans. 12d. 1 gr. $^{6}\!/_{7}$.

If $1\frac{1}{2}d$. per lb. is gained by selling cheese, at 15d. per lb. what did it cost per cwt.? Ans. £6 6s.

If cheese, which cost £4 3s. 6d. per cwt. is sold for $7\frac{1}{2}d$. per lb. what will the gain or loss per cwt.? Ans. 13s. 6d. loss.

If 15s. per ton is gained by selling coal at 10s. 4d. per cwt. what did they cost per ton? Ans. £9 11s. 8d.

These questions, with some others of a similar kind, were arranged on a printed paper, with the sums, or prices, all left blank. I was requested to fill up any of those blanks, privately, with any prices I pleased, and then announce the question. This being done, the boys each strove to give the answer first; and, in almost every instance, two or more of them answered at once, and in less time than a man would take to count six, distinctly. The replies were, *generally, immediate.*

These boys, I believe, were all monitors; and had been for some time under the special instruction of the master, separately from the school.

The desks, or fixtures, in this school, are on iron frames, and the benches are firmly attached to them. Many of the desks are designed both for writers on sand and on slates, by having a lid to fold over the sand. Pieces of tin, with the alphabet stamped upon them, are also employed in teaching beginners their letters, and to spell easy words. The advantages of such institutions as this, more especially in places like Manchester, which so abounds with the children of indigent labourers, all will admit to be incalculable.

The evening was spent greatly to my taste, in a small circle of literary friends, among whom was the philosophic D*****. It was at once amusing and instructive to observe the simplicity and composure with which he listened to my information relative to the many inquiries and remarks respecting him, which were made by some of the most distinguished philosophers of Paris, Geneva, Milan, &c. The integrity and simplicity of his character, are as remarkable as the originality of his mind, and the acuteness of his perceptions on subjects of science and philosophy.

27th. Having no where seen, in England, one of the national, or Bell's schools, in operation, my friend D. conducted me this morning to one of the two which are established in Manchester. The mode of instruction differs essentially from the plan of Lancaster, and certainly possesses some features that are very valuable. It is less mechanical, and it exercises, to a great extent, the judgment and understanding of the pupils. Much stress is laid upon an acquaintance with the Scriptures; and the method of instruction is better devised for making the children thoroughly acquainted with them. It is a more expensive mode than the other. Instead of printed forms, or lessons, which, when suspended, serve a whole class, each pupil, or, at least, every two, must have his book. The system, I should imagine, requires more skill and management on the part of the teacher, and is not so easily reducible to monitorial government. Each of the two schools contain about 300 boys, and as many girls; the sexes being entirely separated by an intervening wall. The children made a very decent appearance. The floor is of brick, to prevent noise, and, probably, to promote cleanliness. The girls are taught in this school not only to sew and knit, but to *cut out* the more necessary parts of wearing apparel. This is an important feature in this charity; for too many females, especially among the labouring classes, are totally ignorant of the art of making the most simple article of dress. . . .

## II. VICTOR COUSIN

Selections from

## REPORT ON THE STATE OF PUBLIC INSTRUC-
## TION IN PRUSSIA

Addressed to the Court de Montalivet, Peer of France,
Minister of Public Instruction and Ecclesiastical Affairs;
by M. Victor Cousin, Peer of France, Councilor of State,
Professor of Philosophy, Member of the Institute, and
of the Royal Council of Public Instruction. Translated
by Sarah Austin. Second Edition. Effingham Wilson,
London, 1836.

## II. VICTOR COUSIN (1792–1867)

### and his

### *REPORT ON THE STATE OF PUBLIC INSTRUCTION IN PRUSSIA* [1]

VICTOR COUSIN was born in Paris, November 28, 1792. His early education was received at the *Lycée Charlemagne,* and, at the age eighteen, he entered the Normal School where he later became a lecturer on philosophy. During these years he was influenced by Royer-Collard (a teacher of Scottish philosophy), by Laromiguiere (a follower after the philosophy of Locke and Condillac), and by Maine de Biran, a teacher of psychology. Later, he studied German philosophy and had an opportunity to become acquainted with Hegel, Schelling, and Jacobi. In 1824, while he was in Germany, he was imprisoned for a brief period on some political charge and remained under suspicion for more than three years. During this time, however, his philosophy took definite shape, and in 1826 he published the *Fragmens philosophiques.* Between 1825 and 1840, he was engaged in editing the works of Proclus and Descartes and in translating the works of Plato.

Cousin's greatest work came as the result of an appointment with François Pierre Guillaume Guizot (1787–1874)

[1] Only brief selections could be reproduced in the present volume. The original spelling and punctuation are followed.

to the University of Paris in 1828. He attained high distinction as a lecturer, and, in 1832, was appointed as a member of the Council of Public Instruction in Guizot's ministry, after making a trip to Germany (in 1831) to study the public-school system of that country. The results of this study were published in 1831 under the title *Rapport sur l'etat de l' instruction publique en Prusse.*

Cousin's report dealt especially with elementary education, teacher training, and the organization and administration of public education. It was a very convincing document. Cousin considered the Prussian school law a very excellent and comprehensive legislative enactment regarding primary education and stated that such a law for France was absolutely necessary. It was largely due to the influence of Cousin's report that the French law of 1833 was enacted. Under that legislation, provision was made for organizing primary and higher primary instruction in France, for additional schools for the training of teachers, for school inspectors representing the State, and for other educational reform. This act became the foundation upon which a national system of elementary education was developed in France.

The report of Cousin was translated into English and published in England in 1834 and a part of it, dealing especially with the administrative organization of education in Prussia, was reprinted in New York in 1835. The publication of the report in this country was made at the beginning of the period of wide interest in state school support and control and seems to have had considerable influence, although it probably led to legislation in only one or two states. The report served, however, to emphasize the importance of state control of education and the training of teachers in normal schools supported by the state. Its influence is widely apparent, especially in Michigan and Massachusetts.

In Michigan, the report impressed John D. Pierce, who became the first head of the public-school system of that state, and Isaac E. Crary, who served as chairman of the committee on education in the Michigan constitutional convention of 1835. These men worked to make education a distinct branch of the new state government, to create a chief state school office, and to establish schools upon the basis of state support and state control rather than local support and local control. Pierce became the first superintendent of public instruction in that state. Later, a superintendent of public instruction in Michigan said that the system which the framers of the constitution of that state intended to establish, and the conception, powers, and duties of the office of state superintendent of public instruction "were derived from Prussia." The report of Cousin also seems to have had influence upon Charles Brooks, James G. Carter, and Horace Mann in Massachusetts, particularly in the matter of the establishment of state normal schools. The descriptions of the teacher-training institutions in Prussia, which were praised by Cousin and other reporters of European conditions during this time, apparently promoted in this country the movement for training teachers.

Cousin became minister of public instruction in France in 1840, continuing at the same time as director of the Normal School. He later retired from public life and died January 13, 1867.

The report of Victor Cousin is among the most important of all the reports on educational conditions in Europe during the second quarter of the nineteenth century. It was made to the Count de Montalivet, Minister of Public Instruction and Ecclesiastical Affairs of France, in 1831. Cousin seems to have had ready access to all sources of information on the schools of Prussia. He bore from the Minister of Public Instruction in France a letter to the Baron von Altenstein, the Minister of Public Instruction in Berlin, whom Cousin had previously met. Cousin had interviews with the Minister who assigned to the Frenchman "one of his confidential councillors to give me, not only every possible information, but whatever documents, whether printed or manuscript, I might desire. . . . Nothing that I had the least desire to know was concealed from me." . . . By his own observation, he was able to verify the statements and explanations of the educational officials. After procuring and mastering the laws and regulations dealing with all phases of education in Prussia, Cousin then set out "to verify them by accurate and detailed inspection." His report was made in four sections: (1) general organization of public instruction, (2) primary instruction, (3) secondary instruction (the gymnasium), and (4) higher instruction (the universities). In the present study, consideration is confined chiefly to the first and second parts.

Sarah Austin's preface to her translation, the text used here, is uncommonly significant. It reveals a growing interest in public education in England among the "enlightened and benevolent men",—an interest which Cousin's report apparently had helped to widen. The report had been favorably commented on in the foremost journals of the country, in the pulpit, and by leading men in public life.

Such "cheering symptoms of a general tendency of the public mind of England towards the subject of National Education, have been watched with solicitude and hailed with delight by all who are impressed with its importance." Moreover, the Factory Commission, the Poor Law Commission, and other public and private inquiries and reports had "tended more and more to reveal the extent and urgency of our own intellectual and moral wants." Especially significant were the favorable opinions of "a system of education in full activity among a whole people," such as Cousin had described as having been developed and maintained in Prussia, opinions which were strongly expressed by such journals as the *Foreign Quarterly Review, Edinburgh Review, Quarterly Review, Eclectic Review, Journal of Education,* and others.

The *Foreign Quarterly Review* viewed Cousin's report as an incontestable proof, "by the solid and substantial argument of complete practical success," that a system of national education was not visionary, not merely a chimera, "not a phantom of the brain, imagined by dreaming philosophers; but a mode of insuring the elementary instruction of all children, which may be established and maintained not less than any army or navy." The *Edinburgh Review* approved the report from beginning to end, as a work of "the most unbiased wisdom." This journal expressed the belief that the report established principles and conclusions to which England might well appeal in attempts to improve its educational arrangements. The *Spectator* also recommended the work of Cousin. "The public mind has been for some time tending towards considering the propriety of national education. There are signs abroad which ought to stimulate thought into action." The *Leeds Mercury* rejoiced that Englishmen now had the description of the Prussian system before them and believed that "it will soon begin to be duly appreciated, and that some attempt worthy of a free and enlightened people and a liberal legislature will be made to naturalize among us." *Bell's New Messenger* expressed surprise and delight with the account of the Prussian school system. The *Athenæum* said that Mrs. Austin, in translating the report, deserved the gratitude of the country, not merely because of the ability and fidelity with which she had performed the undertaking, but also because she had drawn "the attention of her countrymen to their most important interests."

Mrs. Austin had done her task well and with honest zeal. The report moved her, and she thought it must "touch any human heart." It had merit not only as the account of a legislative plan for education but as the account of "a system living and working" in the lives of the German people. She saw the need in England for such a system. The times were ready for it, she believed. "The men who, in their several classes, were content to tread step by step in the paths wherein their fathers trod, are gone. Society is no longer a calm current, but a tossing sea. Reverence for tradition, for authority, is gone. In such a state of things, who can deny the absolute necessity for national education?"

She wrote fervidly and with compelling logic in behalf of compulsory school attendance legislation, which was an important feature of education in Prussia, although she was fully aware of the deep and prevalent belief in England at the time "that the prime excellence of a government is to let alone." Compulsory school attendance would be an infringement of liberty, it was believed. But Mrs. Austin appealed for the children. Is exemption from compulsion to attend school salutary or pernicious? she asked. Shall the whole future lives of the children be sacrificed to the present interests of the persons who have the disposal of them? She argued that government should secure to the children "for life the blessings of physical, moral, and intellectual health."

She maintained also that the interference which the government had lately exercised in behalf of children in manufacturing areas had settled an important principle, had shown the right of the state "to interpose to rescue children from influences believed to be detrimental to their moral and intellectual character." Twice had this right been formally recognized and proclaimed in the Court of Chancery—the right to remove the child wholly out of the selfish power of the parent. Parental authority was subject to abuse and should be checked. If that authority could be invaded for the purpose of protecting children from one class of evils it could in another, she believed. Children should be sheltered from "the rudeness and the apathy of the fathers." She pointed to the antiquity of *Schulpflichtigkeit*—the obligation to send children to school—and its beneficent influences, and sought to correct "the erroneous notion prevalent here, that the legal obligation to educate children is a modern invention of the 'military and despotic government' of Prussia." She undertook also to refute the popular view that a national system of education was antireligious and to answer those "guilty of great inconsistency as to the ends and objects of education." Zealous champions of education had pointed to it as the way to advancement, to knowledge as power, to learning as the means of personal betterment, and yet they complained or feared that education would set the people "above their station, disgust them with labour, make them ambitious, envious, dissatisfied!" The same claims for and the same fears of education were being made and expressed in the United States at the same time that the inconsistency in English thought was being pointed out by Mrs. Austin. She also laid particular emphasis upon the necessity of an unfailing supply of trained teachers and pointed to the need for schools for the training of teachers.

## REPORT ON THE STATE OF PUBLIC
## INSTRUCTION IN PRUSSIA

In Prussia, the minister of public instruction enjoys a
rank and authority equal to those of any of his colleagues;
the care of all affairs connected with the public exercise of
religion falls also within his department, as in France;
and as the secondary schools of medicine, and all establishments relative to public health, belong to this ministry, it
bears the official denomination of Ministry of Public Instruction, of Ecclesiastical and Medical Affairs (*Ministerium
des öffentlichen Unterrichts, der geistlichen-und medicinal-
Angelegenheiten*).

In Prussia, as in other states, public instruction long
formed a part of the business of the Minister of the Interior.
It was not until 1819 that a special department of administration was consecrated to this object, with Baron von Altenstein at its head. I regard this change as of the highest
importance. In the first place the service is much better
performed, there being more complete unity in the central
point, from which all emanates and to which all is addressed; and the authority, being more cogent, is better
obeyed. In the next place, the high rank assigned to the
head of public instruction marks the respect in which everything relating to that important subject is held by the government; hence science assumes her proper place in the
state. Civilization, the intellectual and moral interests of

society, have their appointed ministry. This ministry embraces everything relating to science, and consequently all schools, libraries, and kindred institutions,—such as botanic gardens, museums, cabinets, the lower schools of surgery and medicine, academies of music, &c. Indeed it is perfectly natural that the minister who has the faculties of medicine under his control, should also direct the inferior schools and institutions relating to that science; that the minister who presides over the faculties of letters and science, should also preside over scientific and literary academies; that the minister who is the guardian of public instruction, should be guardian of the great collections and libraries, without which instruction is impossible.

Unquestionably all classification must be in some degree arbitrary; and there are consequently some establishments at Berlin and in the provinces, which are claimed both by the minister of the interior and by the minister of public instruction. In general, however, the line of demarcation which separates their provinces is distinctly traced. The ministry of the interior, in principle, comprehends all those institutions which relate to the *application* of science,—to manufacturers, commerce, public works, &c., even when instruction is connected with such institutions. The ministry of public instruction comprehends everything of a moral and intellectual character. All establishments which bear this character, from the highest to the lowest, even when they touch on those in the department of the minister of the interior, belong to the province of the minister of public instruction, and depend directly or indirectly on him. I am well aware, Sir, that this is not the case with us. The greater part of the institutions connected with art, science, and literature are not within the limits of your authority. I regret it extremely; not for the sake of the increase of that authority, but for the manifest interest of art, science, and letters, as well as for that of public education, which is thus, as it were, without a base, and deprived of the instruments it needs. My opinion on this head is known to you: it is founded on reasons I have often laid before you. I withhold them here, where my only business is to make you acquainted with the whole extent of the legal powers of the minister of public instruction in Prussia.

Here, as in France, the superintendence of ecclesiastical affairs is united to that of public instruction. This union is founded on the very nature of things, and on the relation of the two services, which touch at all points, and often are blended in the same persons; many learned divines being useful professors, and the faculties of theology, which form an integral part of public instruction, being at the same time amenable to religious authority. God be praised, the affairs of religion are no longer consigned, as the arts are, to a place in the same department with manufactures and horse-breeding; they have found their proper station by the side of science and letters. The functions of Baron von Altenstein, in Prussia, are in this respect precisely yours as minister of public instruction and ecclesiastical affairs.

It remains for me to show how this ministry is organized in its centre of action at Berlin.

The organization is the same which I have found everywhere from the time I entered Germany. A council, more or less numerous; under a president, a director or a minister, according to the extent of the district. In fact, as I have elsewhere remarked, this institution arises from the nature of things, and the necessities of the service.

In those departments in which the administration is, if I may so speak, rather material than moral, we can understand that a minister may do without a council; but when his ministry is essentially moral, like that of public instruction, which requires not only attention to laws and regulations, but a mass of rare, various and profound knowledge, in which business almost always resolves itself into questions of science, it is evident that the minister must have the aid of councillors, to perpetuate the principles and the spirit which become traditionary in public bodies, and which a single and variable head might constantly overthrow; to make new rules or modify old ones; to aid the judgement of the minister as to what establishments to found, or what to suppress; above all, to guide him in the appreciation and the choice of men, and to serve as a rampart to ward off solicitation and intrigue. Let us suppose the best-intentioned minister; let us suppose that he has to make regulations for a faculty of theology, of law, of medicine, of science, or of letters, or to choose a professor for one of these faculties; suppose he has to decide some question of this kind, relating to things or to persons,—to whom is he to apply? To the faculty itself? But this were to check all progress; this were to constitute corporations, stagnant, because judges in their own cause; this were to nourish that *esprit de corps* so fatal to science, to abdicate the government, to renounce the right of judging for himself. Shall he apply to some celebrated individual? But this person, who is entirely irresponsible, may consult his own private views, his own peculiar system, or the interest of that branch of science for which he is personally distinguished. We may safely affirm that, in the end, solicitation, importunity, persistency will carry it. A thousand secret springs will be set in motion about the minister; recommendations from above, intrigues from below; in all directions, irresponsible and extraneous influences will surround and prevail over him. I have already said, and I repeat with the fullest conviction, that unchecked ministerial power is desired only by intriguing mediocrity, which despairs of deceiving a council composed of men versed in all parts of the service. Without doubt this council must be organized in such a manner as to answer its end; but this organization is very simple; it consists merely in putting at the head of each important branch of the service, that is to say, of the kinds of knowledge taught in each stage of public instruction, a man known by his labours,—by a long course of eminent and successful teaching. This councillor, who in my opinion ought still to remain a professor or teacher, and only to receive a more or less considerable salary as councillor, should be bound to make a report of all the affairs, real and personal, belonging to his department. He should make this report to the other councillors; it would be discussed; the intelligence and information of all the other members of the council would enlighten and modify the conclusions of the reporter, whose views might be warped by prejudices of system and by exclusive tastes. The discussion being gone through, the council would pronounce an opinion. The minister who has heard the report, and the discussion upon it, decides as he pleases, since he is responsible; but he decides as advised.

If the minister learns from his correspondence that things

are not going on well in any establishment, he sends the inspector best qualified for the particular case. If it relates to a law faculty, he takes a lawyer; if to a faculty of science, a man of science; and so on for all the other faculties. If it concerns a gymnasium, he selects a professor (teacher) of a gymnasium. In general he chooses one of the members of one of the three sections of the council. This councillor, chosen for the particular occasion, instantly repairs to the place where his presence is needed; makes an inspection, the more accurate and profound because it is special; returns to Berlin, makes his report immediately, and a prompt and efficacious decision follows. This takes place only on great occasions, which are extremely rare. For ordinary circumstances, and the general course of affairs, the correspondence and the intervention of the provincial authorities, immediately connected with the ministry of public instruction, suffice.

It is of the nature of aristocratical governments to have a great number of gratuitous offices, as we see in the example of England; but governments which are at once popular and monarchical, like Prussia and France, cannot admit of such a system; and if it were pushed far in either country, it would end in nothing short of gradually changing the form of the government. In fact, it would be vain to attempt to intrust these gratuitous employments to all the citizens eligible to them on the score of merit: persons of small fortune would soon tire of them, and it must end in their falling into the hands of persons of large property, who would soon virtually govern. In Prussia, all public servants are paid; and as no post whatever can be obtained without passing through the most rigorous examinations, all are able and enlightened men. And as, moreover, they are taken from every class of society, they bring to the exercise of their duties the general spirit of the nation, while, in that exercise, they contract habits of public business. This must be the system of every popular monarchy.

I do not attempt here to go into details. I have confined myself wholly to the endeavour to make the machinery of public instruction in Prussia intelligible to you, as a whole. To sum up all; primary instruction is parochial and departmental, and at the same time is subject to the minister of public instruction; which double character appears to me consequent on the very nature of establishments which equally require the constant superintendence of local powers, and the guidance of a superior hand, vivifying and harmon, izing the whole. This double character is represented by the *Schulrath,* who has a seat in the council of the department, and is responsible, both to the ministry of the interior, and to that of public instruction.

On the other hand, all secondary instruction is under the care of the *Schulcollegium* (school-board), which forms part of the provincial consistory, and which is nominated by the minister of public instruction. All higher instruction, that of universities, has for its organ and its head the royal commissary, who acts under immediate authority of the minister. Thus nothing escapes the eye and the power of the minister, yet at the same time each of these departments of public instruction enjoys sufficient liberty of action. The universities elect their own officers. The school-board proposes and overlooks the professors of gymnasia, and takes cognisance of all the more important points of primary instruction. The *Schulrath,* with the council of regency, (or rather the council of regency, on the report of the *Schulrath,*) and in pursuance of the correspondence of the inspectors and committees, decides on the greater part of the affairs of the lower stage of instruction. The minister, without entering into the infinite details of popular instruction, is thoroughly informed as to results, and directs everything by instructions emanating from the centre, which tend to diffuse a national unity throughout the whole. He does not interfere minutely with the business of secondary instruction; but nothing is done without his sanction, and this is never given but on full and accurate reports. The same applies to universities: they govern themselves, but according to fixed laws. The professors elect their deans and their rectors, but they are themselves nominated by the minister. In short, the end of the entire organization of public instruction in Prussia is, to leave details to the local powers, and to reserve to the minister and his council the direction and general impulse given to the whole.

## Duty of Parents to Send Their Children to the Primary Schools

This duty is so national, so rooted in all the legal and moral habits of the country, that it is expressed by a single word, *Schulpflichtigkeit* (school-duty, or school-obligation.) It corresponds to another word, similarly formed and similarly sanctioned by public opinion, *Dienstpflichtigkeit* (service-obligation, i. e. military service). These two words are completely characteristic of Prussia: they contain the secret of its originality as a nation, of its power as a state, and the germ of its future condition. They express, in my opinion, the two bases of true civilization,—knowledge and strength. Military conscription, instead of voluntary enlistment, at first found many adversaries among us: it is now considered as a condition and a means of civilization and public order. I am convinced the time will come when popular instruction will be equally recognized as a social duty imperative on all for the sake of all.

In Prussia, the state has long imposed on all parents the strict obligation of sending their children to school, unless they are able to prove that they are giving them a competent education at home. This duty has been successfully defined and regulated with precision for the different seasons of the year (see in Neigebauer's Collection, pp. 186 and 187, the circular of Frederic the Great, dated Jan. 1, 1769); it has been subjected to a severe supervision. Lastly, in the great attempts at codification which took place in 1794, it assumed its place among the fundamental laws of the state. The two articles of the general code relating to this obligation are as follows: *Allgemeines Landrecht,* Part II. title xii.

"Art. 43. Every inhabitant who cannot, or will not, cause the needful instruction to be given to his children at home, is bound to send them to school from the age of five years.

"Art. 44. From that age no child shall omit going to school, nor absent himself from it for any length of time, unless under particular circumstances, and with the consent of the civil and ecclesiastical authorities."

Lastly, the legislative project of 1819, which has the force of law, and regulates the present order of things throughout the country, devotes an entire title or chapter (Title IV.) to this obligation, which it follows out into its most minute applications. I cannot do better than quote the exact text of this title of the law of 1819, with the whole array of regulations, at once rigorous and prudent, which it contains. You will thus be made acquainted with both the letter and the spirit of the Prussian law on this important point.

"Parents or guardians are bound to send their children or wards to the public school; or to provide in some other manner that they receive a competent education.

"Parents, or those on whom children are dependent, (and under this head are comprehended masters or manufacturers who have children as servants or as apprentices, at an age when they should go to school,) shall be bound to give them a suitable education, from their seventh year to their fourteenth inclusive.[1] The schoolmaster shall judge whether a child gives proof of sufficient precocity to enter the school before that age, and the school-committee (*Schulvorstand*) shall grant an authority for its admission. A child who shall have gone through the whole course of elementary instruction before the age of fourteen, cannot be taken away from school by its parents without the permission of the committee, nor till after the members of the committee charged with the inspection of the school shall have proceeded to an examination of the pupil, which must be fully satisfactory as to morals and health. It is desirable that children who have quitted school, and have been confirmed and admitted to the communion, should attend the catechizing on Sundays at church for at least a year. This

[1] Five is the age fixed by the fundamental law; but seven is that at which education is rigidly enforced.

custom, which was formerly general, must be re-established wherever it has fallen into disuse.

"Parents and masters who do not send their children, or those entrusted to their care, to a public school, must point out to the municipal authorities or school-committees, whenever they are required, what means they provide for the education of such children.

"Every year after Easter or Michaelmas, the committees and the municipal authorities shall make an inquiry concerning all the families lying within their jurisdiction who have notoriously not provided for their children that private education which they are bound to give them, in default of public education. For this purpose they shall make a census of all the children of age to go to school. The baptismal registers, and those of the civil authorities, shall be open to them at the commencement of every year, and the police must afford them every possible facility and assistance.

"It is recognized as a principle, that in the country every child shall be sent to the school of the parish (*Gemeinde*), village, or school-association (*Schulverein*) to which its parents belong. If the parents wish to send their children to any other school, or to give them a private education, they must declare the same to the school-committee; and the permission cannot be refused them; provided always, that they pay the charges imposed on them for the support of the school to which they would naturally belong.

"Parents and masters are bound to see that the children under their care regularly follow the school courses for the time prescribed by law. On the other hand, schoolmasters shall keep lists of attendance, according to a prescribed formula, which must be submitted to the school-committee every fortnight.

"In order to facilitate to parents the execution of this law, and, at the same time, not to deprive them entirely of the assistance which their children might afford them in their labours, the hours of lessons in the elementary schools shall be arranged in such a manner as to leave the children several hours daily for domestic work.

"Schoolmasters are forbidden, under very heavy penalties, to employ their scholars in the work of their own household.

"All schools shall be shut on Sundays. The afternoons, between divine service and the catechism, may be devoted to gymnastic exercises.

"Care is everywhere to be taken to furnish necessitous parents with the means of sending their children to school, by providing them with the things necessary for their instruction, or with such clothes as they stand in need of.

"It is to be hoped that these facilities and helps, the moral and religious influence of the clergy, the wise counsels of members of the school-committees and of the municipal authorities, will gradually lead the people to appreciate the benefits of a good elementary education, and will spread among the young that wish and thirst for knowledge, which will lead them to seek every means of acquiring it.

"If, however, parents and masters neglect sending their children punctually to school, the clergymen must first explain to them the heavy responsibility which rests upon them; after that, the school-committee must summon them to appear before it, and address severe remonstrances to them. No excuse whatever shall be deemed valid (exclusive of the proof that the education of the child is otherwise provided for), except certificates of illness signed by the medical man or the clergyman; the absence of the parents and masters which had occasioned that of the children; or, lastly, the want of the necessary clothing, funds for providing which had not been forthcoming.

"If these remonstrances are not sufficient, coercive measures are then to be resorted to against the parents, guardians, or masters. The children are to be taken to school by an officer of the police, or the parents are to be sentenced to graduated punishments or fines; and in case they are unable to pay, to imprisonment or labour, for the benefit of the parish. These punishments may be successively increased, but are never to exceed the maximum of punishment of correctional police.

"The fines are to be awarded by the school-committee; to be collected, if necessary, with the aid of the police, and paid into the funds of the committee. The execution of the other punishments rests with the police.

"Whenever it shall be necessary to pass sentence of imprisonment, or of forced labour for the benefit of the parish, care shall be taken that the children of the persons so condemned are not neglected while their parents are undergoing the penalty of the law.

"The parents who shall have incurred such sentences may, on the request of the school-committees, and as an augmentation of punishment, be deprived of all participation in the public funds for the relief of the poor.

"Nevertheless, that part of the public relief which is given for the education of children, shall not be withdrawn from them; though it shall cease to pass through their hands.

"They can have no share of any public relief, so long as they persist in not fulfilling the duties of Christian and conscientious parents towards their children.

"They shall be equally incapable of taking any part in the administration of the parish, or of holding any office connected with the church or the school.

"If all these punishments are found intellectual, a guardian shall be appointed specially to watch over the education of the children, or, in case they are wards, a co-guardian.

"Jewish parents, who obstinately refuse obedience to the competent authorities, may be deprived of their civil rights in the provinces in which the edict of the 11th of May, 1812, is in force.

"Cases of marked negligence on the part of entire parishes, or of particular families, may be mentioned in the published reports, without, however, naming individuals.

"The protestant or catholic pastors are to judge for themselves how far to use their influence, according to the circumstances of the case. But they are earnestly to endeavour, especially in their sermons at the opening of schools, to persuade parents to give great attention to the education of their children, and to send them regularly to school; they may even make allusion to any striking instances of a neglect of these duties. Lastly, they shall admit no children to the conferences preparatory to confirmation and communion, who do not present certificates, attesting that they have completed their time at school; or that they are still in punctual attendance upon it; or that they are receiving, or have received, a private education."

## Duty of Each Parish to Maintain a Primary School at Its Own Cost

It would be manifestly absurd to require of parents that they should send their children to school, if there were not schools enough to enable them to fulfill this duty. Now private schools afford but an uncertain resource. It is therefore the duty of the state to provide for the accomplishment of the law it has enacted: hence the following regulations, which had already passed into common usage, and were almost universally in practice, but were first formally sanctioned by Titles III. and V. of the law of 1819, of which I have spoken, and which I shall now continue to extract from, or, frequently, to translate entire.

"Every parish, however small, is bound to have an elementary school, complete or incomplete; that is to say, accomplishing the whole scheme of instruction prescribed by the law, or, at least, the most indispensable parts of the scheme.

"Every town is bound to have at least one burgher or middle school, or more, according to its population.

"Small towns, of less than fifteen hundred inhabitants, which cannot support the expense of a burgher school, are bound to have at least elementary schools. Above all, they must have elementary schools of the lower class, in proportion to the number of children of both sexes of an age to go to school.

"In case a town be not able to maintain separately, and

in distinct buildings, an elementary school and a burgher school, it shall be permitted to use the inferior classes of the burgher school as elementary school: in like manner, in case of necessity satisfactorily proved, the inferior classes of the gymnasium may be used as burgher school.

"In every town or city in which there are several elementary schools, they shall be distributed over the several quarters of the town: nevertheless, the inhabitants shall not be bound by their place of residence to send their children to one school rather than another.

"In towns which have several schools of the several gradations or stages, the authorities shall be careful to organize them all conformably to the instructions given above, so that they may be connected together, and form a coherent whole.

"Jewish residents in towns may establish schools at their own expense, on condition that they be organized, superintended and administered by them conformably with the present law. They may equally send their children to other schools; but they are not permitted to have any share in the management of those schools.

"The first care should be to furnish the country with the needful elementary schools. Wherever there exist incomplete schools, they must be improved, and must be changed as quickly as possible into complete elementary schools: this must invariably take place when a school has, or is in a condition to have, two masters. In order that all country places may have sufficient elementary schools within their reach, the inhabitants of each rural parish shall form an association for country schools (*Landschulverein*), under the direction of the public authorities. This association is to consist, first, of all the landed proprietors, without distinction, whether they have or have not children; secondly, of all householders domiciliated in the parish, even if they be not land-owners.

"Each village, including the neighbouring farms, may form an association of this kind of itself. The same applies to a combination of a number of isolated farm-houses.

"Every village ought to have its school; but in certain cases, and as exceptions to the general rule, several villages may unite together into one school-association, under the following conditions:

"1. The absolute impossibility for a parish to furnish the means of an elementary school of itself.

"2. The villages which associate must be so near that the children can punctually attend the common school. The distance allowed shall not exceed half a mile (2¼ English miles) in flat country, and a quarter of a mile in hilly country.

"3. No such combination can be formed among villages separated by marshes or rivers, which would render attendance on school difficult, or even impracticable, at certain seasons of the year.

"4. The number of children collected must not be too great. For one master, it must not exceed a hundred. More may be admitted if there are means of maintaining two masters, and if the building is large enough; but in that case the villages would be very nearly able to support each its own school, which is always preferable.

"Leave to form such combinations shall only be granted temporarily to villages which are likely to be able to maintain their own schools; and such establishments shall be gradually reformed.

"If a village, from its extent and population, or from difference in the religious persuasions of the inhabitants, had already two schools, and could provide for their maintenance, they shall on no account be united, especially if they be of different confessions of faith. On the contrary, separate schools shall be encouraged wherever circumstances permit.

"Difference of religion alone ought not, however, to be an obstacle to the formation of an association for a country school; but in forming such an association of catholics and protestants, regard must be had to the numerical proportion of the inhabitants of each communion. If it be possible, there shall, in this case, conjointly with the head master professing the faith of the majority, be a second master, professing that of the minority.

"Jews scattered about the country may enjoy all the advantages of the school-associations, but must not take part in their management. They must provide for the religious education of their children themselves.

"Wherever the union of two schools of different communions be judged expedient, it must take place by common agreement between the two parties. Moreover, in case of a union of this kind, or of the establishment of schools for various sects (*Simultanschulen*), provision must be made that each of these sects have within reach all that may be necessary for the religious education of the scholars belonging to it. And in order that no sect may have anything to fear, and that all it brings into the common fund may be secured to it, an authentic document shall be drawn up every year, setting forth the respective rights of each, and the particular terms of the association.

"If a union cannot be effected, or if it is found impracticable to form a school common to both religions, the authorities shall interfere, and shall take the measures best suited to the necessities and the circumstances of the place."

We have now, Sir, seen the establishment of primary schools throughout Prussia. I shall proceed to show with what care and forethought the government which commands them has provided for their support. This is done in Title V. of the law of 1819. I give it, with some few abridgements.

The law begins by defining what is required for the complete maintenance of a school, in order that it may answer its end.

"1. A suitable income for schoolmasters and mistresses, and a certain provision for them when they are past service.

"2. A building for the purposes of teaching and of exercise, properly laid out, kept in repair and warmed.

"3. Furniture, books, pictures, instruments, and all things necessary for the lessons and exercises.

"4. Pecuniary assistance for the necessitous scholars."

The first is the essential point. If you would have good masters, you must first of all ensure them a maintenance. The Prussian law expresses itself on this head in the most solemn manner. "It is our firm will," says the king, in whose name it speaks, "that in the maintenance of every school, this be regarded as the most important object, and take precedence of all others."

"It is neither possible nor necessary to fix a general and uniform rule on this head for the whole monarchy. The condition of the different places, and the particular circumstances can alone determine the salary attached to each school. The inspectors and the committees of schools must take care that this salary be as high as possible. But there shall be a minimum fixed for the salaries of schoolmasters in towns and villages, proportioned to the state of prosperity of each province, and determined by the provincial consistories. The salaries which are below this minimum must be raised to it as speedily as possible. Lastly, in order that this salary may always be in proportion to the real value of the school and the existing price of provisions, it shall be revised from time to time.

"As a principle, every school should have a building specially appropriated to it: whenever it is necessary to hire a house, it must, if possible, be isolated, and have no connexion with other buildings.

"The conditions which are essential in a schoolhouse, and must be rigidly enforced, are, a healthy situation, rooms of a sufficient size, well boarded, well aired, and kept with the greatest neatness, and, whenever it is possible, a good lodging for the master. In schools which have several masters, one at least is, if possible, to lodge in the school-house. The provincial consistories shall cause plans to be drawn of school-houses of different sizes, for villages and small towns, with an approximating estimate of the cost of building, and of the necessary furniture, in order that there may be some fixed standard for new buildings and for the greater repairs.

"Every school in a village or small town shall have a garden, cultivated according to the nature of the country, either as kitchen-garden, orchard, nursery-garden, or laid out for raising bees; and this garden shall be made available for the instruction of the scholars.

"Wherever the nature of the spot will admit, there shall be a gravelled plain or court, in front of the school, for the children's exercises.

"The materials necessary for instruction consist, above all, in a sufficient collection of books for the use of the master, and as many as possible for that of the scholars.

"There shall be, according to the degree of every school, a collection of maps and geographical instruments, models for drawing, writing, music, &c.; the instruments and collections necessary for studying mathematics and natural history; lastly, according to the extent of the system of instruction, there shall be the apparatus necessary for gymnastic exercises, and the tools and implements suited to the teaching of the mechanical arts or manufactures in the schools in which that branch of knowledge is introduced. The provincial consistories shall fix the minimum of the moveables required for the inferior schools.

"As to the necessitous scholars, wherever there is no free school, called a poor's school (*Armenschule*), every public school is bound, whatever be its general rules concerning the sum paid by the scholars, to give them instruction gratuitously, or partly so. Parents who send many children to school shall have all necessary indulgence as to the payment of the *Schulgeld* (school-money, or fee); at the same time the master's regular salary must in no way suffer. Moreover, every school is bound to furnish gratuitously to poor scholars, books and other necessaries, a part of which shall be given to them as their own property, and part shall remain as belonging to the stock of the school."

But to meet the demands of a school established on these four bases, and embracing such a system of instruction, considerable funds are necessary; and to raise these funds every variety of means presented by the local circumstances must be called into action. The following are the most general rules laid down by the law on that point.

"Schools or houses for education which possess funds arising from endowments, of whatever kind, shall be maintained, and if needful improved, out of these funds. In case they are insufficient, they shall have a right to assistance from other sources.

"It is a principle, that as the gymnasia, and other establishments for public instruction of the same degree, are mainly supported by the general funds of the state, or of the province, so the inferior schools in towns and villages are supported by the towns and by the school-associations in the country.

"On the other hand, if a town cannot, out of its own resources, support the lower grade of instruction of which it stands in need, every department shall have school-funds, from which it shall assist the necessitous parish; but this aid shall only be temporary, and shall be diminished or withdrawn in proportion as the place becomes more able to support its school.

"If, for instance, a village cannot, from its position, unite in a school-association with other villages, nor, from poverty, maintain a school by itself, the department shall give it assistance.

"In towns, public education and the maintenance of it are not to be postponed to any other of the parochial necessities or claims whatsoever. They are to be reckoned among the objects to be provided for in the first place.

"When schools are to be organized in a town, it must first be exactly determined what are the most urgent expenses to be incurred; then the disposable funds, or those appropriated to education, must be carefully examined, to see whether they are sufficient, or can be made so by a better management; care being had that the income of funds belonging to any particular establishments be used for their sole benefit, and not for that of all the schools of the place. An account must be taken of all funds obtainable from pious donations and other local and parochial sources, from the increase of the sum paid by each child (*Schulgeld*), and from the aids the department can furnish. If all these means are insufficient, then the funds rigorously necessary shall be levied on the householders (*Hausväter*, literally housefathers).

"The assessment shall be made by the parochial authorities, with the participation of the school-committees.

"No one shall refuse to pay the rate levied upon him under pretext that the schools of his parish, or of his religious persuasion, are flourishing; since it is necessary to provide for the general education of the parish, and all schools are open to all, and may be equally profitable to every individual.

"By the word householders (*Hausväter*) is meant all the inhabitants of a parish who keep house for themselves. All who are rated to the other necessities of the parish are to be rated in the same proportion to the school-rate.

"The persons exempted from these rates are:—

"Hired servants, or those who are boarded by others; excepting always such as keep house, and must therefore be considered as householders.

"Military men of every rank in active service, unless they exercise a civil profession, or possess property in the funds.

"As ecclesiastics and schoolmasters render essential services to public education, either gratuitously or for a very small remuneration, they also shall be exempted from paying the school-rate; but they shall pay the *Schulgeld,* or sum paid by each child attending school, unless usage or some special agreement have freed them from that obligation.

"If the repairs of a school-house become impossible, from the poverty of the inhabitants of the place, or the charges they have already to bear, or if the rates imposed do not cover the necessary expense, assistance shall be asked from the departmental funds.

"The higher sort of girls' schools shall have no claim to assistance from these funds, and shall be maintained by the persons or associations which establish them. When a town shall have made sufficient provision for its elementary boys' and girls' schools, it may set on foot higher girls' schools.

"The maintenance of schools peculiar to Jewish communities shall be entirely at their charge; but this shall not exempt the members of such communities from the rate levied for the general instruction of the town.

"The maintenance of village schools rests on the country school-associations. Thus all landowners, tenants and householders, without distinction, contribute in proportion to the income of their respective properties lying within the circle of the association, or to the product of their industry; and are to pay this contribution or rate either in money or in kind; or, if they can do so no otherwise, in building-materials, or even in labour.

"The instructions given above as to the liability to pay this rate (*Beiträgspflichtigkeit*) are applicable to country as well as to town. On every occasion the question of the necessity of levying a rate shall be examined and determined by the departmental authority responsible for the schools; and the assessment of such rate shall be made by the parochial authorities, in conjunction with the school-committees.

"The portion of the rate assessed on any estate shall be attached to it as a real charge; so that if the property should be dismembered, each portion shall remain charged with its share of the rate without any fresh assessment.

"When village schools possess any revenues from bequests, endowments, aid from the church funds, or the payment of the scholars, then the rate chargeable on the members of the association to which such schools belong shall not be levied further than is necessary to improve the schools, or to add to the revenues, if they are insufficient. But every fresh bequest or donation in favour of the schools shall be devoted to the improvement of the school, or of the master's income, and not to the diminution of the rate, unless such is the express will of the donor or testator.

"If two or more schools of the same communion exist in a village, the whole village shall be considered as forming one single school-association, and each school shall be maintained by the product of the general rate.

"If these schools are of different communions, the householders of each communion form an association for their own school, and pay their rate to that alone.

"But in case a school-association shall comprehend the members of several sects, no regard is to be had to the different sects in the assessment of the rate for the maintenance of the school.

"If the members of small Christian sects choose to separate themselves from the association to which they naturally belong, and to establish distinct schools, they shall be at liberty to do so, on condition of proving that they have means sufficient for the maintenance of such schools, and that they thoroughly fulfill the duties of the association to which they belong.

"The particular obligations attached to ecclesiastical endowments for the support of certain schools, even when these endowments have lapsed to the state, shall continue to be scrupulously fulfilled. The same will apply to high-schools, or gymnasia.

"Among the special means of providing for the maintenance of schools, schoolmasters in small towns and villages may be allowed to receive in kind a part of the remuneration from the scholars (*Schulgeld*), fixed by the provincial consistories. But no arrangement to this effect can be made without the consent of the schoolmaster.

"If the garden, which ought to be attached to every country school, cannot be paid for out of the funds of the school, the members of the association shall be obliged to hire or buy one."

Further, a cabinet order, dated Berlin, September 28th, 1810; the edict for the advancement of the civilization of the country, dated September 14th, 1811; and a cabinet order, dated November 5th, 1811,—decree, "that on occasion of any divisions or allotments which the parishes may make, sufficient land shall be allotted to the schoolmaster for the cultivation of his vegetables, and for the feed of a cow; about two acres of good land, or more if the land is bad."

"In places where right of common still exists, the schoolmaster shall have the right of feeding a fixed number of cattle, and shall share in all other benefits of the common.

"Wherever the schoolmasters have been accustomed to receive certain fixed allowances out of the collections at christenings, marriages and funerals, this custom may be continued.[1] But these sources of income must be calculated and valued, on an average, among the general receipts of the schoolmaster; and care shall be taken that the services thus imposed on the schoolmaster, such as the attending the body to the grave, &c., do not interfere with the duties of his office.

"In places where allowances of this kind do not exist, or have been abolished, they shall neither be introduced nor restored.

"Among the schoolmaster's sources of income, it will not be permitted to reckon his place at the table of every family in the commune in rotation (an ancient custom, for which there is an appropriate word, *Wandeltisch,* moveable table). If he can thus have his board gratuitously, it can only be as an accessory to his other income, and shall be put an end to the moment it appears that his dignity or his duties are likely to suffer from it.

"No schoolmaster shall henceforward be allowed to col-

[1] I have not chosen to omit these provisions, though they belong to a state of society so unlike our own; as they all tend to show how everything may be turned to account by a truly provident administration.—TRANSL.

lect gifts or fees, whether in money or in kind, from door to door, whether in person, or by his scholars.

"Nevertheless, the sums collected by schoolmasters, and the presents the pupils of the gymnasia receive for singing in choruses on certain solemn occasions, shall not be suppressed; but in making these collections, care must be taken to avoid whatever may tend to lower the dignity of master or scholars. The same observation applies to the poor scholars who go about singing choruses from door to door, to collect money (*Kurrenden*), in places where this custom still subsists. In places where it is abolished, and replaced by choirs of scholars in the churches, they shall receive compensation for the product of the collections they used to make in person, by collections at private houses or at churches, or even by the parish, such collections being regarded as forming part of the school-funds.

"The general rate levied on the householders for the support of schools having no other object than that of facilitating their establishment for the benefit of all, it is just that those who actually profit by these establishments should support them by a special payment, (*Schulgeld,* school-money,) which may also serve to encourage the masters. This payment may be raised in schools of all degrees in the following manner:—

"The school-committees in towns shall, with the approbation of the departmental authorities, fix the amount of the payment in the lower schools; but the towns may entirely suppress the special payment in certain schools, on condition that they make up for this source of income from the general school-fund, or from some other source.

"In particular cases it is reserved for the provincial consistories to decide whether the *Schulgeld* for country schools shall be kept up where it already exists, or whether it shall be established at the desire of the country school-associations, and in what manner.

"No master shall be allowed to collect the *Schulgeld,* or money paid by the scholars; this must be done by the school-committee.

"In some schools, a fixed portion of the scholars' payment may be employed in the maintenance of the school; but a greater or less portion of it must be reserved exclusively for the masters, and must be divided among them, by way of encouragement: wherever there is no such payment, some means or other must be devised to add to the general funds of the school, an extraordinary fund for such rewards to the masters.

"In places where the maintenance of the school is fixed, all charges on the children for those things which ought to be included in that maintenance, as firing, light, furniture, &c., are abolished.

"The children shall be permitted to form a fund, by voluntary contributions, for the assistance of their necessitous schoolfellows: they shall take part in the management of it, under the direction of the schoolmaster.

"No schoolmaster whatever, although reduced to the minimum of the income allowed by law, can be permitted to increase that income by any occupations which might lower his dignity or his morality, or divert his attention from his functions, and expose him to punishment for that cause. No schoolmaster can undertake any additional employment without the permission of the school-committee, or of the departmental authority; and this permission shall be granted only on condition that the schoolmaster in question shall give up that employment whenever the departmental authority shall judge and declare that it is incompatible with the business of a teacher.

"If a master holds any office about the church, such as clerk, organist, or other, measures must be adopted to prevent the service of the school from being in any way interrupted or impeded by them.

"The income which the schoolmaster derives from his functions about the church shall not be reckoned as forming part of his income from the school.

"In like manner, no schoolmaster or mistress shall try to increase his or her means of subsistence by the exercise of any trade or handicraft, without the permission of the above-mentioned authorities: and this permission shall be refused if the occupation is dirty, or if it is likely to interfere with the punctual performance of the duties of schoolmaster or mistress,—agriculture not even excepted.

"The exemption from parochial and other charges attached to the office of schoolmaster shall not be withdrawn without full indemnification.

"The allowance to infirm schoolmasters shall be drawn, as has been said above, from the fund for the maintenance of the schools to which they have belonged. The pensions of masters of schools whose support depends on the parochial funds of towns or villages, shall, if it be found impossible to pay them otherwise, be added to the general rate levied on householders. In cases where the urban parishes or the country school-associations shall be reduced to a state of great poverty, the king reserves to himself the power of assisting them by extraordinary grants.

"It shall be shortly determined, by a general regulation concerning the pensions of functionaries, under what circumstances, and in what proportion, schoolmasters can become entitled to pensions.

"With regard to the monthly or quarterly allowance granted to the widow and children of a deceased schoolmaster, the particular rules and usages of the place must be followed. The places of masters, which it is important to fill up immediately, must not remain vacant until these quarterly allowances to survivors are paid off; if necessary, the allowances in question must be taken from other sources.

"The orphan children of schoolmasters shall have a special right to all the benefits of establishments for education; always supposing that they fulfill the conditions necessary to obtain them.

"But as the establishment of a provincial fund for pensions to infirm schoolmasters, or widows and orphans of schoolmasters, affords the most expedient sort of provision for this sort of claims, the provincial consistories shall take the measures necessary to establish such funds in all places.

"The collection and administration of the revenues of schools must be conducted according to a form which may render them easy to the committee of each town or village; they must be under the supreme direction of the public authorities; must secure to schools the entire portion due to them; and must in no way lower the dignity of the teacher.

"The local authorities, under the superintendence of the

provincial consistories, shall take measures in accordance with this principle, for the collection and administration of the general revenues of schools, as well as for those of each particular school in the same parish.

"The committees are legally responsible towards schools and schoolmasters for the punctual and full payment of their incomes.

"The school treasuries, of which every department ought to have one, shall be composed of the revenues which already belong to them of right, or which may hereafter accrue to them from the funds long ago created for the benefit of schools by the kings of Prussia; of such sums as, at the time of the secularization of church property, were, or may hereafter be, appropriated to schools; and sometimes also of extraordinary grants from the royal treasury, till it can be decided how each department shall maintain the schools which are not supported by the parishes, or shall assist the parochial schools.

"In provinces where there are general funds, destined specially to the support of protestant or of catholic schools, these funds shall not be blended and confounded in the departmental school-treasury. In like manner, funds arising from endowment, and intended for a particular establishment or establishments, must be under a management distinct from the departmental school-funds, though under the superintendence of the departmental authorities. Endowments or bequests in favour of poor scholars, of schoolmasters, of their widows and orphans, or of any like objects, shall in all cases be rigorously administered according to the intention of the donors, and must not be confounded with other school-revenues.

"The contributions or rates (*Beiträge*), in money or in kind, assessed upon householders for the maintenance of schools, as well as the money paid by the children (*Schulgeld*), are obligatory under the same sanctions and with the same privileges as the general taxes of the state.

"School-buildings shall in all cases enjoy the same exemptions and privileges as churches.

"Donations by will, or in any other manner, to schools, shall not be subject to the usual claims of the church."

### GENERAL OBJECTS AND DIFFERENT GRADATIONS OF PRIMARY INSTRUCTION.

I continue to analyse and quote the law of 1819. The portion of it to which I now come is comprised in Titles I. and II. of that law.

It distinguishes two stages or gradations in primary instruction,—elementary schools and burgher schools.[1]

"The elementary schools (*Elementarschulen*) have for object the regular development of the faculties of man, by more or less extended instruction in the branches of knowledge indispensable to the lower classes, both in town and country.

"The burgher schools (*Bürgerschulen, Stadtschulen,*) bring the child to that point at which peculiar aptitude for classical studies, properly so called, or for some particular profession, may manifest itself.

"The gymnasia carry on education to the point at which boys, after having received a classical and liberal culture,

[1] Or, as we may call them, schools for the middle classes.—TRANSL.

enter on a course of practical studies in ordinary life, or scientific, superior and special, or professional, studies at the universities."

These different stages concur to form, if I may use the expression, a single great establishment of national education, the system of which is *one,* and the different branches of which, (while each pursues its own peculiar end,) must yet be intimately connected together.

The primary instruction in question is the basis of the entire system: though divided into two degrees or stages, it has its unity, its general rules; and even the distinctions which localities, circumstances, or the spirit of the founders, may have introduced into schools of the same stage or class, can neither affect their fundamental constitution, nor the conditions of the admission of the pupils.

Nevertheless the sex, language, religion and future vocation of the pupils require consideration. The particular rules laid down by the law to that end are as follows:

"1. Establishments for girls must be, as much as possible, formed separately, corresponding, as to their course of instruction, to the elementary schools, or to the burgher schools. The general principles of instruction and discipline laid down for boys' schools are the same for girls', with modifications appropriate to their sex.

"2. The general constitution of schools is the same for all those portions of the population, composing the Prussian monarchy, which are of a different origin. If a few schools should deviate from this rule," says the law of 1819, "they must gradually be brought back to it. In all those, without exception, wherein a foreign language is spoken, the pupils, according to the rank of the school, shall receive, besides the lessons in the dialect of the province, complete instruction in the German language; and both masters and pupils may use that language in common conversation.[1]

"3. Difference of religion in Christian schools necessarily produces some difference in the religious instruction. This instruction shall always be adapted to the spirit and the dogmas of the church to which the school belongs. But as, in every school of a Christian state, the dominant spirit, common to all modes of faith, ought to be piety and a profound reverence for God, every school may receive children of another communion. Masters and inspectors must most carefully avoid every kind of constraint or annoyance to the children on account of their particular creed. No school shall be made abusively instrumental to any views of proselytism; and the children of a persuasion different from that of the school, shall not be obliged, against the will of their parents, or their own, to attend the religious instruction or exercise in it. Private masters of their own creed shall be charged with their religious instruction; and in any place where it would be impossible to have as many masters as there are forms of belief, parents must the more sedulously perform those duties themselves, if they do not wish their children to follow the religious instructions given in the school.

"Christian schools may admit children of the Jewish persuasion on precisely the same terms as children of all other religions; but Jewish schools may not receive any child of Christian parents."

Generally speaking, no institution established by par-

[1] This relates to the Polish provinces of the Prussian monarchy.

157

ticular classes of society is permitted to depart essentially from the principles which rule the general spirit of the national schools. This does not, of course, apply to schools created for a special or professional education; such as those for soldiers, farmers, miners, manufacturers, seamen, artists, &c., which fall under the department of the minister of the interior, and not under that of public instruction, and are not consequently included under the law in question.

The fundamental character of that law is the moral and religious spirit which pervades all its provisions.

"The first vocation of every school," says the law of 1819, "is, to train up the young in such a manner as to implant in their minds a knowledge of the relation of man to God, and at the same time to excite and foster both the will and the strength to govern their lives after the spirit and the precepts of Christianity. Schools must early train children to piety, and must therefore strive to second and complete the early instructions of the parents. In every school, therefore, the occupations of the day shall begin and end with a short prayer and some pious reflections, which the master must contrive to render so varied and impressive that a moral exercise shall never degenerate into an affair of habit. Moreover the masters shall take care that the children punctually attend divine service on Sundays and holidays. All the solemnities of schools shall be interspersed with songs of a religious character. Lastly, the admission of the scholars to the communion should be made an occasion for strengthening the ties which ought to unite master and pupil, and of opening their minds to the most generous and sublime sentiments of religion.

"Care shall likewise be taken to inculcate on youth the

duty of obedience to the laws, fidelity and attachment to the sovereign and state, in order that these virtues may combine to produce in them the sacred love of country.

"Though in establishments which admit no boarders, the authority of the masters does not extend beyond the precincts of the school, they are nevertheless not to remain indifferent to the behaviour of the pupils out of school hours. In boarding-schools, the whole authority of the parents is delegated to them.

"The paternal attachment of the masters, their affectionate kindness towards all their pupils, will be the most powerful means of preserving them from immoral influences, and of inclining them to virtue.

"No kind of punishment which has a tendency to weaken the sentiment of honour shall, on any pretence, be inflicted: corporal punishments, in case they be necessary, shall be devoid of cruelty, and on no account injurious either to modesty or to health.

"Incorrigible scholars, or those whose example or influence may be pernicious to their schoolfellows, after all the resources of paternal authority, joined to that of the masters, shall have been exhausted, shall be expelled, in compliance with the judgement of the school-committees.

"By making the pupils themselves, as they advance in age, assist in maintaining order in the school, they will be accustomed to feel themselves useful and active members of society.

"Primary instruction shall have for its aim to develope the faculties of the soul, the reason, the senses, and the bodily strength. It shall comprehend religion and morals, the knowledge of size and numbers, of nature and man;

corporeal exercises, singing, and lastly, imitation of form, by drawing and writing.

"In every school for girls, without exception, the works peculiar to their sex shall be taught.

"Gymnastics shall be considered as a necessary part of a complete system of education, and shall be taught by simple rules favourable to the promotion of the health and bodily strength of children.

"Every complete elementary school necessarily comprehends the following objects:—

"1. Religious instruction, as a means of forming the moral character of children according to the positive truths of Christianity.

"2. The German language, and, in provinces where a foreign language is spoken, the language of the country, in addition to the German.

"3. The elements of geometry, together with the general principles of drawing.

"4. Calculation and practical arithmetic.

"5. The elements of physics, geography, general history, and especially the history of Prussia.

"Care must be taken to introduce and combine these branches of knowledge with the reading and writing lessons, as much as possible, independently of the instruction which shall be given on those subjects specially.

"6. Singing; with a view to improve the voices of the children, to elevate their hearts and minds, to perfect and ennoble the popular songs and church music or psalmody.

"7. Writing and gymnastic exercises, which fortify all the senses, and especially that of sight.

"8. The simplest manual labours, and some instructions in husbandry, according to the agriculture of the respective parts of the country.

"The instructions in religion, reading, writing, arithmetic and singing are strictly indispensable in every school. No school shall be considered as a complete elementary school, unless it fulfill the whole scheme of instruction just marked out.

"Every burgher school shall afford instruction on the following heads:—

"1. Religion and morals.

"2. The German language, and at the same time the language of the country in the provinces not German; reading, composition, exercises in style, study of the national classics. In all the German part of the country, the modern foreign languages are an accessory branch of study.

"3. Latin is taught to all the children, within certain limits, as means of exercising their faculties and their judgement, whether they be or be not to enter the higher schools.

"4. The elements of mathematics, and especially a thorough course of practical arithmetic.

"5. Physical science, as far as is sufficient to explain the most remarkable phænomena of nature.

"6. Geography and history combined, in order to give some knowledge of the earth, of the general history of the world, of the people who inhabit it, and the empires into which it is divided. Prussia, its history, laws and constitution, shall form the subject of a special study.

"7. The principles of drawing shall be taught to all, concurrently with the lessons in physics, natural history, and geometry.

"8. Writing must be carefully attended to, and the hand trained to write distinctly and neatly.

"9. The singing lessons shall be attended by all the pupils, not only with a view to form them to that art, but to qualify them to assist in the services of the church with propriety and solemnity, by singing the psalms or choral music with correctness and judgement.

"10. Gymnastic exercises, adapted to the age and strength of the scholars."

This entire course of instruction is indispensable to constitute a burgher school. If the funds of the school render it possible to raise it a step higher in the scale, so as to prepare the boys for the learned professions, and qualify them to enter the gymnasia immediately, such school then takes the title of *höhere Stadtschule* (higher town-school), or Progymnasium.

The following are also important regulations relating to the general subject of this chapter.

"Masters must take pains to know the particular character and qualities of each pupil, and must give the greatest possible attention to the periodical examinations.

"Every scholar of an elementary school shall, when he leaves it, receive a certificate as to his capacity, and his moral and religious dispositions, signed by the masters and the school-committee. These certificates shall always be presented to the clergyman before admission to the communion, to master-manufacturers or artisans on being bound apprentice, or to housekeepers on entering service.

"The certificates shall not be given to the scholars till the moment of their finally quitting school; and in both the burgher schools and the gymnasia, this shall always give occasion to a great solemnity.

"There shall be particular regulations, fixing the number of lessons which are to be given weekly and daily, in each department, and for each gradation.

"The grand divisions of the courses shall be from Easter to Easter, or, when local circumstances make it more expedient, from Michaelmas to Michaelmas.

"Every school may admit scholars, change its classes, or close its course of studies half-yearly.

"On Sundays and days of high festival the schools shall be shut; with the exception of the Sunday schools for adults who have been neglected in their youth, or for children who would otherwise be deprived of all instruction in the summer, in parts of the country where there are insurmountable obstacles to keeping school during that season.

"In order to impose no shackles on the constant onward course of improvement no special books shall be prescribed for the different branches of instruction in the primary schools. They shall be free to adopt the best books as they appear.

"For religious instruction, which in protestant schools is founded mainly on the Holy Scriptures, the Bible and the catechisms generally adopted shall be used. The New Testament shall be given to children who can read. Those who approach the time of communicating shall have the whole Bible in Luther's translation. This book shall also be used for the religious instruction in all the classes of the gymnasia, to which shall be added the New Testament in Greek.

"The lesson-books shall be carefully selected by the school-committees, with the concurrence of the higher authorities, without whose approbation no book can be admitted. The ecclesiastical authorities are, in like manner, to be consulted on the choice of religious works.

"The bishops, in concert with the provincial consistories, shall choose the religious books for the use of catholic schools. In case these two authorities should not agree in their choice, the matter must be referred to the minister of public instruction, who shall decide.

"If there is a deficiency of elementary books in any branch of learning, the minister shall see that proper ones be written or compiled.

"The masters of the public schools must choose the methods best adapted to the natural growth and improvement of the human mind; the methods which gradually and constantly enlarge the understandings of the children, and not such as instill merely mechanical knowledge.

"It will be the duty of the school-committees to inspect the methods adopted by the masters, and to aid them with their advice; they are never to tolerate a bad method; and they shall refer the matter to a higher authority if their advice is disregarded.

"Parents or guardians have a right to inquire into the system of education pursued in the school, and into the progress made by their children. In order, however, to avoid continual applications of this sort, measures shall be taken for giving a public report of the state of the school from time to time.

"Parents may address any complaints to the higher authorities charged with the superintendence of schools, and these complaints must be examined into with the greatest care.

"On the other hand, those who entrust their children to a public school are bound not to oppose any obstacle to their conforming exactly to the rules established in the school. They are bound, on the contrary, to second the views of the masters, to fulfill all their obligations towards them, and to furnish the children with everything necessary for their studies.

"It is essential to the general order that every pupil in every public school should be obliged to go through the whole course of fundamental instruction, of the degree or stage to which that school belongs; and parents shall not be allowed to withhold a pupil at pleasure from any branch of instruction. Dispensations from any branch must be asked of the higher authorities, who will judge of the validity of the reasons.

"Every public school, inasmuch as it is a national institution, ought to afford the greatest publicity possible. Consequently, in every boy's school, besides the private examinations on passing from one class to another, there must be public examinations calculated to show the nature and the excellence of the studies.

"Besides this, the director (or chairman) of the committee, or one of the masters, shall give an account of the state and progress of the school in a written report. Lastly, from time to time a general report on the state of education in each province shall be published.

"Every establishment shall be at liberty to choose the days on which to give the public the means of knowing the state of the school, by speeches or other exercises. But the anniversaries of the most remarkable days in the national history are to be selected in preference.

"As girls are destined by nature for a quiet and retired life, these exercises or trials are never to be public in their schools. The examination shall take place only in the presence of the masters and parents.

"But if, on the one hand, it is incumbent on those charged with the conduct of the public schools to strive to accomplish the duties the state imposes on them for the training of citizens, they, on their part, have a right to expect that every one should pay the respect and gratitude to which they are entitled as labourers in the sacred work of education. Masters and mistresses ought, therefore, to be the objects of the general esteem due to their laborious and honourable functions.

"Institutions for the public instruction have a right to claim from all, even those who do not send their children to them, assistance and support wherever or whenever needed. All public authorities are required to protect the public schools, each in his sphere of action, and to lend their aid to schoolmasters in the exercise of their functions, as to any other servants of the state.

"In all the parishes of the kingdom, without exception, the clergymen of every Christian communion shall seize every occasion, whether at church, or during their visits to schools, or in their sermons at the opening of classes, of reminding the schools of their high and holy mission, and the people of their duties towards the schools. The authorities, the clergy, and the masters shall unite their efforts to strengthen the ties of respect and attachment between the people and the school, so that the people may accustom themselves more and more to regard education as one of the essential conditions of public life, and may daily take a deeper interest in its progress."

## THE TRAINING OF PRIMARY TEACHERS, MODE OF APPOINTMENT, PROMOTION AND PUNISHMENT

The best plans of instruction cannot be executed except by the instrumentality of good teachers; and the state has done nothing for popular education, if it does not watch that those who devote themselves to teaching be well prepared; then suitably placed, encouraged and guided in the duty of continued self-improvement; and lastly, promoted and rewarded in proportion to their advancement, or punished according to their faults. Such is the object of Title VI. of the law of 1819. We translate that, as we did those which preceded.

"A schoolmaster, to be worthy of his vocation, should be pious, discreet, and deeply impressed with the dignity and sacredness of his calling. He should be thoroughly acquainted with the duties peculiar to the grade of primary instruction in which he desires to be employed; he should possess the art of communicating knowledge, with that of moulding the minds of children; he should be unshaken in his loyalty to the state, conscientious in the duties of his office, friendly and judicious in his intercourse with the parents of his pupils, and with his fellow-citizens in general; finally, he should strive to inspire them with a lively interest in the school, and secure to it their favour and support.

*"Of the Training of Schoolmasters.*

"In order gradually to provide schools with masters of this character, the care of their training must not be abandoned to chance; the foundation of primary normal schools (*Schullehrer-Seminarien,*) must be continued. The expenses of these establishments shall be defrayed partly by the general funds of the state, and partly by the departmental funds for schools.

"To repair the annual loss of schoolmasters, each department should have, as far as possible, a corresponding number of young men, who have been well trained, and are of acknowledged aptitude for the office (*Candidaten*); that is, each department will need a primary normal school. The following regulations will serve as the groundwork of such establishments.

"1. No primary normal school shall admit more than sixty or seventy pupils (*Präparanden*).

"2. In each department peopled by a nearly equal number of protestants and catholics, there shall be established, if resources and circumstances permit, a primary normal school for each religion. But where the inequality in this respect is great, the schools of the less numerous sect shall be supplied with masters from the primary normal school of the same sect in a neighbouring department, or from small establishments annexed to a primary school of the ordinary class. Normal schools, common to protestants and catholics, shall be permitted, when each pupil can receive the religious instruction appropriate to his faith.

"3. In order, without rigorous confinement, to preserve the pupils from the dissipation, allurements, and habits of

a kind of life which does not accord with their future condition, the primary normal schools shall, as far as practicable,
be established only in towns of moderate size. On the other
hand, it is desirable that the town be not so small as to deprive them of the advantages derived from the neighbourhood of schools of different grades. Regard also must be had
to the character, to the mode of life and the manners of the
inhabitants of the town.

"4. That the primary normal schools may be able to select
and train their own recruits, they shall, if possible, be placed
near to houses of education for orphans and paupers; but
their choice of pupils must be limited to such boys as exhibit
a decided talent and a natural aptitude for teaching, never
diverting any from the pursuit he would have preferred.
The asylums for orphan girls will contribute in like manner to the supply of schoolmistresses.

"5. It is not necessary that there should be two kinds of
primary normal schools, one for training the masters of
elementary schools and another the masters of burgher
schools; because, in the first place, the latter are based on
the former, and in the next, those who aim at the mastership of a burgher school will be the better able to prepare
themselves for that end in a single establishment, as they
will have access to burgher schools, where they will be able
to practise the appropriate exercises.

"6. The studies of the primary normal schools are, however, essentially different from those of the simply primary
schools. Their pupils are expected to possess already all the
knowledge communicated in the primary schools; and their
special object is to add to the information thus acquired just
and enlarged notions on the art of teaching, and on the edu-

cation of children considered as a whole, or in the details of its different branches. But since, from a deficiency of boys sufficiently well prepared, it is seldom possible to proceed immediately to that which constitutes the main object of those schools, they will be permitted to receive pupils who are deficient in some parts of primary instruction, and to make these the subjects of their first labours.

"No one, however, shall be admitted to the primary normal schools who does not possess elementary knowledge of the lowest grade, or of whose morality there is the least doubt.

"The age of admission shall be from sixteen to eighteen years.

"7. The principal aim of the primary normal schools should be to form men, sound both in body and mind, and to imbue the pupils with the sentiment of religion, and with that zeal and love for the duties of a schoolmaster which is so closely allied to religion.

"The course of instruction and exercise shall comprehend all the branches which, according to the present law, are to be taught in primary schools.

"In the provinces where German is not spoken, the masters of primary normal schools must be especially careful thoroughly to familiarize the pupils with it, without however neglecting the language of the country.

"In all normal schools singing and playing on the organ shall be cultivated with the most sedulous and serious application.

"The gymnastic exercises in most general use shall form part of the system.

"With respect to methods of teaching, the endeavour shall

be, not so much to inculcate theories on the pupils, as to lead them by enlightened observation and their own experience to simple and lucid principles; and with this view, to the normal schools shall be attached others, in which the pupils may exercise themselves by practice.

"Towards the close of their course, the pupils of the normal schools shall be instructed in all the duties of schoolmasters towards their ecclesiastical and temporal superiors, towards the church, the parish or district, and the parents of the scholars.

"8. In each primary normal school the length of the course shall be three years, of which the first is devoted to supplemental primary instruction, the second to specific and more elevated studies, and the third to practice and occasional experiments in the primary schools annexed and in other schools of the place. When the supplemental instruction is not required, the course may be reduced to two years.

"9. As the preparation for so important a function as that of public teacher will admit of no interruption during this term of three or two years, no pupil, even when he shall have reached the age of military service, shall be called out to active service in the army. But pupils above twenty years of age shall be enrolled in the *Landwehr* of the first levy (*Aufgebot*); and those between seventeen and twenty may join in the drill of the *Landwehr* of the second levy.

"10. In every primary normal school certain allowances or exhibitions (*Stipendia*) shall be distributed among a fixed number of the poor scholars of good promise, but in such a manner as not to habituate them to too much ease and indulgence, or unfit them for the least lucrative of the masterships.

"11. Every pupil of a normal school receiving such allowance from the establishment, is obliged, at the expiration of the term, to accept the mastership to which the provincial consistories may appoint him; the prospect of advancement being, however, always set before him as the consequence of continued good conduct.

"12. The regulations of every primary normal school must be sanctioned by the minister of public instruction and ecclesiastical affairs, who, by reason of the great importance of these establishments to the civilization of the people, ought to be constantly informed of all that concerns them. The immediate superintendence will be exercised by the provincial consistories, and, in what relates to the religious instruction of each communion, more particularly by the ecclesiastical authorities.

"But preparation for teaching need not be confined to the primary normal schools. The great primary schools also present means of training boys to the business of a schoolmaster.

"Moreover, clergymen, or skilful schoolmasters, may train up masters for either village or town schools; only they must have the permission of the provincial consistory, which will have the power of withdrawing its sanction if the end seems not to be attained, or of sending the pupils to a primary normal school, there to finish their education, should the mode of preparation, though good as far as it goes, appear incomplete.

"The superintendence of these small preparatory establishments may be confided to the inspectors of circles (*Kreis-inspectoren*).

"Where these small establishments are annexed to girls' schools, they will serve to train schoolmistresses.

## Of the Appointment of Schoolmasters.

"As a general rule, any man of mature age, of irreproachable morals and sincere piety, who understands the duties of the office he aspires to fill, and gives satisfactory proofs that he does, is fit for the post of public teacher. Foreigners, who satisfy all these conditions, are eligible as public teachers in Prussia.

"But the places of schoolmaster belong by preference to the pupils of the primary normal schools, who shall have gone through the course of two or three years in those establishments, who shall have been found qualified at the half-yearly or yearly examinations in the theory and practice of all branches of tuition in use in the town or country schools, and who shall be furnished with a certificate of capacity.

"In order to conduct these examinations, commissions of competent men shall be nominated, composed of two clerical and two lay members. The clerical members for the examinations of protestant teachers shall be nominated by the ecclesiastical authorities of the province; those for the catholic teachers, by the bishop of the diocese. The lay members shall be nominated by the provincial consistory.

"The members of these commissions are not nominated for a permanency; they may be removed every three years.

"The examination of catholic teachers, concerning religion and all subjects connected with it, is conducted separately, under the superintendence of an ecclesiastic of high rank, delegated by the archbishop; the examination concerning instruction, under that of a councillor of the provincial consistory.

In the case of protestant teachers, the two parts of the examination are likewise separated; the first takes place under the superintendence of a clergyman, the second under that of a lay councillor of the provincial consistory.

"But the two parts of the examination, though distinct, are considered as forming one whole; all the members of the commission assist at them, and the result is announced in one and the same certificate.

"These examinations must equally be passed by those who have been trained out of the normal schools, on which account the time of the examinations must be early announced by the provincial consistories in the official prints of the province.

"Every young man whose competency is admitted shall receive a certificate, delivered and signed by the whole commission, his examiners, by their president, and by the head master of the primary normal school or other establishment in which he was trained to his calling. It must state his moral character, and his degree of aptitude for teaching. The certificates of capacity will therefore bear the title of 'excellent' (*vorzüglich*), 'good or sufficient' (*hinläglich*), 'passable' (*nothdürftig*): they should also specify and positively define the degree of fitness of the person, whether for the higher primary schools, or for those which are elementary. Such as prove incompetent shall, by a formal decree, be wholly rejected, or sent back to continue their studies.

"Those who, not having been educated in the primary normal schools, or in any similar establishment, wish to obtain situations as teachers, must present themselves for examination to the competent authority, when they will generally be transferred to the grand and solemn examinations of the normal schools. But if urgent reasons demand an examination extraordinary, two judges, one ecclesiastical and one lay, may be named for the purpose, who shall, jointly, examine them in all the branches of primary instruction.

"The religious examination of the young men intended for the separate schools of small Christian sects, or Jewish communities, shall be left to the principals of those schools.

"All teachers who have been found on examination fit for the duties of master, shall be placed, with the index of the degree of their certificate, upon the list of the candidates of each department, and shall have a claim to an appointment. That they may obtain situations as soon as possible, the names of the eligible candidates shall be published every six months in the official papers of the departments, and the order of their classification shall be regulated by that of their certificates.

"The mistresses of public schools must equally give proof of their fitness for teaching, in examinations appointed by the provincial consistories.

"At the expiration of three years from the promulgation of this law, no masters shall be appointed to the schools which are not German, but such as know the German language and are capable of teaching it.

*Mode of Appointment; with whom rests the Choice and Appointment of the Schoolmasters.*

"With respect to the associations for the country schools organized conformably to this law, the election and nomination of the schoolmasters resides in the committees of such associations; and the ecclesiastical inspectors of the school shall, as members of these committees, present the individuals esteemed fit for the office.

"In town schools already founded and endowed, for the maintenance of which the rate levied on the householders of the place is not necessary, the right of election and nomination is exercised by the founders, with the co-operation of the persons invested with power by the state.

"In schools which depend entirely, or in part, on the above-mentioned rate, the municipal authorities of the parish take part in the election and nomination of masters, and exercise this right by deputies, whom they nominate for that purpose.

"In all schools and houses of education in towns founded by the king, the election and nomination to the masterships are conducted by the provincial consistories; except when they are particular authorities in whom this right is vested.

"But when the schools are partly supported by the funds of the town, or the rate levied on householders, the municipal authorities of the town have by right a voice in the election.

"In the particular establishments of small Christian sects, or Jewish communities, this same right is given to the trustees of the community.

"When assistant-masters (*Hülfslehrer*) are wanted in a

school for a short time only, they are appointed directly by the provincial consistories, subject, for the catholic schools, to the approbation of the bishops.

"A brevet (*Anstellungsurkunde,*—testimonial of appointment,) shall be delivered to every regular master, whether for the superior or inferior schools, by the authorities by whom he was nominated. The extraordinary and assistant teachers receive only a simple nomination from the authorities who appoint them.

"No schoolmaster's brevet shall be granted, unless the person has been, previously to his election, inscribed upon the list of candidates, or unless he has subsequently submitted to the required examination.

"In every brevet the duties of the individual named should be enumerated as exactly as possible. In the case of masters of inferior schools, regard shall in general be had to the more precise instructions which should be given by the provincial consistories respecting the duties of masters. All the emoluments of the office must also be exactly stated and guarantied to the master.

"No contract for a determinate time shall be made with the schoolmasters, except for the situation of teacher extraordinary, or of assistant in the superior or inferior schools.

"The schoolmaster's brevets shall have no validity or legal force till they have obtained the royal ratification (*landesherrlichc Bestätigung*).

"The ratification of the appointment to a schoolmastership shall, in general, be claimed by those who deliver the brevet of nomination to the provincial consistories, which, according to the extent of their powers, shall grant this ratification, or shall obtain it from the ministerial authorities.

"For the masterships to which the provincial consistories have the immediate appointment, the ratification of the brevet of nomination shall be necessary only when it must be granted by the ministerial authorities; in all other cases, the brevets given by the consistories shall be sufficient.

"The brevets of catholic teachers shall be sent to the bishops, who shall declare if there be no objection on their part to the nomination; and they shall forward this declaration, together with the brevet, to the provincial consistories, who will give the ratification and send it to the nominee.

"If any difference of opinion arise between the provincial consistories and the bishops which they cannot settle, the question shall be decided by the ministerial authority.

"The brevets of the public teachers of the small Christian sects, or Jewish communities, must likewise, to acquire legal validity, receive the ratification of the provincial consistories.

"Brevets sent to be ratified, must always be accompanied by a certificate of examination, and by one from the candidates' superiors, attesting their morality and good conduct.

"The authorities who nominate and ratify should carefully examine whether the candidates be eligible according to the forenamed conditions; whether the office have a regular stipend properly secured, and whether the brevet be according to legal form.

"Should a doubt arise on any of these points, or if the opportunity seem favourable for regulating other affairs relating to the school, the ratification of the brevet of nomination must not be given till all such matters are arranged.

The above-mentioned authorities are responsible for any neglect of which they may be guilty on this head.

"It is understood that they have the right of refusing the ratification to incompetent candidates, and of proceeding to a new election.

"They are also at liberty, if they find that the vacant places might be made a means of rewarding and encouraging persons of greater merit, to call the attention of the electors to them; but if these persist in the choice they have made, the ratification, if nothing can be alleged against the fitness of the person elected, must be granted.

"The brevets of new masters for primary schools, inferior or superior, must be sent for ratification within two months at furthest after the occurrence of the vacancy.

"If, from peculiar obstacles, this interval prove insufficient, a prolongation of it may be obtained on a statement of the reason; if not, the right of nominating devolves on the authorities whose business it is to ratify the brevet. In such cases, the nomination to the catholic masterships will be made by the bishop; and the ratification, in the ordinary way, by the provincial consistories.

"The brevets of nomination must be ratified by the royal authority, and returned to the hands of the schoolmaster elect, before he can be installed in his office, or be entitled to its revenues.

"The selection of an appropriate and solemn mode of installation (*Einsetzung*) is left at the discretion of those who immediately superintend each school; but the following rules are to be observed:—

"1. All those who enter for the first time upon the office of ordinary schoolmaster shall take oath, and those who are removed from one school to another shall promise, to perform with fidelity the duties of the post, of which they shall be informed beforehand, and to submit to the authority of their spiritual and temporal superiors.

"2. At the installation, the master shall be presented not only to the scholars, but also to the municipal body in the church. These presentations shall be conducted by the ecclesiastical members of the committee of superintendence, and accompanied by appropriate exhortations.

"In schools of a higher order, the teachers newly nominated shall, according to their rank, be presented to the more considerable bodies, either at solemnities appointed for the occasion, or on some regular public day of the school.

"3. At each installation an exact account of the ceremony shall be drawn up, signed by those whose duty it is to take part in it, and by the teacher himself; and the document shall be deposited with the official records of the school, and an authentic copy sent to the provincial consistories.

"4. Teachers shall enter upon possession, on the month of their installation, of the revenues secured to them in their brevet of nomination. Every deviation from this rule must have the especial approbation of the authorities who give the ratification.

"5. Schoolmasters in town or country, who are elected and confirmed, may require of the school-associations that they provide a conveyance for themselves, their family, and effects, free of expense, for the distance of twenty-five miles, or indemnify them for the expenses of removal. But if a master accept another situation within ten years from the time his nomination was ratified, he shall, in order that the school-associations or special school funds may not suffer from too heavy charges, be called upon for an idemnity, proportioned to the length of his service, for the outlay occasioned by his installation.

"That public teachers may devote themselves entirely to the performance of their duties and to the work of self-improvement, their liability to military service in time of peace is thus ordered: No master legally elected, nominated, confirmed and installed, though of an age to serve, shall be liable to active service, but shall be forthwith registered in the *Landwehr* of the first levy. Masters of less than twenty-five years of age, whose place can be supplied by their colleagues or by assistant masters, shall take part in the annual drill of the *Landwehr* of the first levy; but all those who, according to the certificate of the inspector of the school, cannot be so replaced, shall be registered for the exercise of the second levy, from which no master of an age to serve in the *Landwehr* can be exempted. In time of war, all these modifications cease, and every schoolmaster must submit to the unalterable regulations of the law of the third of September 1814, on the obligation to serve.

"It is the duty of the enlightened persons to whom the superintendence of the schools is confided, to watch over the progress of the masters in attainments.

"The directors and rectors of the gymnasia and town schools shall especially attend to the younger masters, give them advice, set them right, and excite them to aim at perfection, by attending to the plans of more experienced masters, by frequenting their society, by forming school-conferences or other meetings of schoolmasters, and by studying the best works on education.

"Every ecclesiastic, every inspector of a circle, is expected to show the same solicitude for the progress and improvement of the masters of the elementary schools which come under their cognizance.

"Moreover, the provincial consistories shall choose ecclesiastics and inspectors, zealous and skilful in popular instruction, and shall induce them to form and direct grand associations of town and country schoolmasters, for the purpose of keeping alive a sense of the dignity and sanctity of their vocation, of continuing their own improvement by regular meetings, by consultations, conversations, practical essays, written theses, dissertations on particular branches of tuition, by reading together well-selected works, and by the discussions to which they give rise.

"Those who direct such associations with remarkable industry and success shall be encouraged and supported, and have a claim to a recompense proportioned to the trouble they take.

"By a judicious selection of the inspectors of the schools of the circle, each district will in time have its schoolmasters' society.

"Moreover, masters of the lower schools, of good capacity but small attainments, shall be sent by the provincial consistories, for a certain time, to a primary normal school, to receive the instruction they may still need; and their schools shall in the mean time be supplied with temporary masters. The provincial consistories may even from time to time recall a certain number of masters, though of competent ability, to a primary normal school, or any other educational establishment of renown, there to go through a more complete course of tuition both in theory and practice; and particularly that they may make themselves acquainted with the latest improvements in the art of teaching; and also that they may effect a stricter union among themselves, and establish a beneficial interchange of learning, experience and opinions. In parts which are not German, the chief object of these courses and societies should be to give teachers already placed additional instruction in the German language.

"Liberty to form these societies, and to re-enter the primary normal schools, since they occasion expenses which fall upon the public funds, shall be asked every time from the ministerial authorities, to whom an account must be given of the progress and results of these conferences.

"The most eminent masters, those who are destined for the direction of the primary normal schools, shall also, with the consent, or even at the suggestion, of government, be enabled from the public funds to seek by travel, both in Prussia and other countries, more exact and extended information on the organization of primary schools, and their wants both internal and external.

"Able schoolmasters, who are faithful in their vocation and unremitting in self-improvement, shall be encouraged by promotion to places of a higher class, and even, on particular occasions, by extraordinary rewards. With a view to preserve the utmost possible regularity in the advancement of the numerous class of schoolmasters, and to order so that no superior teacher shall be below one who is inferior, the provincial consistories shall prepare tables of the masterships of town and country schools, classed according to their revenues, and shall take care that, in general, promotions are made according to these tables.

"Length of service alone shall not constitute a claim, nor

establish an absolute right, to advancement; but a teacher who petitions to be removed to a situation superior to that for which he has received a certificate, in whatever school he may be, shall undergo a new examination.

"This examination for promotion shall be conducted by the same persons as the former. It is always proportioned to the rank of the situation sought for. Masters proposed as directors, or headmasters, will be examined chiefly as to their knowledge of the business of teaching in general, and of the organization and good management of a school, suitably to its superior or inferior rank.

"When the competency of the individual proposed is so well known as to render a new trial unnecessary, the authorities who ratify for the post in question can dispense with the examination.

"Nothing shall be paid at any examination but the cost of the stamp of the certificate, whether for the candidateship, for appointment, or for promotion. In like manner, all charges for brevets of nomination and of ratification of masters recently appointed or promoted are abolished, except the stamp and postage.

"At the end of each year, the departmental authorities shall remit to government a list of all the schoolmasters recently appointed or promoted in the department, with a statement of the income of their situations; and these authorities shall not be held excusable if they suffer individual merit to be unemployed or unrewarded, or the least service to pass unnoticed.

"On the other hand, incompetent masters must not look for any encouragement or advancement, or to be treated otherwise than with rigour.

"When schoolmasters, who in other respects perform their duties well, manifest a spirit of resistance to their superiors, or live in dissention with their assistants or their school-committee, after reproof, exhortation, and even some disciplinary measures, have been tried without effect, the evil shall be put an end to by removing them to another place; nor must they be surprised if, in promotion to the degree of blame they merit, they sink into places of smaller income: but these changes, when adopted as punishments, must in no case take place without the consent of the supreme ministerial authority.

"If, after their removal, these masters still exhibit a turbulent spirit, or an inclination to oppose established rules, they shall then be deprived of their employment.

"The schoolmaster who, from indolence, carelessness, or bad disposition, neglects his occupation, instructs badly, or uses his power without discernment, shall be admonished first by the inspector of the school, and then by the inspector of the circle. If he does not amend, he shall be reported to the provincial authorities, who, on sufficient evidence, shall impose, amongst other penalties, and according to the income of the delinquent, progressive pecuniary fines, which shall be added to the funds of the school. If reprimands, threats, and punishments have no effect, his employment shall be taken from him.

"But if the want of educational skill in a master arise from an incapacity which might have been known, or which was known, before the ratification of his brevet, he shall be transferred to some occupation for which he is more fit, and the responsibility rests upon the authorities by whom he was so hastily proposed or so inconsiderately confirmed.

"Those teachers who give scandal to their pupils, and to the inhabitants of their neighbourhood, by their principles or conduct, in a moral, religious, or political point of view, shall be deprived, as unworthy of office.

"Gross violations of modesty, temperance, moderation, or any open abuse of his authority as father, husband, or head of a family, shall be punished in a schoolmaster by the loss of his place.

"The punishment of offences against religion is fixed by the members, and according to the constitution, of the church to which the school, district, or master belong.

"As the character of teachers should be pure and irreproachable, the proper authorities shall, as soon as such accusations are made, examine into the case, and when the offence involves the loss of office, shall instantly take the necessary steps.

"Members of school-committees, and inspectors, who in any of these cases are guilty of negligence, shall be held responsible, and, according to circumstances, subjected to a pecuniary fine or to loss of office.

"If a schoolmaster be guilty of an offence which is the subject of criminal proceedings, his superiors shall previously suspend him, and send the case for final judgement to the regular authorities.

"If a schoolmaster be found guilty by a criminal tribunal, he shall also be deprived of his post. The court in passing sentence shall also pronounce his dismissal.

"But if the civil authorities seize the criminal, and commit him for trial, without the preliminary accusation, they shall immediately give notice to the authority which has the immediate charge of the post in question, and which shall forthwith take the requisite measures relating to it.

"If schoolmasters, whose conduct is otherwise good, be sent to prison for a few days for some slight offence of correctional police, and the provincial consistories think that they cannot without degrading the office of teacher suffer them to continue in their present post, they shall remove them as soon as possible to another.

"No master shall be deprived of his place except by a judgement pronounced after an examination and statement of the facts by the provincial consistories.

"Therefore,—

"1. It is expressly recommended to the provincial consistories to proceed with the most rigorous caution. On every occasion they must procure the aid of a lawyer and an inspector, who are bound to receive all documents relating to the question; and when the offence is against religion, they shall ask the advice of the provincial ecclesiastic authorities, and in the case of catholic masters, that of the bishop. When the investigation is finished, they may adopt disciplinary measures, or call in the intervention of a court of justice.

"2. If this latter step be deemed necessary, as soon as all the documents relating to the examination, and to the preliminary statement of the evidence, are given in, the proper tribunal shall be required to pronounce sentence of expulsion, and while the trial is pending the provincial consistory shall suspend the accused.

"The place of a schoolmaster thus or otherwise suspended shall be supplied in the manner which circumstances render most convenient, and half the stipend shall be devoted to the payment of the substitute. If this prove insufficient, the deficiency shall be supplied from the funds of the school, or from those of the parish, or by contributions; or else, if all these fail, recourse shall be had to the provincial school-funds.

"When a teacher is suspended, he shall give up the whole or part of the school-house, if his continued connexion with the school is likely to be dangerous, or if the lodging be required for his substitute. If it be necessary that he leave the school-house entirely, his wants shall be provided for till the close of the judicial inquiry.

"3. In the Rhenish provinces, all such affairs are declared within the competency of the correctional court, within the jurisdiction of which the accused is domiciliated.

"4. The course to be followed by the courts in this kind of process is the ordinary one; except that, in the other provinces, the provincial consistories have the right of naming a deputy, who shall be heard on the business, and who shall assist in the discussion at the time judgement is given. In the Rhenish provinces, the *Procureur d'état* shall be empowered to demand explanations and information from the provincial consistories whenever he shall think proper. In the said provinces, the necessary deviations from the ordinary course shall be left to the decision of the provincial consistories of that part of the kingdom.

"5. The accused, as well as the authorities, have a right of appealing, either on questions of fact or of law, within the term, and according to the forms prescribed by the judiciary instructions then in force.

"6. The higher ministerial authorities shall decide, from

the reasons of the master's dismissal, and from his subsequent conduct, whether he ought to be excluded for ever from the exercise of his functions, or whether, after a time, he shall be reinstated.

"7. Lastly, whenever schoolmasters are brought to trial, the courts of justice shall instantly communicate the sentence to the provincial consistories, or the authorities presiding over schools, in order that they may immediately proceed to take the measures which the circumstances demand."

OF THE GOVERNMENT OF PRIMARY INSTRUCTION, OR OF THE AUTHORITIES TO WHOM THE SUPERINTENDENCE OF SCHOOLS IS COMMITTED.

Such is the general organization of primary instruction. But to suppose that this mechanism will work of itself, is expecting too much from it and from human nature. It requires an administration whose eye and hand shall watch and animate the whole. I shall now proceed to lay before you the system of government set over primary instruction in Prussia. It has been of necessity referred to in the foregoing chapters, but this is the place for treating it in detail.

The fundamental principle is, that the ancient and beneficial union of popular education with Christianity and the church ought to be maintained in a just and reasonable measure, always under the supreme control of the state, and of the minister of public instruction and ecclesiastical affairs.

I refer again to the law of 1819.

We will begin with the parishes.

## Parish Authorities.

"General rule: As every parish, in town or country, has its primary school or schools, so every primary school, in town or country, shall have its own particular management, its own special committee of superintendence (*Schulvorstand*).

## Primary Schools in the Country.

"1. The committee of each country elementary school shall consist, in places where the church contributes to the support of the school, of the patron of the church, of the clergyman of the parish to which the school belongs, of the magistrates of the *commune* where several villages are associated, and of one or two householders, members of the school-association. In every such association, comprehending persons of different communions, care shall be taken that each communion, according to the number of householders belonging to it, shall have representatives in the managing committee of the school.

"2. The patrons or founders (if there be any), the clergyman and the magistrates of the parish or *commune,* form the managing committee of the school. The other members are elected by the school-association of the *commune;* but they shall be proposed for the approbation of the provincial consistory by the intermediate school-authority; namely, that of the circle, *Kreisschulbehörden* (circle-school-authority), that is, the Kreisschulinspectoren (circle-school-inspectors).

"The members who are elected shall hold their seats four years, with the power of being re-elected.

"No one shall refuse to become one of the managing school-committee; the only legitimate excuse shall be the possession of other offices in the parish.

"3. For schools endowed entirely by the church, the clergy may act as substitutes for the managing committee; but they shall be bound to observe all the obligations and all the duties imposed upon ordinary committees of management.

"4. The managing committees have cognisance of all school matters; the entire superintendence of such, both internally and externally, rests with them. All that belongs to the internal order of the school, as also to the superintendence and direction of the masters, should be the peculiar office of the ecclesiastical members of the managing committee: the pastor or curate of the village, who is one of this committee, is also the natural inspector of the school of the village, and shall visit the school frequently, and attend to the teachers. He takes part, too, in the external management and superintendence of the school; but he shall not be required to interfere in the collection of the revenues, nor in anything relating to them, nor in the special management of the school-funds.

"The committees are the first authorities empowered to receive complaints of the schools or of the teachers from school-associations, or from their individual members; as well as those from the teachers themselves, or from the scholars: they also constitute the medium through which petitions or claims are transmitted to the higher authorities.

"The efforts of these committees ought to be mainly directed to the organizing and maintaining of the schools conformably to the laws and regulations, so that they may accomplish their end: with which view, they shall advise, direct, and support the teachers, try to make the inhabitants of the parish love their schools, excite their interest and their zeal, and finally strive to remove the coarseness and ignorance of the country youth.

"5. Each managing committee shall meet every three months, on a stated day, and as often besides as may be needful, to deliberate on the concerns entrusted to it.

"They shall also, if advised by the ecclesiastical member specially charged with the superintendence of the school, summon the master to attend any of their meetings, and to give his opinion on the affairs of his school.

"6. All the members of the managing committees fill this office gratuitously; but the ecclesiastics charged with the superintendence of the schools shall be fetched and taken home at the expense of the school-society, when they have not horses of their own, and the school they have to visit is out of their parish.

"7. More precise statements of the powers of the committees of management shall be published by the provincial consistories, in accordance with the general provisions of the present law, and with reference to the particular circumstances of the different provinces.

"8. In villages where there are two schools, one common administration shall be formed for the two, composed of the patron of the church, if in this capacity he contribute to the support of the said schools, or of one of them; of the ecclesiastic or ecclesiastics of the place; of the municipal authorities, and of one Christian householder for each school.

"9. Small Christian sects throughout the country shall be permitted to organize, according to their particular constitution and discipline, the management of their own schools; only they must always make known to the district-inspector what that management is, and to whom entrusted. They shall be bound, whensoever called upon, to give all requisite information; and they shall in no way resist, if the provincial consistories think proper to ordain a revision of their schools. The same shall be granted, on like conditions, to the Jews, who take no part in the school-association of the parish they inhabit, and who have their own peculiar schools; but they shall be bound to give all the information necessary for regulating the attendance of the children who are of age to go to these schools.

### Primary Schools in Towns.

"1. In small towns, where there is but one school, the managing committees shall be composed in exactly the same manner, and shall have the same powers as those of the country; only, where there are two or more clergymen, the highest in rank shall belong to the committee; also a member of the municipal magistracy (*Mitglied des Magistrats*), and one of the representatives of the burghers or citizens.

"2. In small or middle-sized towns which contain several primary schools, a common committee of management shall be formed in like manner for all (*Ortsschulbehörde*,—literally, school-authorities of the place); only a Christian householder of each school, and a clergyman of each faith, if the schools are of different communions, shall, of right, have a seat in this council. If it be deemed necessary, a person specially versed in school business (*Schulmann*,—school-man,) shall also be admitted.

"If there be any private schools in such towns, which have already their own peculiar management, they shall not be broken up by the establishment of the higher school-authorities above named.

"3. Large towns shall be divided into school districts, having each its school-committee.

"But in every large town there shall be a central point of superintendence for all the schools except the gymnasia; this central point is the school-commission (*Schulcommission*). The school-commissions shall be composed of the superintendent, of the dean or highest ecclesiastic of the place, and (according to the extent of the town and the number of schools) of one or two members of the municipality, who shall be elected by the body itself; of an equal number of the representatives of the burghers or citizens, and of one or two persons skilled in matters of education. A member of each managing committee shall be added besides, if some such have not already, in virtue of other functions, a seat in the commission. Peculiar circumstances may furnish sufficient cause for deviation from this rule.

"4. All the committees and commissions of town schools shall be confirmed by the provincial consistories. These are bound to exercise vigilant care that none be admitted but upright judicious men, zealous for the good cause of education, and esteemed by their fellow-citizens.

"They shall have the right of refusing the ratification of the nomination of incompetent persons, of demanding new elections, and, if the second nominee for the same place be ineligible, of immediately filling up the place themselves.

"5. The members introduced by election shall be confirmed for six years, and may be re-elected. On the other hand, no elected member shall be obliged to act in these commissions for more than three years.

"No man can refuse to act in these commissions, except for the same reasons which release from the obligation to join the managing committees of village schools, namely, municipal duties.

"6. The authority of the school-commissions extends over all the schools of each town, which they shall preserve in harmony one with the other.

"Throughout the whole extent of their jurisdiction, their duty is,—

"1.) To take care that the town be provided with the necessary schools of different degrees, and properly connected with each other:

"2.) To inquire into the wants of the schools, and the means of supplying them, and to assist in the assessment and collection of the rates or loans of the householders:

"3.) To make themselves well acquainted with the state of all the school-funds and revenues, general as well as particular:

"4.) To take charge of the general fund of the schools of the town:

"5.) To enforce the execution of whatever is ordained by the law, the minister, or the provincial consistories, in order to secure proper instruction to all children of an age to go to school, and to prevent even the poorest among them from growing up neglected and without education, in beggary and all the vices which idleness begets and fosters:

"6.) To apply themselves diligently to the improvement of the schools, and to animate the zeal of their fellow-citizens;

to offer suggestions on this subject to the magistrates and town-authorities, and enable them, from exact information on all that relates to the schools of the place, to judge correctly of their wants, and of the best means of supplying them; to keep alive the zeal of the teachers, and give them advice and direction.

"7. Their immediate jurisdiction shall extend over all the primary schools of the town, and the educational establishments of the same grade; over the orphan-houses, the poor's schools, and those supported by pious endowments in the towns and their suburbs.

"They shall superintend and direct the internal as well as the external affairs of these establishments; and in this respect they represent the whole authority of the town, except in the election of the head master, the administration of the property, and management of the judicial matters of the schools.

"The several committees of the different circles of large towns shall have the superintendence of their several schools; but they are subordinate to the school-commission of the same towns.

"8. Their superintendence shall extend to the primary schools and houses of education of the same grade belonging to the church or to other corporate bodies, only in as far as it shall be necessary to keep these schools within the limits of the law, their management being left to those whom it concerns. The commission can have no cognisance of those schools, except through the reports of the special managing bodies, from which it will derive the required information on the internal and external condition of such schools; it shall, however, have power to procure more exact information by the visits of such of its members as are conversant with these matters.

"9. The school-commission has no other connexion with the gymnasia of the town, than the receiving the information necessary for regulating the attendance of the children who are of an age to go there.

"10. The particular schools of small Christian sects in towns shall hold the same relation to the commission and committees of the town schools, as the same schools in the country do to the inspectors of circles.

"11. Every Jewish school in a town should have a managing body of its own, composed of members of the Jewish community; but such schools shall also be subject to the superintendence of the school-committees, which may not only demand of the managers any information they may need, but by frequent visits may ascertain the actual state of such schools.

"12. All private establishments for instruction or education in large towns are under the superintendence of the school-commission, through the medium of the school-committees; and in small towns, under that of the committees, as we shall see hereafter.

"13. The labours of these committees, and of the commission, shall be so divided amongst the members, that the external affairs of the school shall fall more especially to the charge of the laymen, and the internal arrangements to that of the clergy, and of those peculiarly versed in such matters.

"14. The school-commission and the committees of circles shall regularly meet once a month, and shall hold extraordinary meetings whenever circumstances require. The presidents or chairmen of these meetings shall always be elected for three years by the members, and confirmed by the provincial consistories.

"Questions shall be determined by a majority of voices, except such as relate to the internal affairs of the school, which shall be decided by the opinion of the ecclesiastical members and those familiar with the subject; but no person in the commission shall have two votes, even when he holds two offices.

"15. The committees shall be free to convoke all or part of the clergy and schoolmasters of the circle, to assist in extraordinary meetings.

"16. The servants and officers of the municipal authorities also work for the school-committees and commissions, when the local school-funds are not able to pay officers of their own.

"17. The members of the committees and commissions fill their posts gratuitously. The treasurers (*Rendanten*) alone shall have a claim to remuneration, proportioned to their services.

"18. At the end of each year the school-commissions shall send up to the provincial consistories circumstantial reports of the condition of the schools within their jurisdiction. In small towns, and in the country, this report shall be made through the inspectors of circles,—a new school-authority, whose character and functions must now be explained.

### Authorities or Officers of Circles.

"1. There shall be a general superintendence of the lower schools in the country and in the small towns of a circle, as also of all the managing committees of these schools: and this superintendence shall be exercised by the overseer or inspector of the circle (*Kreisschulaufseher* or *Kreisschulinspector*).

"The school-circles shall be the same as, or shall be commensurate with, the circles of ecclesiastical superintendence for protestants, and the corresponding divisions for catholics.

"Those ecclesiastical circles which are too wide for one range of school-inspection, shall be divided into two or three circles of school-inspection.

"2. In general, the superintendents shall be the circle-inspectors for the evangelical (*i. e.* protestant) schools; and therefore great care shall be taken, at the time of their nomination, to raise to this post none but clergymen who possess, besides the qualities indispensable in their profession, a considerable acquaintance with schools, who enter upon it with zeal and alacrity, and who are fit for their office. Clergymen who are not superintendents, may be appointed inspectors of school-circles, particularly when an ecclesiastical circle shall be divided into several circles of school-inspection; and also when it is desired by the superintendent himself, on account of his age, infirmities, or multiplied occupations; or when the provincial consistory, for other important reasons, shall deem it advisable. In the two first cases, it is necessary to have the assent of the superintendent to the choice of the inspector of the circle; in the last, the opinion of the minister of public instruction and ecclesiastical affairs shall be taken.

"Laymen also, when circumstances require, may be appointed circle-inspectors, with the previous approbation of the minister of public instruction and ecclesiastical affairs; but especial care shall be taken to choose none but such men as are remarkable for good sense, and activity in the cause of education, and who are generally esteemed for the dignity of their character and conduct.

"3. The circle-inspectors for catholic schools are commonly the deans. The appointment of other ecclesiastics, or of laymen, as inspectors of school-circles, is authorised in like cases and on like conditions as in the evangelical (protestant) schools.

"4. The circle-inspectors for protestant schools shall be nominated by the provincial consistories, and confirmed by the minister of public instruction.

"The circle-inspectors for catholic schools shall be proposed by the bishops, and presented, with a statement of the grounds of recommendation, by the provincial consistories to the minister of public instruction, who confirms the appointment. The minister shall have the power to refuse the confirmation, if well-founded objections can be established against the party, and to require the bishop to propose a new candidate.

"Without the previous confirmation of the minister of public instruction, no circle-inspector, protestant or catholic, shall be installed or enter upon his office.

"5. The duties of the circle-inspectors shall be, to examine into the interior of schools, and the conduct of the committees and masters of such schools. The whole system of teaching and of education pursued in the schools shall be submitted to their revision and their superior direction.

"They shall strive to arrange each school in harmony with the present law, with the particular rules of the provincial consistories for each province, and with the instructions those consistories may issue.

"They shall animate and direct the schoolmasters and the ecclesiastical members of the committees, encourage those who do well, admonish betimes those who do ill; and, if these admonitions are insufficient, report them to the higher authorities. The same obligation is imposed upon them with respect to the moral conduct of the schoolmasters. One essential part of their task is, to watch over and promote the continual improvement of the head masters and their assistants.

"6. The inspectors of circles shall take care to be constantly informed on the state of the schools in their circle, by means of the reports which the parochial committees are bound to send them every six months, of all changes and events of any importance occurring in the schools; by attending the examinations; by making as many visits as possible in person and unexpected, and by the solemn revisions which every circle-inspector is to make once every year of all the schools within his district. At these revisions they shall examine the children in public; they shall also inquire into all that concerns the school; they shall exact an account of the internal and external administration from the committee of management; listen to the complaints or the wishes of the members of the association, and take measures to remedy whatever is amiss. They shall send a complete report of the revision to the provincial consistories, which from time to time shall appoint councillors from their own body to assist in these revisions, or order revisions extraordinary.

"7. In what relates to the external affairs of the country

schools, the circle-inspectors shall act in concert with the councillors of the circle included within the range of their inspection. These councillors (*Landräthe*) shall give active attention to all things which concern the external state of the schools, whether their co-operation have been claimed by the inspectors of circles or by the provincial consistories.

"8. The installation of the school-committees of management is conducted by the circle-inspectors; but these shall invariably give notice to the councillor of the circle (*Landrath*), that he may be present at the ceremony.

"9. All orders, all inquiries of the provincial consistories relative to the internal affairs of the schools, shall be addressed to the circle-inspectors; and, on the other hand, it is their place to lay the internal wants of the schools, and of their masters, before the provincial consistories.

"The inspectors of catholic schools shall be bound to give the bishop of their diocese every information required of them on all the religious part of the constitution of schools, and their spiritual discipline; they shall receive the instructions of the bishops on this subject: but their first duty is to make known to the provincial consistories the general state of the schools. On the other hand, they shall communicate to the bishops the report of the annual revision addressed to the provincial consistories.

"10. The protestant inspectors, both in this capacity and in virtue of the places they already hold as ecclesiastics, are in connexion with the synods; but they, as well as the clerical members of the committees of management, shall inform the synods of the condition and wants of the schools, and shall interchange the fruits of their experience and their opinions on primary education at their meetings. Suggestions on this subject may be inserted in the reports of the synods. The lay-inspectors shall give the synods written accounts of the state of the schools in their jurisdiction.

"11. The superintendence of the schools of peculiar churches, such as the scattered members of the smaller Christian sects in the country, is confided to the inspectors of circles.

"12. Private establishments for education in the country shall also be committed to the superintendence of the said inspectors.

"But with respect to general police, they are, like the establishments above mentioned, in the jurisdiction of the ordinary police-authorities of the country.

"13. Every school-inspector shall receive an annual allowance for the travelling expenses of the revisions and visitations made in the course of his duty. The provincial consistories shall determine the sum, as well as the funds from which it shall be drawn.

"At the time of the annual revision of the schools, the school-associations shall fetch and send back the circle-inspectors; but for extraordinary visits out of their districts, they shall (according to the ordinance of the 28th February 1816, relative to allowances for board and travelling,) either travel post with three horses, or hire a carriage, and send in their account to the departmental authorities.

"14. The provincial consistories shall publish more precise instructions, based upon this law, relative to the powers of the circle-inspectors over the schools of both communions.

"But in confirming and determining here anew (says the royal edict of 1819) the share of the clergy in the superintendence of the schools, we at the same time ordain, to the end that they may exercise this superintendence in a more enlightened manner, and that they may thus be enabled to maintain their dignity with the schoolmasters, that every clergyman, whether of the protestant or catholic church, study both the theory and practice of popular instruction; that he strive to render his studies, whether at the university, the catholic faculties of theology, or the primary normal schools, available to this end; and, if he do not himself teach in the public schools whilst he is a candidate for holy orders, that at least he acquaint himself with their organization, and with the subjects there taught.

"At the time of the examinations for a curacy, or for the office of pastor, particular attention shall be paid to the knowledge the candidate possesses on the subject of education and teaching; and, in future, none shall be admitted into holy orders, if at these examinations he do not give proof of the knowledge necessary for the right management and superintendence of schools. In the provinces possessing establishments in which the clerical candidates can acquire such knowledge, this regulation shall come into force in one year after the promulgation of the present law; and at the end of two years, in provinces which have not the same advantages.

"From a just reliance on the religious sentiments and enlightened views of the whole ecclesiastical body, we are confident that the share of salutary superintendence of the lower schools, which is entrusted to them in order to preserve the bond between the church and the schools, will be performed with dignity, but also with gentleness and love; that they will honour the respectable profession of teacher in the persons of all its members; that they will endeavour to secure to them, in their parishes, the consideration which is their due, and will always support them with vigour and firmness."

The law of 1819 concludes with the circle-inspector. But I ought to add, that above this inspector, the departmental councillor to whom he addresses himself, and who, in the business of primary instruction, represents the departmental authorities so often mentioned here, is the school-councillor (*Schulrath*), an officer belonging to the council of civil administration of the department, and who nevertheless is named by the minister of public instruction and ecclesiastical affairs. This administrative council of the department, the regency (*Regierung*), represented by the *Schulrath,* must not be confounded with the provincial consistories, of which the school-board (*Schulcollegium*) forms a part. This high scholastic authority, which is *provincial* and not *departmental,* does not interfere with primary instruction, except on the most important points; as, for example, on all that relates to the primary normal schools, which are above the jursdiction of the several regencies, of the *Schulrath,* and of the circle-inspector. . . .

. . . This law, [of 1819] without going into detail with relation to any particular branch, omits no topic of interest, and is the most extensive and complete law on primary instruction of which I have any knowledge.

It is impossible not to be struck with its profound wisdom. No inapplicable general principles, no spirit of system, no partial or exclusive views govern the legislator. He avails himself of all the means that can conduce to his end, however widely these means may differ. It is a king, and an absolute king, who issued this law; it is an irresponsible minister who advised or who digested it; and yet we find no injudicious spirit of centralization or of official despotism (*bureaucratie ministérielle*); almost everything is left to the parochial, departmental, or provincial authorities; little more than the general supervision and direction are reserved to the minister. The clergy have a great share in the managment of popular instruction, and householders are also consulted in the towns and villages. In a word, all persons or classes who have an interest in the subject, find their appropriate place in this organization, and concur, each in his own manner and degree, to the common end, which is, the civilization of the people.

On these grounds the Prussian law of 1819 appears to me excellent; nor is it to be imagined, that such a law could be conceived and matured by the wisdom of an individual. Baron von Altenstein rather digested than created it. Indeed we may almost say, that it already existed in a vast number of partial and detached ordinances, and in the manners and customs of the country. There is, perhaps, not a single article of this long law to which numerous anterior regulations did not serve as a groundwork; and, in a paper on the history of primary instruction in Prussia inserted in the first number of the second volume of the Journal of Primary Instruction, by Councillor Backendorf, I find rules as old as the years 1728 and 1736 which comprise a number of the provisions of the law of 1819. The obligation of parents to send their children to school is of great antiquity in Prussia. The powerful and active superintendence exercised by the church over the education of the people, dates from the origin of protestantism, of which it is an inherent characteristic. It is evident that the authors of a revolution effected in the name of liberty of conscience must necessarily labour at the emancipation of the popular mind, and the diffusion of knowledge, as the only secure means of defending their cause and rooting it in the minds of the people. Unquestionably the law of 1819 raises education to a sufficiently high pitch in the elementary schools and those for the middle classes; but if the course of instruction seem somewhat too full for some places or districts, it must be remembered that it was already acted up to, and even surpassed, in many others. The boldest measure was the establishment of a grand primary normal school for each department; but there were already similar establishments in most of the old provinces of the monarchy. In short, this law does little more than methodize what already existed, not only in Prussia, but throughout Germany.

It is not, then, a metaphysical, arbitrary and artificial abstraction, like the greater part of our laws on primary instruction; it is founded on reality and experience, and has, for that reason, been carried into execution, and produced the happiest results with extraordinary rapidity. Having taken care to ascertain that it was everywhere practicable, the Prussian minister peremptorily required that it should everywhere be practised; leaving the details to the authorities appointed to execute them, and reserving to himself only the general guidance and supervision. This guidance has been so firm, this supervision has been so vigilant, and the parochial, departmental and provincial authorities (*i.e.* the *Schulcollegium* or school-board in the provincial consistories, the *Schulrath* in each departmental council, or regency, the *Commissions* in the towns, and the *Committees* in each urban or rural parish)—in short all the individuals or bodies entrusted with the management of schools have displayed so steady and well-directed a zeal, that in almost every part of the kingdom the reality actually goes beyond the law; and, on all points at least where zeal alone is required, even more is done than is commanded. Thus, for instance, the law established one great primary normal school in each department; now, not only is this fulfilled to the letter, but in many departments there are, besides, several small subsidiary normal schools;—a result which implies all the others; since primary normal schools can flourish only in proportion to the demand for masters, and the existence of situations affording a decent subsistence to masters says everything that can be said as to the prevalence of primary instruction. Schoolmasters are regarded by the law of Prussia as servants of the state; as such, they have a claim to a retiring pension in their old age; and in every department a society, which the law recommended rather than enjoined, has been formed for the relief of the widows and orphans of schoolmasters. I have before me the regulations of a great number of these societies, and I transmit them for your inspection. The results are the same in all, though the means employed vary more or less. If this report were not already too long, I should have subjoined a translation of one of these lists of regulations, as a sort of model for the associations of the same kind which I wish to see formed in every department of France.

The law required plans of school-houses of different sizes, and commanded that none should be built or repaired except according to such plans. The ministry has shown the most praiseworthy perseverance on this point, and I have now under my eye a general order addressed to all the regencies, containing a detailed description of the best and most economical manner of building school-houses. I send you, together with this order, six plans of houses of different sizes for primary normal schools. I earnestly request that you will have them examined, and, if they are approved, will send similar ones into all our departments; for the construction of school-houses which are to serve both for boys and girls must not be left to inexperience, or to an injudicious economy.

The greatest difficulty was to obtain from the new provinces, and particularly those on the Rhine, so recently annexed to the monarchy, the execution of that article of the law which imposes on parents, under severe penalties, the obligation of sending their children to school. The ministry had the wisdom to suspend this part of the law in these provinces, and to labour to bring about the same results by persuasion and zeal. When the taste for instruction had been thus gradually diffused, and the population of these provinces appeared sufficiently prepared for such a measure, the law was rendered obligatory. This took place in 1825, and from that moment it has been steadily and rigorously enforced. I have now before me an order of the regency of Köln, dated 1827, by which the Cabinet-order of the 14th of May 1825, on the obligation of attending school, is enforced. I have a similar order of the regency of Aachen (*Aix-la-Chapelle*) dated March 7, 1826, and another of that of Düsseldorf of the 20th of July of the same year. The law has everywhere been carried into effect, but with a judicious mixture of gentleness and severity:

thus, in 1826, which was a remarkably bad year, the ministry even saw fit to moderate the zeal of the local administrations, and to enjoin them not to compel the parishes to contribute to the repairs and improvements of schools, but first to have recourse to every means of persuasion. This circular is dated the 12th of May 1826. It appeared to me useful to study the manner in which the government applied the general law of 1819 to the Grand Duchy of Posen, so far behind the Rhenish provinces in civilization. I have accordingly collected a great number of documents, which prove the wisdom of the course pursued by the ministry, and the progress which popular instruction and civilization, over which it presides, have made throughout the Polish part of the kingdom. It would also be desirable that all the instructions which emanated from the ministry, or from the provincial bodies, with a view of applying the law of 1819 to the Jews, should be published in French. It would be seen what measures were taken to diffuse the taste for knowledge among a portion of the Prussian people, who, though numerous and wealthy, are generally unenlightened, and dread the effect which attendance on public schools may have on the faith of their children.

Without question, Sir, in the present state of things, a law concerning primary instruction is indispensable in France; the question is, how to produce a good one, in a country where there is a total absence of all precedent and all experience in so grave a matter. The education of the people has hitherto been so neglected,—so few trials have been made, or those trials have succeeded so ill, that we are entirely without those universally received notions, those predilections rooted in the habits and the mind of a nation, which are the conditions and the bases of all good legislation. I wish, then, for a law; and at the same time I dread it; for I tremble lest we should plunge into vision-ary and impracticable projects again, without attending to what actually exists. God grant that we may be wise enough to see that any law on primary instruction passed now, must be a provisional and not a definitive law; that it must of necessity be re-constructed at the end of ten years, and that the only thing now to be aimed at is, to supply the most urgent wants, and to give a legal sanc-tion to some incontestable points! What are these points? I shall endeavour, Sir, to determine them, following the path marked out by existing facts.

The idea of compelling parents to send their children to school is perhaps not sufficiently diffused through the nation to justify the experiment of making it law; but everybody agrees in regarding the establishment of a school in every *commune* as necessary. It is also willingly conceded that the maintenance of this school must rest with the *commune;* always provided that, in case of inability through poverty, the *commune* shall apply to the depart-ment, and the department to the state. This point may be assumed as universally admitted, and may therefore be-come law. Indeed practice has already anticipated law; for a year past all the municipal councils have voted as large a portion of their funds as they could possibly spare, for the support of popular instruction in their *com-munes*. Nothing further is required, therefore, than to an-nex to this fact, which is nearly universal, a legal obligation.

You are likewise aware, Sir, that many of the councils of departments have felt the necessity of securing a supply of schoolmasters, and a more complete education for them, and have, with this view, established primary normal schools in their departments. Indeed, they have often shown rather prodigality than parsimony on this head. This, too, is a most valuable and encouraging indication; and a law ordaining the establishment of a primary normal school in each department, as well as of a primary school in each *commune*, would do little more than confirm and generalize what is now actually doing in almost all parts of the country. Of course this primary normal school must be more or less considerable according to the resources of each department.

Here we have already two most important points on which the country is almost unanimously agreed. You have also, without doubt, been struck by the petitions of a number of towns, great and small, for the establishment of schools of a class rather higher than the common primary schools; such as, though still inferior in classical and scientific studies to our royal and communal *colléges*, might be more particularly adapted to give that kind of generally useful knowledge indispensable to the large portion of the population which is not intended for the learned professions, but which yet needs more extended and varied acquirements than the class of day-labourers and artisans. Such petitions are almost universal. Several municipal councils have voted considerable funds for the purpose, and have applied to us for the necessary authority, for advice and assistance. It is impossible not to regard this as the symptom of a real want,—the indication of a serious deficiency in our system of public instruction.

You, Sir, are sufficiently acquainted with my zeal for

classical and scientific studies; not only do I think that we must keep up to the plan of study prescribed in our *colléges,* and particularly the philological part of that plan, but I think we ought to raise and extend it, and thus, while we maintain our incontestable superiority in the physical and mathematical sciences, endeavour to rival Germany in the solidity of our classical learning. Indeed, classical studies are, without any comparison, the most important of all; for their tendency and their object is the knowledge of human nature, which they consider under all its grandest aspects; here, in the languages and the literature of nations which have left indelible traces of their passage on earth; there, in the fruitful vicissitudes of history, constantly re-modelling and constantly improving the frame of society; lastly, in philosophy, which reveals the simplest elements, and the uniform structure of that wondrous being, whom history, language and literature successively invest with forms the most varied, yet all connected with some part, more or less important, of his internal constitution. Classical studies keep alive the sacred tradition of the moral and intellectual life of the human race. To curtail or enfeeble such studies would, in my eyes, be an act of barbarism, a crime against all true and high civilization, and in some sort an act of high treason against humanity.

Let our royal *colléges* then, and even a great proportion of our communal *colléges,* continue to lead the youth of France into this sanctuary; they will merit the thanks of their country. But can the whole population enter learned schools? or, indeed, is it to be wished that it should? Primary instruction with us, however, is but meagre; between that and the *colléges* there is nothing; so that a tradesman, even in the lower ranks of the middle classes, who has the honourable wish of giving his sons a good education, has no resource but to send them to the *collége*. Two great evils are the consequence. In general, these boys, who know that they are not destined to any very distinguished career, go through their studies in a negligent manner; they never get beyond mediocrity; and when, at about eighteen, they go back to the habits and the business of their fathers, as there is nothing in their ordinary life to recall or to keep up their studies, a few years obliterate every trace of the little classical learning they acquired. On the other hand, these young men often contract tastes and acquaintances at *collége* which render it difficult, nay, almost impossible, for them to return to the humble way of life to which they were born: hence a race of men restless, discontented with their position, with others, and with themselves; enemies of a state of society in which they feel themselves out of their place; and with some acquirements, some real or imagined talent, and unbridled ambition, ready to rush into any career of servility or of revolt. The question then is, Sir, whether we are prepared to make ourselves responsible to the state and society for training up such a race of malcontents? Unquestionably, as I shall take occasion to say elsewhere, a certain number of exhibitions *(bourses)* ought to be given to poor boys who evince remarkable aptness: this is a sacred duty we owe to talent; a duty which must be fulfilled, even at the risk of being sometimes mistaken. These boys, chosen for the promise they give, go through their studies well and thoroughly, and on leaving school experience the same assistance they received on entering. Thus they are enabled, at a later

period of life, to display their talents in the learned and
liberal professions which are open to them, to the advantage of the state to which they owe their education. As,
however, it is impossible for any government to find employment for everybody, it ought not to furnish facilities
for everybody to quit the track in which his fathers have
trod. Our *colléges* ought, without doubt, to remain open
to all who can pay the expense of them; but we ought by
no means to force the lower classes into them: yet this is
the inevitable effect of having no intermediate establishments between the primary schools and the *colléges*. Germany, and Prussia more especially, are rich in establishments of this kind. . . . The Prussian law of 1819 sanctions
them. You perceive, Sir, that I allude to the schools called
tradesmen's or burghers' schools, or schools for the middle
classes *(Bürgerschulen), écoles bourgeoises,*—a name which
it is perhaps impossible to transplant into France, but
which is accurate and expressive, as contradistinguishing
them from the learned schools *(Gelehrteschulen),* called
in Germany *gymnasis,* and in France *colléges,* (in England,
'grammar-schools'),—a name, too, honourable to the class
for whose especial use and benefit they are provided,—
honourable to those of a lower class, who by frequenting
them can rise to a level with that above them. The burgher
schools form the higher step of primary instruction, of
which the elementary schools are the lower step. Thus there
are but two steps or graduations: 1°. Elementary schools,—
the common basis of all popular instruction in town and
country; 2°. Burgher schools, which, in towns of some size
and containing a middle class, furnish an education sufficiently extensive and liberal to all who do not intend to

enter the learned professions. The Prussian law, which fixes a minimum of instruction for the elementary schools, likewise fixes a minimum of instruction for the burgher schools; and there are two kinds of examination, extremely distinct, for obtaining the brevet of primary teacher for these two gradations. The elementary instruction must be uniform and invariable, for the primary schools represent the body of the nation, and are destined to nourish and to strengthen the national unity; and, generally speaking, it is not expedient that the limit fixed by the law for elementary instruction should be exceeded: but this is not the case with the burgher schools, for these are designed for a class among whom a great many shades and diversities exist,—the middle class. It is therefore natural and reasonable that it should be susceptible of extension and elevation, in proportion to the importance of the town, and the character of the population for whom it is destined. In Prussia this class of schools has, accordingly, very different gradations, from the minimum fixed by the law, with which I have already made you acquainted, to that point where it becomes closely allied with the gymnasium, properly so called. At this point it sometimes takes the name of Progymnasium.

I have now before me a report on the different progymnasia existing in the department of Münster: you will see that these establishments are, as their title implies, preparatory gymnasia, in which classical and scientific instruction stops short within certain limits, but in which the middle or trading class may obtain a truly liberal education. In general, the German burgher schools, which are a little inferior to our communal *colléges* in classical and scientific studies, are incomparably superior to them in religious instruction, geography, history, modern languages, music, drawing, and national literature.

In my opinion, it is of the highest importance to create in France, under one name or another, burgher schools, or schools for the middle classes, which give a very varied education; and to convert a certain number of our communal *colléges* into schools of that description. I regard this, Sir, as an affair of state. I entreat you not to listen to those who will tell you that we have several gradations in primary instruction, and that what I ask for has been already provided. It is no such thing: we have three stages it is true, but they are ill defined, which reduces the distinction to nothing. Besides, three degrees form an arbitary classification, the reason of which I confess myself at a loss to find; whereas the two degrees determined by the Prussian law are founded on the most obvious and natural distinctions. Lastly, while we circumscribe these two degrees within the limits of primary instruction, it is not unimportant to define and characterize them by different names. Those names in use among us—schools of the third, second, and first degree,—mark nothing but abstract differences; they say nothing to the imagination, and therefore do not impress themselves on the mind. In Prussia, the names of elementary school and of burgher school, representing the lowest and the higher degree of primary instruction, are popular and significant; that of *Mittelschule* (middle or intermediate school), instead of *Bürgerschule,* is also in use in some parts of Germany. I beg of you, Sir, to consider whether this name could not be introduced amongst us; middle school and elementary school would comprehend the two essential degrees of primary instruction, and our primary normal schools would equally furnish masters to these two degrees; for which, however, there would be two sorts of examination and two sorts of brevet. You would only have to fix a minimum of instruction for the middle schools, as you would doubtless do for the elementary; having care to let each establishment gradually go beyond this minimum according to its resources, and, above all, according to its success.

This, Sir, appears to me to be substantially the object of all those petitions which the towns are now addressing to you; some, for a change in the scheme of our communal *colléges;* some, for instituting a course of instruction of a more general utility in our royal *colléges,* collaterally with the scientific and classical course now given; some, to have schools for which they know not very well how to find a name, and which have sometimes been called *écoles industrielles,* in contradistinction from our *colléges.* On no account must you reduce or abridge the classical course of our *colléges:* on the contrary, I repeat, it ought to be rendered more profound and extensive. We must not introduce into our *colléges* two sorts of scholars; this would be contrary to all sound discipline, and would infallibly enfeeble the more difficult studies for the benefit of the more easy. Neither must we give the name of *écoles industrielles*—schools for the manufacturing and trading classes[1]—to schools where the pupils are not supposed to have any special calling. The mass of the people are con-

[1] We have the word *commercial* as applied to schools, but these are notoriously so far from approaching the point M. Cousin aims at, that I dislike to employ it.—TRANSL.

scious only of their wants; to you, Sir, it belongs to discover the true means of satisfying those wants. There is a cry raised from one end of France to the other, demanding, on behalf of three fourths of the population, establishments which may fill the middle ground between the simple elementary schools and the *colléges*. The demands are urgent and almost unanimous. Here, then, we have another point of the highest importance, on which it would be easy to come to an understanding. The general wish, and numerous attempts, more or less successful, here call for the intervention of the legislature, and render it at once necessary and easy.

The most difficult point in a law on primary instruction is the determination what are the authorities to be employed. Here also let us consult facts. Since you have been charged with the direction of public instruction, where, Sir, have you found an active, efficient ally in your solicitude for the education of the people? who have assisted you? who have made sacrifices in common with those of the state? who have built schools, paid masters, set on foot normal schools? In all directions it has been the municipal councils, and the councils of the departments, stimulated and represented by the *maires* and the prefects. Wherever the municipal and departmental councils have had the will, wherever the *maires* and the prefects have had it too: and these latter have invariably followed the impulse of the superior authority which appoints them, and to which they are responsible. Here, then, is the clue you must follow. You must look for support and assistance from that quarter where you have always found them,—the quarter, I will add, in which the whole force and vitality of France resides. The French administration is the glory and the masterwork of the imperial government. The organization of France in *mairies* and prefectures, with municipal and departmental councils, is the foundation of government and of social order. This foundation has stood firm amidst so much ruin, that prudence and policy seem to point to it as the best and safest prop. Moreover, this organization has just been reformed and vivified by rendering the municipal and departmental councils elective and popular. Thus the French administration unites all that we want, activity and popularity. The administration, then, is what you must call to your aid. Recollect, also, that it is these local councils that pay, and that you cannot fairly expect much from them unless they have a large share in the disbursement of the money they have voted. These councils are chosen out of the body of the people, and return to it again; they are incessantly in contact with the people; they *are* the people legally represented, as the *maires* and the prefects are these councils embodied, if I may so say, in one person, for the sake of activity and despatch. I regard, then, as another incontestable point, the necessary intervention of the municipal and departmental councils in the management of public instruction. As there ought to be a school in every *commune,* so there ought to be for every communal school a special committee of superintendence, which ought to be formed out of the municipal council, and presided over by the *maire.* I shall perhaps be told, that men who are fit to conduct the business of the *commune* are not fit to superintend the communal school. I deny it: nothing is wanted for this superintendence but zeal, and fathers of families cannot want zeal where their dearest interests are concerned. In Prussia no difficulty is found in this matter, and every parish-school has its *Schulvorstand,* in great part elective. Over the heads of these local committees there ought to be a central committee in the chief town of each department, chosen out of the council of the department, and presided over by the prefect. The committee of each *commune* would correspond with the committee of the department; that is to say, in short, the *maire,* with the prefect. This correspondence would stimulate the zeal of both committees. By it, the departmental committee would know what is the annual supply of schoolmasters required for the whole department, and consequently, the number of masters the normal school of the department ought to furnish, and consequently, the number of pupils it ought to admit. It would have incessantly to urge on the zeal of the local committees in establishing and improving schools, for the sake of providing as well as possible for the pupils it sends out of its normal school. Nothing can be more simple than this organization. It is, applied to primary instruction, what takes place in the ordinary administration: I mean, the combined action of the municipal councils and the departmental councils,—of the *maires* and the prefects.

After the administrative authorities, it is unquestionably the clergy who ought to occupy the most important place in the business of popular education. How is it possible they could neglect, nay even repugn, such a mission? But that they have done so is a fact, which, however deplorable, we are bound to acknowledge. The clergy in France are generally indifferent, or even hostile, to the education of the people. Let them blame themselves if the law does not give them great influence over primary instruction; for it was their duty to anticipate the law, and to take up a position which they must necessarily have continued to occupy. The law, offspring of facts, will therefore place small reliance on the clergy; but if it rejected them altogether, it would commit an egregious fault; for it would set the clergy in decided opposition to primary instruction, and would engage in a conflict, open, scandalous and perilous. The rational middle course is to put the *curé* or the pastor,[1] and if need be both, on every communal committee; and the highest dignitary of the church in each department, on the departmental committee. To make ecclesiastics presidents of these committees, as the restored government did with regard to its committees of cantons, would be neither more nor less than to intend what that government intended, viz. that these committees should never meet at all, or should meet to no end. On the other hand, to exclude ecclesiastics from our committees, as certain persons who fancy themselves great philosophers would fain do, would be a reaction very pernicious in various ways. We must neither deliver over our committees into the hands of the clergy, nor exclude them; we must admit them, because they have a right to be there, and to represent the religion of the country. The men of good sense, good manners, and of consideration in their neighbourhood, of whom these committees ought to be, and will be, composed, will gradually gain ascendancy over their ecclesiastical colleagues, by treating them with the respect due to their sacred functions. We must have the clergy; we must neglect nothing to bring them into the path to-

---

[1] *i. e.* the catholic and the protestant clergyman.—TRANSL.

wards which everything urges them to turn,—both their obvious interest, and their sacred calling, and the ancient services which their order rendered to the cause of civilization in Europe. But if we wish to have the clergy allied with us in the work of popular instruction, that instruction must not be stripped of morality and religion; for then indeed it would become the duty of the clergy to oppose it, and they would have the sympathy of all virtuous men, of all good fathers of families, and even of the mass of the people, on their side. Thank God, Sir, you are too enlightened a statesman to think that true popular instruction can exist without moral education, popular morality without religion, or popular religion without a church. Christianity ought to be the basis of the instruction of the people; we must not flinch from the open profession of this maxim; it is no less politic than it is honest. We baptize our children, and bring them up in the Christian faith and in the bosom of the church; in after-life, age, reflection, the breath of human opinions, modify their early impressions, but it is good that these impressions should have been made by Christianity. Popular education ought therefore to be religious, that is to say, Christian; for, I repeat it, there is no such thing as religion in general; in Europe, and in our days, religion means Christianity. Let our popular schools then be Christian; let them be so entirely and earnestly. By degrees the clergy will open their eyes, and will lend us efficacious assistance. Indeed, it seems to me impossible that poor priests, scattered through remote villages, dependent on the people, to whom they owe their subsistence, and among whom they live, should long escape the enlightened influence of a power at once national, strong and benevolent. The higher clergy are yours by your power of nomination, and by their temporal interests. By degrees they will come into your views. Meantime, let us watch them; but treat them with respect, and with regard for their interests and their office. Let us throw open our schools to them, for we have nothing to conceal; let us call upon them to cooperate in the holy work we are undertaking. If, after all we can do, they refuse their assistance, we shall have vindicated our prudence and fulfilled our duty. The rest is in the hand of Providence, veiled amid the impenetrable destinies of European society.

But, Sir, you will have remarked that I have not alluded to the share which the university should have in public instruction. In the first place, I profess myself ignorant of what the university now is; I know no university but the imperial university; and that, after having rendered eminent services, expired in 1815. It was succeeded, first, by the royal commission of public instruction, and afterwards by the ministry of public instruction and ecclesiastical affairs. That is the law of the land as at present established. Now nobody contests that the proceedings of the communal and departmental committees, the *maires,* sub-prefects and prefects, ought, like all the other parts of the administration, to refer to one common centre, from which a vigorous impulse and a supreme guidance may emanate, and upon whom all the responsibility before the chambers may rest.

This centre, in France, as in Prussia, is, the ministry and council of public instruction. This is not only according to law, but to nature and reason. It is perfectly consistent to leave primary instruction to the minister who has all the rest of public instruction, as well as ecclesiastical affairs, in his hands; that is to say, the two things with which the education of the people is the most intimately connected. What could be gained by consigning primary instruction to the office of the minister of the interior? If the arts have been put there, that is a capital error which must on no account be repeated. Has any evil resulted from the present order of things? Far from it: everybody is agreed that the minister and his council have done a great deal for primary instruction since the revolution of July. As you, Sir, would have been able to effect nothing without the municipal and departmental councils, the *maires* and prefects, so those authorities acknowledge that they could have done little or nothing without your cooperation and direction. It is you who excited their zeal, who supported and encouraged them; you who, as the enlightened dispenser of the funds placed in your hands by the two chambers, have given vigour to public instruction, by giving proportionate aid to necessitous places. You will render an account to the chambers, and I do not think your statements will induce them to reverse the actual division of public business, or to abridge your powers, which they ought rather to extend. Reasonable men do not wish to take primary instruction out of your hands; they know that it properly falls within your department.

So far there are no difficulties; but difficulties will arise as soon as you seek to govern primary instruction by means of your ordinary agents, the academical rectors and inspectors. Here you have to encounter an almost universal resistance. We must inquire into the causes of this resistance. People in general do not see what primary instruction has to do with academical or university education or discipline: they think that this instruction being essentially communal and departmental, the authorities under whose superintendence it naturally falls are those of the *commune* and the department. They think, too, that primary instruction demands constant, and therefore local, superintendence; and they think that the rector and the inspectors of an *académie,* which often embraces three, four, or five departments,—as for instance that of Britanny,—are incapable of such superintendence, seeing that in Germany there is a special inspector not only for every regency, but for every circle. And besides, between ourselves, with some few exceptions, your academical inspectors inspect very little more than your inspectors-general. In short, I shall never cease to repeat,—no inspections are good for anything that are not special. The same man cannot, to any purpose, inspect faculties, royal and communal *colléges,* a countless mass of institutions, boarding-schools, and establishments of primary instruction, all differing very widely. These different stages of instruction demand different inspectors. I therefore strongly recommend the creation of a special inspector of primary instruction for each department. Our academical inspectors should be reserved for schools of the second class, which will suffice, and more than suffice, to employ all their powers and all their diligence. Your natural agents and correspondents for primary instruction are the prefects, who would preside over the departmental committees, and to whom the correspondence of *maires* and communal committees, as well as the report of the departmental inspector, would be addressed.

The prefects would correspond officially with you, as they have hitherto done extra-officially; and there would be a councillor in the central council of public instruction, specially charged with the reports to be made on that portion of the business, as in fact there is now. This machinery is very simple, and would produce quick results; being less complex, it would work more freely. The only thing in which I would employ agents taken from the body of teachers would be, the commission of examination appointed for granting schoolmasters' brevets. No one disputes that professors have peculiar qualifications, and all the necessary impartiality, for that office. I should wish, then, that the examination-commission should be appointed by you, and composed of masters or professors of the royal or the communal *colléges* of the department; adding, for the religious part, a clergyman proposed by the bishop.

As to private teachers, and what people are pleased to call liberty of primary tuition, I can only repeat what I have said elsewhere,—we must neither oppose it, nor reckon upon it. There are branches of the public service which must be secured against all casualties by the state, and in the first rank of these is primary instruction. It is the bounden duty of government to guarantee it against all caprices of public opinion, and against the variable and uncertain calculations of those who would engage in it as a means of subsistence. On this principle are founded our primary normal schools in each department, bound to furnish annually the average number of schoolmasters required by the department. We must rely exclusively on these normal schools for the regular supply of communal teachers.

But if, in the face of our primary communal schools,

there are persons who, without having passed through the normal schools, choose to establish schools at their own risk and peril, it is obvious that they ought not only to be tolerated, but encouraged;—just as we rejoice that private institutions and boarding-schools should spring up beside our royal and communal *colléges*. This competition cannot be otherwise than useful, in every point of view. If the private schools prosper, so much the better; they are at full liberty to try all sorts of new methods, and to make experiments in teaching, which, on such a scale, cannot be very perilous. At all events, there are our normal schools. Thus all interests are reconciled,—the duties of the state, and the rights of individuals; the claims of experience, and those of innovation. Whoever wishes to set up a private school must be subject to only two conditions, from which no school, public or private, can on any pretext be exempt, —the brevet of capacity, given by the commission of examination, and the supervision of the committee of the *commune* and of the inspector of the department. I would very readily give up the certificate of moral character, as illusory, and as implicitly contained in that of fitness, especially if there be, as there ought to be, a clergyman on the commission.

Here, much more than in Prussia, the privation of a schoolmaster's brevet ought to be pronounced only after a judicial sentence, and by an ordinary court of justice; only, that court must admit special proceedings for special offences. Indeed, everybody understands well enough that a man may be a very bad schoolmaster without having committed any of the crimes or misdemeanours provided against by the law.

All these measures, on which I will not enlarge, are more or less founded on existing facts; they have the sanction of experience;—it would be simply advantageous to add that of law. On all the points concerning which the law is silent, experiments might be made. Among these experiments some would probably be successful: when sufficiently long practice had confirmed them, they might be inserted in a new law; or *ordonnances* and instructions, maturely weighed by the royal council, would convert them into general and official measures. Nothing must pass into a law which has not the warranty of success. Laws are not to be perilous experiments on society; they ought simply to sum up and to generalize the lessons of experience. . . .

## The Normal Schools.

I have now lying before me a great number of general measures taken by the minister of public instruction for the progressive amelioration of the normal schools, both as to moral discipline and instruction. I shall describe some of these measures, for the sake of making known the spirit which presides over the management of these important establishments.

The discipline is generally very severe. Thus music, so natural and so dear to Germans, is doubtless cultivated with great assiduity; but the government does not suffer the students to regard this acquirement as a source of mere amusement, nor allow them to display it in public concerts, which, though innocent, are of a light character. It permits them to join publicly in church-music alone. I find this restriction in a ministerial circular of the 8th of June 1814.

I also find quoted, in a report of the normal school of Soest, an order of the minister of public instruction, declaring that any out-pupil of a normal school who should be seen in a public-house (*cabaret*) should be instantly expelled. Indeed, it is obvious that the conduct of those students who do not lodge in the school-house must be subject to a special police, and that is, in fact, everywhere the case. One of the most useful things in the primary schools, and particularly those in towns, is the gymnastic training; consequently it is necessary to introduce it into the normal schools. Though the recollections attached to the gymnastic exercises of the celebrated Jahn were not calculated to render the Prussian government favourable to them, it had the good sense to overcome this natural repugnance, and to institute regular gymnastic exercises in all the primary schools of the monarchy, as we see from the following circular.

*"Circular of the royal ministry of public instruction and ecclesiastical and medical affairs, to all schoolboards, concerning the gymnastic exercises in primary normal schools.*

February 26, 1827.

"It is by no means the intention of the ministry to introduce into primary normal schools, (and especially those which have not annexed schools,) gymnastic exercises classed among the regular objects of study, systematically taught with the aid of a special apparatus in halls or places set apart for the purpose, and with a particular costume, all of which would lead to the belief that the old gymnastic exercises (*Turnen*) were re-established. This would be wholly contrary to the intention of the ministry, to the object of the primary normal schools, to the destination of the students, to the station and character of the masters and teachers, and to the system of those establishments, as well with relation to the course of study, as to the habits of life which are desirable for the pupils.

Nevertheless, it is expedient to take into consideration, and to provide for, the physical training of the pupils.

*In the first place, on account of the health.* Experience proves that the change in the manner of living to which the pupils who enter these schools must habituate themselves, is unquestionably detrimental to the health. Most of them, coming from the country, are accustomed to live in the open air, and have not been used to very assiduous mental labour. At an age when the growth is not complete, they must accustom themselves to a sedentary life, to long and uninterrupted study, to change of diet; they must give up the indulgences of home. They are, moreover, exposed to trials which are really severe and painful. They must curtail themselves of sleep; work ten hours and more a day, in classes and rooms full of people; sleep in hot rooms in summer, and in cold ones in winter; go to work immediately after meals, and employ even their hours of recreation in occupations in which the mind is still on the stretch. Such a life must needs be unfavourable to health; and for that very reason it is necessary to contrive bodily exercises which prevent exhaustion, promote the free action of all the organs, and preserve the elasticity, gaiety and freshness of the mind. Nothing, moreover, can be worse for a schoolmaster than to habituate himself to too sedentary a life. In the first place the taste for such a life would be extremely injurious to the school, where the example of a masculine and sustained activity is absolutely indispensable; secondly, it would favour an air of retirement and grandeur incompatible with the position of a country schoolmaster, who is usually forced to go through severe bodily labour for the support of his family.

2. *For the deportment and good carriage of the body.* Awkward and embarrassed manners justly make an unfavourable impression, because they generally prove that a man is coarse and ignorant, or at least, ill-assured in the use of his faculties and his powers. And as presence of mind, courage and firmness are shown by physical address and ability, pure moral sentiments by a decorous air, an amiable and gracious temper by politeness and good manners; so, a good and graceful carriage of the body re-acts on the moral part, and strengthens the good qualities of the soul. Moreover, physical address gives a man invaluable advantages in the inevitable accidents of life, both for his own defence and the assistance of others in times of danger. But it is above all things urgent that a schoolmaster should have a decent and engaging exterior, joined to physical strength, whereby he may gain the esteem and confidence of the parents, and the affection of the children.

3. *Also on account of his calling.* The future master ought to be familiar with all that contributes to the development of the body, and with all salutary exercises. As master, he is bound to watch over the physical accomplishments and the health of his pupils. He ought therefore to know, at least, what are the means proper for the preserva-

tion of the health, and in what way bodily exercises may be combined with the games and employments of children. It follows, that bodily exercises must form a part of every system of education of schoolmasters.

But how are these exercises to be arranged, so as to fulfill their end in accordance with the three objects indicated above? This is a question which cannot be answered in a precise and general manner. It must be left to the judgement of the master and teachers, and to the local capabilities of each individual school.

Establishments like those of Bunzlau, Jenkau, Neuzelle, to which are attached small charity schools for children, are in a most advantageous position. There, children may be trained more regularly and strictly to bodily exercises, and the students of the normal school be made to superintend, and even take an active part in them; the exercises may even be made according to military rules.

But in the primary normal schools to which no such institutions are annexed, bodily exercises must be the more carefully combined with all the ordinary occupations of the pupils,—with their labours in the garden and their excursions. In the evening when they return from bathing and swimming, they shall exercise themselves at their pleasure in running and leaping. When they go out botanizing, or are occupied in household employments, they shall take every occasion of increasing the agility, suppleness and strength of their bodies.

But all will depend on the manner in which the masters manage this. If they contrive that these exercises, established in reality for purposes of utility, appear to the pupils an agreeable and healthful amusement; if they equally avoid a pedantic formality and a scornful indifference; if they have the art of inspiring a taste for these exercises, yet of keeping them always subordinate to the main object,—moral and intellectual education; lastly, if they can observe a just measure in the whole conduct of the matter, —not only is there no danger to be feared, but several advantages may be hoped for. Among others, this: that the pupils, preserved in a certain vigour and agility of frame, may be kept from falling into a heavy gravity, or a melancholy ill suited to their time of life, and above all to be dreaded in men destined to pass their lives among children.

Every possible arrangement must therefore be made in all normal schools for favouring the physical development. It is not to be imagined that there can be any want of time for these exercises; and if there really were, according to the present distribution of the lessons, this would afford a sufficient reason for making such alterations as would leave time.

The minister leaves to the school-boards the care of making known the resolution contained in this circular, to the directors of primary normal schools; whether by communicating it to them entire or abridged, or by means of special circulars founded on the peculiar situation of each school; and at the same time, of charging the said directors, in all their future annual reports, to state the manner in which the bodily exercises are practised at their establishment.

One of the most interesting documents I have obtained is the circular of the 21st of March, 1827, which regulates the course to be followed by schoolmasters recalled for a time to the primary normal schools with a view to perfect themselves in their art. The following is an abridgement of it:—

The circular of the 1st of June 1826 decrees that acting masters may be recalled to the normal school, with a view to their improvement, when it shall be judged necessary; and that they are there to go through a course of methodology (*methodologischer Lehrcursus,*—methodological teaching-course); or to exercise themselves in any particular branches of teaching; or, lastly, to acquire the art of keeping a class in good order, by practising in the school attached for that purpose to the normal school.

According to the observations furnished by experience, and the different suggestions made on this head by the competent authorities, the minister of public instruction hereby makes known, that these measures are not applicable to all the normal schools, which as yet have not complete and methodical courses on all the principal branches of primary instruction. Indeed it cannot be required of the masters of normal schools that they should repeat their regular annual courses, for the benefit of the young masters recalled for improvement; nor would much advantage result from compelling such masters to follow the ordinary courses for the short time they have to spend there. It will therefore be more expedient to form small societies or meetings of schoolmasters, for three or four weeks, in order that they may go over, methodically and in concert, some special portion of what they have to teach, as, for instance, arithmetic, singing, the German language, or religion.

This plan will have the advantage of always bringing together men of equal attainments on one single point, which will thus be studied more fundamentally; and of taking off the attention of only one master of the normal school; namely, of the one who habitually presides over that branch, and who can easily submit to this slight increase of work for a few weeks.

After going over all the several branches of instruction with the same individuals, (who will have been annually recalled for some years,) a general and more extensive course may be arranged, which will find its natural place during the four weeks before the close of the annual labours of the students of the highest class, when they go through the general repetition of the courses of *Didaktik, Methodik,* and *Pädagogik*.[1] The acting schoolmasters may be present at these repetitions, and indeed their presence will be advantageous to the pupils of the normal schools.

If necessary, the vacations may be given up to this purpose, one every three or four years.

Indemnities may, in such cases, be granted to the most zealous masters of the normal schools, as also to the most

[1] As we have no single words approaching to these, I have determined to put the original German, or rather Greek, and to give the definitions in a note. M. Cousin's words are, *de didactique, de méthode, et de pédagogie. Méthodique* would seem more analogous: it is not *method,* but the science of *methods.*

"*Pädagogik.* The *science* of education (or training); the still more difficult *art* of education."

"*Didaktik.* A part or division of *Pädagogik,* namely, the art of teaching."

"*Methodik.* The theory or science of methods; *i. e.* a guide to the discovery of the best possible methods in any science or art." —*Krug's encyclopädisch-philosophisches Lexicon.*—TRANSL.

necessitous of the schoolmasters recalled for these studies.

The superintendents and inspectors, on their part, shall take care to provide temporary substitutes for these schoolmasters. If, however, a school were to be shut a month, (which, if possible, must always be avoided,) the children under their care would still be the gainers, from the increase of knowledge and of skill the master would acquire during his absence.

The principal aim of these measures is to stimulate the zeal and emulation of the masters, and to keep them all in a state to diffuse education throughout the country in a uniform manner, and to participate in the progress which time gradually brings, so as to render the normal school the centre of all primary instruction. This excellent measure recalls to me another of the same kind, which, though it forms no part of the internal regulations of normal schools, has equally in view the improvement of the acting masters; I mean those conferences of the schoolmasters of a circle or district, in which each communicates to his brethren his own methods and experience, and all are enlightened by the interchange of views and thoughts. These conferences are voluntary, it is true; but the government encourages them, counsels them, and often arranges them itself by means of the school-inspectors. We may judge of the importance of these periodical meetings by the regulations for one of them, which I translate here.

1. From the 1st of May to the end of August, the meetings are held once a week on Wednesday afternoon,[1] from

[1] Wednesday afternoon is a holiday in Germany, as Thursday is in France.

two to six o'clock; from the 1st of September to the end of October, once a fortnight, from two to five; from the 1st of November to the end of February, once a month, from two to five, after the moon's first quarter; and from the 1st of March to the end of April, once a fortnight.[1]

The chief subject of discussion at these meetings is, *method*. The best, it is true, must ever reside in the accuracy of judgement, the zeal and activity, of the master, which alone can give interest and life to his school. Nevertheless, it is desirable that similarity of method should, as far as possible, prevail throughout a district; order and regularity in teaching must be promoted by it. The masters shall examine, therefore, what is the best known method for teaching reading, arithmetic, and singing; and what the best elementary books. They shall pass in review all the new works which have appeared on any of the branches of instruction: Dr. Harnisch's method of reading, Pestalozzi's Elements of Arithmetic, or those of Kawerau, Mucke, Schellenberg, Fischer, Rennschmidt, and others; or Scholz's excellent work on arithmetic. They will inquire whether Rothweil's or Natorp's methods of teaching singing are satisfactory? Which is preferable for singing, music written in cipher or with notes? What are the best pieces to give pupils? What is the best reading-book for the second class of country schools? And, among many good works, is Wilmsen's *Children's Friend* to be preferred, or Dr. Harnisch's *Second Reading Book*?

Religious instruction, as the foundation of all popular education, shall form the first object of the deliberations of the conference. Ought the catechetical method to be

[1] No other conferences meet more than once a month.

neglected, as it has been of late years? What are the works necessary to the master, besides the Bible and Luther's Catechism? Does he find sufficient directions in Hoffmann, Geisser, Handel, Hänel, and Kohlrausch? In consequence of the recent extension of the instruction given in our village schools, the conference shall discuss how far the elements of geometry and of drawing may be expediently pursued; within what limits the lessons in geography, history, and the natural sciences are to be circumscribed, and whether these additions are likely to be really useful, or only a barren work of memory.

Discipline is one of the prime conditions of the success of a school; and here the question presents itself as to the employment of rewards and punishments. Experience has proved that this is the part of education the most difficult to handle. Special attention must be paid to it, and all difficulties will be overcome by those who, filled with the spirit of the Gospel, are convinced they owe to their pupils whatever is enjoined by a religious love and a boundless devotion to the holy office they hold.

It is no less the object of these conferences, to furnish the masters with an opportunity of gaining new lights and of extending their own knowledge. Questions in grammar, in the German tongue, in arithmetic, &c., will therefore always form part of the business of the meeting; as likewise, the reading of works on education, and other books which are likely to furnish matter useful to schoolmasters; the practice of singing, and reciprocal communication of the experience of each.

Among the works on education (*ouvrages pédagogiques*) particularly recommended, they will have the journals on primary instruction published in Prussia and throughout Germany.

The pastors charged with the inspection of the conferences may propose questions, which shall be treated in writing, and afterwards discussed at the conference.

A report shall be made of all the meetings.

> (*Extract of the report of Mr. Falk, of Landeshuth,*
> *superintendent of the conferences of schoolmas-*
> *ters, within the range of his school-inspection.*
> Beckedorff's Journal, Vol. ii. No. 2.) . . .

## III. CALVIN E. STOWE

## *REPORT ON ELEMENTARY PUBLIC INSTRUC-*
## *TION IN EUROPE*

Made to the Thirty-sixth General Assembly of the
State of Ohio, December 19, 1837. By C. E. Stowe. Reprinted by order of the House of Representatives of
the Legislature of Massachusetts, March 29, 1838. Boston, Dutton and Wentworth, State Printers. 1838.

## III. CALVIN E. STOWE (1802–1886)

### and his

### *REPORT ON ELEMENTARY PUBLIC INSTRUCTION IN EUROPE* [1]

CALVIN E. STOWE was born at Natick, Mass., April 6, 1802, into a poor but industrious and frugal family whose ancestors had emigrated from England in 1634. While still a small boy, his father died, and it was only through hard work and careful management that his mother kept him in attendance at the district school. Calvin is said to have made good use, however, of a small parish library which was available. When he was twelve years of age, he was apprenticed to a papermaker and he remained in that situation for four years. During that time, he was able to save enough money to pay his expenses for two years at Bradford Academy. Later, he continued his schooling at Gorham Academy and entered Bowdoin College, where he graduated in 1824 with high honors. He remained at Bowdoin after graduation for one year as librarian and tutor and then entered Andover Theological Seminary, where he was graduated in 1828. During a part of this later period, he edited the *Boston Recorder*, a re-

[1] Reprinted in full here except for a short section on education in Russia. The original spelling and punctuation are followed.

ligious paper. From 1830 to 1832, he was professor of languages at Dartmouth College and, from 1832 to 1850, he served as professor of Biblical Literature at the Lane Theological Seminary, in Ohio. From 1850 to 1852, he was professor of Divinity at Bowdoin College and later he became professor of Sacred Literature in the Andover Theological Seminary. While at the Lane Theological Seminary he married (January, 1836) Harriet E. Beecher, daughter of Rev. Lyman Beecher, and sister of Catherine Esther Beecher, the well-known author and lecturer, and of Henry Ward Beecher, the celebrated pulpit orator and lecturer. Mrs. Stowe is better known as Harriet Beecher Stowe, author of "Uncle Tom's Cabin."

Stowe was also active in other fields of educational work. He was one of the founders of the Western Literary Institute, one of the earliest of the American associations of professional teachers. As early as 1835 he had prepared a report on the education of immigrants in which he advocated a liberal system of public schools through which native and foreign-born children could be educated together. In 1839, he published a paper for teachers on seminaries, which is said to have had a wide influence. So highly was Stowe regarded as an educational thinker and leader that he was frequently sought after for service in the normal schools of Massachusetts.

In 1836, Stowe was sent to Europe to purchase a library for the Lane Theological Seminary. Just before he left Ohio, he received from the governor of the state a resolution which the Legislature had passed, requesting Stowe to collect while in Europe "such facts and information as he may deem useful to the state in relation to the various systems of public instruction and education, which have been adopted in the several countries through which he may pass, and make report thereof, with such practical observations as he may think proper, to the next General Assembly." As a result, Stowe made, in December, 1837, a report to the Governor and the Legislature of Ohio under the title *Report on Elementary Public Instruction in Europe*. In this report, he contrasted conditions in Prussia particularly with those in Ohio, discussed the direction and thoroughness of instruction, the training of teachers, and the elementary course of study which had been enriched through the influence of Pestalozzian reforms.

The report of Stowe, which is a very readable document, requires little comment here. Except for a brief section on education in Russia, it is reproduced in full in this volume and speaks for itself. The reader of the report will soon observe, however, that Stowe found in the Prussian school system many features which were to his liking. He was full of praise for the Prussian plan. Moreover, as may be seen from the latter part of the report, Stowe believed that the principles of the school system which he had examined and reported upon could be applied in the organization of public education in the United States. The following paragraph reveals his conviction:

"But perhaps some will be ready to say, the scheme is indeed an excellent one, provided only it were practicable; but the idea of introducing so extensive and complete a course of study into our common schools is entirely visionary and can never be realized. I answer, that it is no theory which I have been exhibiting, but a matter of fact, a copy of actual practice. The above system is no visionary scheme emanating from the closet of a recluse, but a sketch of the course of instruction now actually pursued by thousands of schoolmasters in the best district schools that have ever been organized. It can be done, for it has been done, it is now done, and it ought to be done. If it can be done in Europe, I believe it can be done in the United States: if it can be done in Prussia, I know it can be done in Ohio. The people have but to say the word and provide the means, and the thing is accomplished; for the word of the people here is even more powerful than the word of the king there; and the means of the people here are altogether more abundant for such an object than the means of the sovereign there. Shall this object, then, so desirable in itself, so entirely practicable, so easily within our reach, fail of accomplishment? For the honor and welfare of our state, for the safety of our whole nation, I trust it will not fail; but that we shall soon witness in this commonwealth the introduction of a system of common school instruction, fully adequate to all the wants of our population."

If Stowe's theme failed to stir the emotions of multitudes as did his wife's drama of the abolitionist creed, the report was less narrow in range and more permanent in appeal than "Uncle Tom's Cabin," the sensation which a dozen years later ran into millions of copies. The report aroused the interest of legislators as well as of educators, and much of the educational advancement of the remainder of the *ante-bellum* period can be traced to its influence. The legislature of Ohio ordered ten thousand copies printed and distributed to every school district in the state, and, later, the report was ordered reprinted by the Legislatures

## CALVIN E. STOWE

of Massachusetts, Michigan, North Carolina, Pennsylvania, and Virginia.[1]

[1] The text used in this volume is that of the reprint ordered by the House of Representatives of the Legislature of Massachusetts, March 29, 1838. Boston, Dutton and Wentworth, 1838.

The Massachusetts reprint was compared with the reprint of the report ordered made by the Legislature of North Carolina January 7, 1839, and the two reprints were found to be identical.

# REPORT ON
## ELEMENTARY PUBLIC INSTRUCTION

*To His Excellency the Governor, and the Honorable the
General Assembly of the State of Ohio:*

In March, 1836, just before I embarked for Europe, I
received a communication from Governor Lucas, with the
great seal of the State, enclosing the following resolves of
the General Assembly, *to wit*:

*"Resolved by the General Assembly of the State of Ohio,*
That C. E. Stowe, Professor in one of the Literary Institutions of this State, be requested to collect, during the progress of his contemplated tour in Europe, such facts and
information as he may deem useful to the State, in relation to the various systems of public instruction and education, which have been adopted in the several countries
through which he may pass, and make report thereof, with
such practical observations as he may think proper, to the
next General Assembly.

*"Resolved,* That His Excellency the Governor be requested to transmit a certified copy of the foregoing proceedings to Professor Stowe."

In pursuance of the above resolutions, I communicated
the intention of the General Assembly to Hon. A. Steven-
son, the American Minister near the British Court, and he
very readily furnished me with the credentials necessary

for the most satisfactory attainment of the object of my inquiries. I am also happy to remark, that the communication of Governor Lucas was a ready passport to my free admission to every public institution in Europe to which I applied—and that my endeavors were seconded in the most encouraging manner by all the gentlemen connected with the educational establishments in the several countries through which I passed; and the warmest expressions of approbation were elicited of the zeal manifested by so young a state as Ohio, in the great cause of general education. Particularly in some of the old communities of central Europe, where it happened to be known that I was born in the same year in which Ohio became a sovereign State, it seemed to be matter of amusement as well as gratification, that a man who was *just as old as the State in which he lived,* had come with official authority to inquire respecting the best mode of education for the growing population of his native land; and they remarked, that our Governor and Legislators must be very enlightened and highly cultivated men. When in one instance I informed them that our Governor was a plain farmer, and that a majority of our Legislators were of the same occupation, the well known line which a Latin poet applies to husbandmen was applied to us:

"O fortunatos nimium si sua bona norint."
"Oh happy people, if they do but appreciate their own blessings."

In the progress of my tour I visited England, Scotland, France, Prussia, and the different States of Germany; and had opportunity to see the celebrated Universities of Cambridge, Oxford, Edinburg, Glasgow, Paris, Berlin, Halle, Leipsic, Heidelberg, and some others; and I was everywhere received with the greatest kindness, and every desirable facility was afforded me for the promotion of my inquiries. But knowing that a solid foundation must be laid before a durable superstructure can be reared, and being aware that, on this principle, the chief attention of our Legislature is, and for the present must be, directed to our common schools, my investigation of the Universities was comparatively brief—and the most of my time was spent in visiting the best district schools I could hear of, and also the high schools intended for the business education of young men, and the institutions for the education of teachers.

Before I proceed to the result of my inquiries on these topics, I would call the attention of the Legislature to some facts of a more general nature, which strongly impressed themselves upon my mind during the progress of my tour —and which, it seems to me, have a very important bearing upon the successful maintenance, if not the very existence, of free institutions in our country. I allude particularly to the wonderful change which has taken place in the policy of monarchial governments in respect to the education of the people. Formerly it was supposed that despotism could be maintained only by a sovereign with an army devoted to his interests, and dependent only upon himself for subsistence; an aristocracy which should monopolise the wealth and the intellectual culture of the entire nation; and a mass of people held in entire ignorance of their rights and privileges as men, and condemned to drudge for life for a bare and precarious subsistence—the mere dependents and slaves of the higher orders. But what is the aspect which the sovereignties of Europe now present?— and what is the change which is forcing itself along, even into the despotisms of Asia and Africa? Ever since the revolution which separated this country from the British Empire, the idea of popular rights has been working its way irresistibly throughout the civilized world: and sovereigns who have had the sagacity to see the unavoidable results, have adapted their measures to the new aspect of the times. A new era in the history of civilization has evidently commenced. A despotic king of the Protestant faith, dreading the evils of an ignorant and unbridled democracy, such as was witnessed in the French revolution, has now for forty years been pursuing a course of instruction for his whole people, more complete, better adapted to develope every faculty of the soul, and to bring into action, every capability of every kind that may exist, even in the poorest cottage of the most obscure corner of his kingdom, that has ever before been imagined. Men of the highest order of intellect and most extensive attainments are encouraged to devote themselves to the business of teaching: the best plans for the furtherance of this object are immediately received and generously rewarded; talent and industry, wherever they exist, are sought out and promoted; and nothing is left undone that can help forward this great design.

The introduction of this system was preceded by political changes, which, considered as emanating from the government itself, have scarcely a parallel in the history of nations. When Frederick William III. ascended the throne of Prussia in 1797, the condition of the people was in many respects truly deplorable. But immediately upon his accession he set about reforming abuses, and introducing improvements. The odious religious edict was abolished— the administration of justice was thoroughly reformed, and rigid economy introduced into the royal household. The exclusive privileges of the nobles were taken away, and their power so completely broken, that there is now no hereditary aristocracy which can interfere with the sovereign, or oppress the people.

In 1810, the peasantry, who before had no ownership in the soil which they cultivated, and consequently no independence of character, by a royal decree, became freeholders on the following terms, namely: those who held their lands on perpetual lease, by giving up one-third, and those who held them on limited or life leases, by giving up one-half, to the landlord, became the owners in fee simple of the rest. The military is now so modelled that every citizen between the ages of 18 and 21 is in actual service in the standing army, where he is instructed in all that pertains to military life, and then returns to his peaceful occupations. Thus the army is made up entirely of citizens—and every citizen is a soldier; and there is no such thing as a standing army at the entire devotion of the sovereign, and independent of the people.

The prime minister, Hardenberg, in a circular published at the time when these reforms were in progress, declares, that "the new system is based upon the principle, that every subject, personally free, be able to raise himself, and develope his powers freely, without let or hindrance from any other; that the public burdens be borne in common and in

just proportions; that equality before the law, be secured
to every subject; that justice be rigidly and punctually administered; that merit in whatever rank it may be found,
be enabled to rise without obstacle; that the government
be carried on with unity, order, and power; that, by the
education of the people, and the spread of true religion,
the general interests, and a national spirit be promoted, as
the only secure basis of the national welfare."

Another European king of the Roman Catholic faith,
Louis of Bavaria, who is connected by marriage with the
royal house of Prussia, moved by this example, and excited
by emulation in behalf both of his church and kingdom,
is now zealously pushing forward the same experiment
among his own people, and already the Bavarian schools
begin to rival the Prussian; and the University of Berlin
finds its only equal in that of Munich. Louis has in one
thing gone even beyond his brother of Prussia, in that he
has granted to his people a real constitutional representation in the government, a privilege and a right which the
Prussians have labored in vain to extort from Frederick
William.

Even the Autocrat, Nicholas of Russia, (married to a
daughter of the Prussian monarch, who inherits much of
her father's spirit,) has been induced to commence a similar
system throughout his vast dominions; and from the reports to the emperor of M. d'Ouvaroff, the Russian Minister of Public Instruction, it appears, that already from
Poland to Siberia, and from the White Sea to the regions
beyond the Caucasus, including the provinces so recently
wrested from Persia, there are the beginnings of a complete

system of common school instruction for the whole people, to be carried into full execution as fast as it is possible to provide the requisite number of qualified teachers.

Thus three sovereigns, representing the three great divisions of Christendom, the Protestant, the Romish, and the Greek, are now zealously engaged in doing what despotic sovereigns have seldom done before—enlightening and educating their people; and that too with better plans of instruction, and a more efficient accomplishment in practice than the world has ever before witnessed. Nor is the spirit of education confined to these nations. The kingdom of Wirtemberg, and the grand duchy of Baden, are not behind Prussia or Bavaria. The smaller states of Germany, and even old Austria, are pushing forward in the same career; France is all awake; Spain and Italy are beginning to open their eyes; the government of England—which has hitherto neglected the education of the common people more than any other Protestant country of Europe—is beginning to bestir itself; and even the Sultan of Turkey, and the Pacha of Egypt, are looking around for well qualified teachers to go among their people. In London and Paris I saw Turks, and Arabs, and Greeks, who had been sent by their respective governments to these cities, for the express purpose of being educated for teachers in their native countries, if not for the whole people, at least for the favored few. At Constantinople a society has been formed for the promotion of useful knowledge, which publishes a monthly journal edited by one of the Turks who studied in Paris; and the Sultan now employs a French teacher in his capital, whom he especially invited from France. And here too in our own country, in the movements of New

England, New York, Pennsylvania, Ohio, Michigan, and several other of the states, we are strongly reminded of the educational zeal of the age.

In short the world seems to be awake and combining in one simultaneous effort for the spread of education; and sad indeed will be the condition of that community which lags behind in this universal march.

But I wish to direct your attention to the influence which these wide spread systems of education in the sovereignties of Europe, emanating from Prussia, must exert on our own institutions. The sovereigns to whom I have alluded, are not only educating the people, but they are laying aside the pomp, the trappings, and the lavish expenses of royalty, and by simplicity, by rigid economy, by an energetic and impartial administration of the government, are endeavoring to establish their thrones in the hearts of their people.

Frederick William, in his dress, appearance, and whole deportment, is as simple and unostentatious as an Ohio farmer; and few of our wealthy merchants ride in so plain a carriage, or sleep on so homely a bed as the monarch of Prussia. After witnessing the pageantry, the pomp and ostentation of the limited monarchy of England, one is astonished at the rigid simplicity of the great military despotism of central Europe.

In every stage of instruction it is made a prominent object, and one which is repeatedly and strenuously insisted on in all the laws pertaining to education, to awaken a *national spirit*—to create in the youthful mind a warm attachment to his native land, and its institutions, and to fix in his affections a decided preference for the peculiarities of his own country. Indeed the whole plan (which is well understood to have originated in Prussia, when the rapid spread of republican principles first began to threaten the thrones of Europe,) evidently is to unite with the military force which always attends a despotism, a strong moral power over the understanding and affections of the people. In view of this fact, an able English writer denominates the modern kingdom of Prussia, "that wonderful machine of state-craft—as a mere machine the most remarkable in existence—on the model of which most European governments are gradually proceeding to reform themselves." Already has this plan so far succeeded, that there is evidently in these countries a growing disregard for the *forms* of free government, provided the *substance* be enjoyed in the security and prosperity of the people.

Republicanism can be maintained only by universal intelligence and virtue among the people, and disinterestedness and fidelity in the rulers. Republics are considered the natural foes to monarchies; and where both start up side by side, it is taken for granted that the one must supplant the other. Hence their watchful jealousy of each other. Now when we see monarchies strengthening themselves in the manner described, are not republics exposed to double danger from vice, and neglect of education within themselves? And do not patriotism and the necessity of self-preservation, call upon us to do more and better for the education of our whole people, than any despotic sovereign can do for his? Did we stand alone—were there no rival governments on earth—or if we were surrounded by despotisms of degraded and ignorant slaves, like those of the ancient oriental world; *even then,* without intelligence and virtue in the great mass of the people, our liberties would pass from us. How emphatically must this be the case *now,* when the whole aspect of things is changed, and monarchies have actually stolen a march upon republics in the promotion of popular intelligence? . . . [At this point in the Report occurs the omitted section on education in Russia.]

### Internal Arrangements of the Prussian Schools.

I will now ask your attention to a few facts respecting the internal management of the schools in Prussia and some other parts of Germany, which were impressed on my mind by a personal inspection of those establishments.

One of the circumstances that interested me most was the excellent order and rigid economy with which all the Prussian institutions are conducted. Particularly in large boarding schools, where hundreds, and sometimes thousands of youth are collected together, the benefits of the system are strikingly manifest. Every boy is taught to wait upon himself—to keep his person, clothing, furniture, and books, in perfect order and neatness; and no extravagance in dress, and no waste of fuel or food, or property of any kind is permitted. Each student has his own single bed, which is generally a light mattrass, laid upon a frame of slender bars of iron, because such bedsteads are not likely to be infested by insects, and each one makes his own bed and keeps it in order. In the house, there is a place for every thing and every thing must be in its place. In one closet are the shoe-brushes and blacking, in another the lamps and oil, in another the fuel. At the doors are good mats and scrapers, and every thing of the kind necessary for neatness and comfort, and every student is taught, as carefully as he is taught any other lesson, to make a proper use of all these articles at the right time, and then to leave them in good order at their proper places. Every instance of neglect is sure to receive its appropriate reprimand, and if necessary, severe punishment. I know of nothing that can benefit us more than the introduction of such oft-repeated lessons on carefulness and frugality into all our educational establishments; for the contrary habits of carelessness and wastefulness, notwithstanding all the advantages which we enjoy, have already done us immense mischief. Very many of our families waste and throw away nearly as much as they use; and one third of the expenses of housekeeping might be saved by system and frugality. It is true, we have such an abundance of every thing that this enormous waste is not so sensibly felt as it would be in a more densely populated region; but it is not *always* to be so with us. The productions of our country for some years past have by no means kept pace with the increase of consumption, and many an American family during the last season has felt a hard pressure, where they never expected to feel one.

Especially should this be made a branch of female education, and studied faithfully and perseveringly by all who are to be wives and mothers, and have the care of families.

The universal success also and very beneficial results, with which the arts of drawing and designing, vocal and instrumental music, moral instruction and the Bible, have been introduced into schools, was another fact peculiarly interesting to me. I asked all the teachers with whom I conversed, whether they did not sometimes find children who were actually incapable of learning to draw and to sing. I have had but one reply, and that was, that they found the same diversity of natural talent in regard to these as in regard to reading, writing, and the other branches of education; but they had never seen a child who was capable of learning to read and write, who could not be taught to sing well and draw neatly, and that too without taking any time which would at all interfere with, indeed which would not actually promote his progress in other studies. In regard to the necessity of moral instruction and the beneficial influence of the Bible in schools, the testimony was no less explicit and uniform. I inquired of all classes of teachers, and men of every grade of religious faith, instructors in common schools, high schools, and schools of art, of professors in colleges, universities and professional seminaries, in cities and in the country, in places where there was a uniformity and in places where was a diversity of creeds, of believers and unbelievers, of rationalists and enthusiasts, of Catholics and Protestants; and I never found but one reply, and that was, that to leave the moral faculty uninstructed was to leave the most important part of the human mind undeveloped, and to strip education of almost every thing that can make it valuable; and that the Bible, independently of the interest attending it, as containing the most ancient and influential writings ever recorded by human hands, and comprising the religious system of almost the whole of the civilized world, is in itself the best book that can be put into the hands of children to interest, to exercise, and to unfold their intellectual and moral powers. Every teacher whom I consulted, repelled with indignation the idea that moral instruction is not proper for schools; and spurned with contempt the allegation, that the Bible cannot be introduced into common schools without encouraging a sectarian bias in the matter of teaching; an indignation and contempt which I believe will be fully participated in by every high-minded teacher in christendom.

A few instances, to illustrate the above mentioned general statements, I here subjoin:—Early in September I visited the Orphan House at Halle, an institution founded by the benevolence of Franke, about the year 1700, and which has been an object of special favor with the present king of Prussia. It now contains from 2700 to 3000 boys, most of them orphans sustained by charity. After examining its extensive grounds, its commodious and neat buildings, its large book store, its noble printing establishment, for printing the Bible in the oriental and modern languages, its large apothecary's shop, for the dispensation of medicine to the poor, and the exquisitely beautiful statue of its founder, erected by Frederic William III; I was invited by Drs. Guerike and Netto to go into the dining-hall and see the boys partake of their supper. The hall is a very long and narrow room, and furnished the whole length of each side with short tables like the mess tables on board a man of war, each table accommodating about twelve boys. The tables were without cloths, but very clean, and were provided with little pewter basins of warm soup, and just as many pieces of dark and coarse, but very wholesome, bread, as there were to be boys at the table. When the bell rang, the boys entered in a very quiet and orderly manner, each with a little pewter spoon in his hand. When they had arranged themselves at table, at a signal from the teacher one of the boys ascended a pulpit near the cen-

tre of the hall, and in the most appropriate manner suppli-
cated the blessing of God upon their frugal repast. The
boys then each took his bit of bread in one hand, and with
his spoon in the other, made a very quiet and healthful
meal. They then united in singing two or three verses of
a hymn, and retired in the same quiet and orderly manner
in which they had entered. It being warm weather, they
were dressed in jackets and trowsers of clean, coarse brown
linen; and a more cheerful, healthy, intelligent set of youthful faces and glistening eyes I never saw before; and notwithstanding the gravity with which they partook of their
supper and left the hall, when fairly in the yard, there was
such a pattering of little feet, such a chattering of German,
and such skipping and playing, as satisfied me that none
of their boyish spirits had been broken by the discipline
of the school.

At Weisenfels, near Lutzen where the great battle was
fought in the thirty years' war, there is a collection of various schools, under the superintendence of Dr. Harnisch,
in what was formerly a large convent. Among the rest there
is one of those institutions peculiar to Prussia, in which
the children of very destitute families are taken and educated at the public expense, to become teachers in poor villages where they can never expect to receive a large compensation; institutions of a class which we do not *need
here,* because no villages in this country *need* be poor. Of
course, though they have all the advantages of scientific
advancement enjoyed in the most favored schools, frugality and self-denial form an important part of their education. Dr. Harnisch invited me to this part of the establishment to see these boys dine. When I came to the room,

they were sitting at their writing tables, engaged in their studies as usual. At the ringing of the bell they arose. Some of the boys left the room, and the others removed the papers and books from the tables, and laid them away in their places. Some of the boys who had gone out, then re-entered with clean, coarse table cloths in their hands, which they spread over their writing tables. These were followed by others with loaves of brown bread, and plates provided with cold meat and sausages, neatly cut in slices, and jars of water, which they arranged on the table. Of these materials, after a short religious service, they made a cheerful and hearty meal; then arose, cleared away their tables, swept their room, and after a suitable season of recreation, resumed their studies. They are taught to take care of themselves, independent of any help, and their only luxuries are the fruits and plants which they cultivate with their own hands, and which grow abundantly in the gardens of the institution.

## Institutions for Reformation.

At Berlin, I visited an establishment for the reformation of youthful offenders. Here boys are placed, who have committed offences that bring them under the supervision of the police, to be instructed, and rescued from vice, instead of being hardened in iniquity, by living in the common prison with old offenders. It is under the care of Dr. Kopf, a most simple-hearted, excellent old gentleman; just such an one as reminds us of the ancient christians, who lived in the times of the persecution, simplicity and purity of the christian church. He has been very successful in reclaiming the young offender, and many an one, who would otherwise have been forever lost, has, by the influence of this institution, been saved to himself—to his country—and to God. It is a manual labor school; and to a judicious intermingling of study and labor, religious instruction, kind treatment and necessary severity, it has owed its success. When I was there, most of the boys were employed in cutting screws for the rail-road which the government was then constructing between Berlin and Leipsic; and there were but few who could not maintain themselves by their labor. As I was passing with Dr. K. from room to room, I heard some beautiful voices singing in an adjoining apartment, and on entering I found about twenty of the boys, sitting at a long table, making clothes for the establishment, and singing at their work. The Dr. enjoyed my surprise, and on going out, remarked—"I always keep these little rogues singing at their work, for while the children sing, the devil cannot come among them at all; he can only sit out doors there and growl; but if they stop singing, in the devil comes." The Bible and the singing of religious hymns, are among the most efficient instruments which he employs for softening the hardened heart, and bringing the vicious and stubborn will to docility.

A similar establishment in the neighborhood of Hamburg, to which I was introduced by Dr. Julius, who is known to many of our citizens, afforded striking examples of the happy influence of moral and religious instruction, in reclaiming the vicious and saving the lost. Hamburg is the largest commercial city of Germany, and its population is extremely crowded. Though it is highly distinguished for its benevolent institutions, and for the hospitality and integrity of its citizens, yet the very circumstances in which it is placed, produce among the lowest class of its population, habits of degradation and beastliness, of which we have but few examples on this side of the Atlantic. The children, therefore, received into this institution, are often of the very worst and most hopeless character. Not only are their *minds* most thoroughly depraved, but their very senses and bodily organization seem to partake in the viciousness and degradation of their hearts. Their appetites are so perverted, that sometimes the most loathsome and disgusting substances are preferred to wholesome food. The Superintendent, Mr. Wichern, states, that though plentifully supplied with provisions, yet when first received, some of them will steal and eat soap, rancid grease that has been laid aside for the purpose of greasing shoes, and even catch May-bugs and devour them; and it is with the utmost difficulty that these disgusting habits are broken up. An ordinary man might suppose that the task of restoring such poor creatures to decency and good morals was entirely hopeless. Not so with Mr. Wichern. He took hold with the firm hope that the moral power of the word of God is competent even to such a task. His means are prayer, the Bible, singing, affectionate conversation, severe punishment when unavoidable, and constant steady employment, in useful labor. On one occasion, when every other means seemed to fail, he collected the children together, and read to them, in the words of the New Testament, the simple narrative of the sufferings and death of Christ, with some remarks on the design and object of his mission to this world. The effect was wonderful. They burst into tears of contrition, and during the whole of that term, from June till October, the influence of this scene was visible in all their conduct. The idea that takes so strong a hold when the character of Christ is exhibited to such poor creatures is, that *they are objects of affection;* miserable, wicked, despised as they are, yet Christ, the son of God, loved them, and loved them enough to suffer and to die for them—and still loves them. The thought that *they can yet be loved,* melts the heart, and gives them hope, and is a strong incentive to reformation.

On another occasion, when considerable progress had been made in their moral education, the Superintendent discovered that some of them had taken nails from the premises, and applied them to their own use, without permission. He called them together, expressed his great disappointment and sorrow that they had profited so little by the instructions which had been given them, and told them that till he had evidence of their sincere repentance, he could not admit them to the morning and evening religious exercises of his family. With expressions of deep regret for their sin, and with promises, entreaties, and tears, they begged to have this privilege restored to them; but was firm in his refusal. A few evenings afterward, while walking in the garden, he heard youthful voices among the shrubbery; and drawing near unperceived, he found that the boys had formed themselves into little companies of seven or eight each, and met morning and evening in different retired spots in the garden, to sing, read the Bible and pray among themselves; to ask God to forgive them the sins they had committed, and to give them strength to resist temptation in future. With such evidence of repentance he soon restored to them the privilege of attending morning and evening prayers with his family.—One morning soon after, on entering his study, he found it all adorned with wreaths of the most beautiful flowers, which the boys had arranged there at early day-break, in testimony of their joy and gratitude for his kindness. Thus rapidly had these poor creatures advanced in moral feeling, religious sensibility, and good taste.

In the spring, Mr. Wichern gives to each boy a patch of ground in the garden, which he is to call his own, and cultivate as he pleases. One of the boys began to erect a little hut of sticks and earth upon his plot, in which he might rest during the heat of the day, and to which he might retire when he wished to be alone. When it was all finished, it occurred to him to dedicate it to its use by religious ceremonies. Accordingly, he collected the boys together. The hut was adorned with wreaths of flowers, a little table was placed in the centre on which lay the open Bible, ornamented in the same manner. He then read with great seriousness the 14th, 15th, and 24th verses of the cxviii. Psalm:

"The Lord is my strength and my song, and is become my salvation."
"The voice of rejoicing and salvation is heard in the tabernacles of the righteous."
"This is the day which the Lord hath made. We will rejoice and be glad in it."

After this, the exercises were concluded by singing and prayer. Another boy afterwards built him a hut, which was to be dedicated in a similar way; but when the boys came together, they saw in it a piece of timber which belonged to the establishment, and ascertaining that it had been taken without permission, they at once demolished the whole edifice, and restored the timber to its place. At the time of harvest, when they first entered the field to gather the potatoes, before commencing the work, they formed into a circle, and much to the surprise of the Superintendent, broke out together into the harvest hymn:

"Now let us all thank God."

After singing this, they fell to their work with great cheerfulness and vigor.

I mention these instances, from numerous others which might be produced, to show how much may be done in reclaiming the most hopeless youthful offenders by a judicious application of the right means of moral influence. How short-sighted and destructive, then, is the policy which would exclude such influence from our public institutions! The same effects have been produced by houses of reformation in our own country. I would mention, as one instance, the institution of Mr. Welles in Massachusetts.

Now, laying aside all considerations of benevolence and of religious obligations, is it not for the highest good of the State, that these minds should be withdrawn from vice and trained up to be enlightened and useful citizens, contributing a large share to the public wealth, virtue and happiness; rather than that they should come forward in life miserable criminals, of no use to themselves or the public, depredating on the property and violating the rights of the industrious citizens, increasing the public burdens by their crimes, endangering the well being of society, and under-mining our liberties! They can be either the one or the other, according as we choose to educate them ourselves in the right way, or leave them to be educated by the thieves and drunkards in our streets, or the convicts in our prisons. The efforts made by some foreign nations to educate this part of their population, is a good lesson for us. All the schools and houses of reformation in Prussia, do not cost the government so much as old England is obliged to expend in prisons and constables for the regulation of that part of her population, for which the government provides no schools but the hulks and the jails; and I leave it to any one to say which arrangement produces the greatest amount of public happiness.

When I was in Berlin I went into the public prison, and visited every part of the establishment. At last I was introduced to a very large hall which was full of children, with their books and teachers, and having all the appearance of a common Prussian school-room. "What," said I, "is it possible that all these children are imprisoned here for crime?" "Oh no," said my conductor, smiling at my simplicity, "but if a parent is imprisoned for crime, and on that account his children are left destitute of the means of education, and liable to grow up in ignorance and crime, the government has them taken here, and maintained and educated for useful employment." The thought brought tears to my eyes. This was a new idea to me. I know not that it has ever been suggested in the United States; but surely it is the duty of government, as well as its highest interest, when a man is paying the penalty of his crime in a public prison, to see that his unoffending children are not left to suffer, and to inherit their father's vices. Surely it would be better for the child, and *cheaper* as well as better, for the State. Let it not be supposed that a man would go to prison for the sake of having his children taken care of, for they who go to prison usually have little regard for their children; and if they had, discipline like that of the Berlin prison would soon sicken them of such a bargain.

Where education is estimated according to its real value, people are willing to expend money for the support of schools; and if necessary, to deny themselves some physical advantages for the sake of giving their children the blessings of moral and intellectual culture. In the government of Baden, four per cent of all the public expense is for education—they have a school with an average of two or three well qualified teachers to every three miles of territory, and every one hundred children; and that too, when the people are so poor that they can seldom afford any other food than dry barley-bread, and a farmer considers it a luxury to be able to allow his family the use of buttermilk three or four times a year. In Prussia, palaces and convents are every where turned into houses of education; and accommodations originally provided for princes and bishops are not considered too good for the schoolmaster and his pupils. But, though occupying palaces, they have no opportunity to be idle or luxurious. Hard labor and frugal living are every where the indispensable conditions to a teacher's life, and I must say, that I have no particular wish that it should be otherwise; for it is only those who are willing to work hard and live frugally, that ever do much good in such a world as this.

I pass now to the consideration of a question of the deepest interest to us all, and that is, can the common schools in our State be made adequate to the wants of our population? I do not hesitate to answer this question decidedly in the affirmative; and to show that I give this answer on good grounds, I need only to state the proper object of education, and lay before you what is actually now done towards accomplishing this object in the common schools of Prussia and Wirtemberg.

What is the proper object of education? The proper object of education is a thorough developement of all the intellectual and moral powers—the awakening and calling forth of every talent that may exist, even in the remotest and obscurest corner of the State, and giving it a useful direction. A system that will do this, and such a system only, do I consider adequate to the wants of our population; such a system, and such a system only, can avert all the evils and produce all the benefits which our common schools were designed to avert and produce. True, such a system must be far more extensive and complete than any now in operation among us—teachers must be more numerous, skilful, persevering, and self-denying—parents must take greater interest in the schools and do more for their support—and the children must attend punctually and regularly, till the whole prescribed course is completed. All this can be done, and I hope will be done; and to show that the thing is really practicable, I now ask your attention to the course of instruction in the common schools of Prussia and Wirtemberg, and other European States, which have done the most in the matter of public instruction.

# CALVIN E. STOWE

## *Course of Instruction in the Common Schools of Prussia and Wirtemberg.*

The whole course comprises eight years, and includes children from the ages of six till fourteen; and it is divided into four parts, of two years each. It is a first principle, that the children be well accommodated as to house and furniture. The school-room must be well constructed, the seats convenient, and the scholars made comfortable, and kept interested. The younger pupils are kept at school but four hours in the day—two in the morning and two in the evening, with a recess at the close of each hour. The older, six hours, broken by recesses as often as is necessary. Most of the school-houses have a bathing place, a garden and a mechanics' shop attached to them, to promote the cleanliness and health of the children, and to aid in mechanical and agricultural instruction. It will be seen by the schedule which follows, that a vast amount of instruction is given during these eight years—and, lest it should seem that so many branches must confuse the young mind, and that they must necessarily be but partially taught, I will say in the outset, that the industry, skill and energy of teachers regularly trained to their business, and depending entirely upon it; the modes of teaching; the habit of always finishing whatever is begun; the perfect method which is preserved; the entire punctuality and regularity of attendance on the part of the scholars; and other things of this kind, facilitate a rapidity and exactness of acquisition and discipline, which may well seem incredible to those who have never witnessed it.

The greatest care is taken that acquisition does not go beyond discipline; and that the taxation of mind be kept entirely and clearly within the constitutional capacity of mental and physical endurance. The studies must never weary, but always interest—the appetite for knowledge must never be cloyed, but be kept always sharp and eager. These purposes are greatly aided by the frequent interchange of topics, and by lively conversational exercises. Before the child is even permitted to learn his letters, he is under conversational instruction, frequently for six months or a year; and then a single week is sufficient to introduce him into intelligible and accurate plain reading.

Every week is systematically divided, and every hour appropriated. The scheme for the week is written on a large sheet of paper, and fixed in a prominent part of the schoolroom, so that every scholar knows what his business will be for every hour in the week; and the plan thus marked out is rigidly followed. As a specimen I present the following study sheet given me by Dr. Diesterweg, of Berlin, and which was the plan for his school when I visited it in September, 1836.

Through all the parts of the course there are frequent reviews and repetitions, that the impressions left on the mind may be distinct, lively and permanent. The exercises of the day are always commenced and closed with a short prayer; and the bible and hymn book are the first volumes put into the pupil's hands, and these books they always retain and keep in constant use during the whole progress of their education.

The general outline of the eight years' course is nearly as follows:

# CALVIN E. STOWE

I. *First part, of two years, including children from six to eight years old—four principal branches, namely:*

1. Logical Exercises, or oral teaching in the exercise of the powers of observation and expression, including religious instruction and the singing of hymns:
2. Elements of Reading;
3. Elements of Writing;
4. Elements of Number, or Arithmetic.

II. *Second part, of two years, including children from eight to ten years old—seven principal branches, namely:*

1. Exercises in Reading;
2. Exercises in Writing;
3. Religious and Moral Instruction, in select Bible Narratives;
4. Language, or Grammar;
5. Numbers, or Arithmetic;
6. Doctrine of space and form, or Geometry;
7. Singing by note, or Elements of Music.

III. *Third part, of two years, including children from ten to twelve years old—eight principal branches:*

1. Exercises in Reading and Elocution;
2. Exercises in Ornamental Writing, preparatory to drawing;
3. Religious Instruction in the connected Bible history;
4. Language, or Grammar, with parsing;
5. Real Instruction, or knowledge of nature and the external world, including the first elements of the sciences and the arts of life—of geography and history;

273

## WEEKLY COURSE OF STUDY

*In the Teachers' Seminary and Boys' School, under the care of Dr. Diesterweg, at Berlin, in the summer term, 1836.*

The Teachers' Seminary is divided into three classes, which are designated by the Roman numerals on the left hand of the columns, and the Boys' School into six, designated by the Arabic figures in the same column. The students in the Teachers' Seminary are employed as instructors in the Boys' School, under the inspection of their teachers. The capital letters at the right hand of the columns are the initials of the teachers who superintend the class in the particular branch mentioned. The whole number of instructors, exclusive of the pupils in the teachers' department, is six.

| Hrs. | | Monday | Tuesday | Wednesday | Thursday | Friday | Saturday |
|---|---|---|---|---|---|---|---|
| 7 to 8. | II. | Arithmetic . R. | Religion . B. | Theory of Music . E. | Botany .. G. | Religion .: B. | Arithmetic . R. |
| | III. | Theory of Music .: E. | Botany .: G. | Religion .: B. | Geometry . S. | Arithmetic . G. | Religion .: B. |
| | 1. | Arithmetic . G. | Latin ...: O. | Arithmetic . G. | German . R. | Latin ...: O. | Arithmetic . G. |
| | 2. | } Latin | Religion .: B. | } Latin | } Latin | } Religion .: B. | } Latin |
| | 3. | } D. and R. | | } J. and R. | } Q. and R. | | } Q. and R. |
| 8 to 9. | II. | Drawing . F. | School keeping . B. | German .: B. | Botany .: G. | School keeping . B. | German .: B. |
| | III. | Arithmetic . G. | Botany .: G. | Violin ...: E. | Singing .: E. | Singing . E. | Singing .: E. |
| | 1. | Latin ...: O. | Religion .: R. | Latin ...: O. | Latin ...: Q. | Religion .: B. | Latin ...: Q. |
| | 2. | History ...: R. | German ..: R. | German .: R. | History .: R. | Geography . G. | } Arithmetic |
| | 3. | Singing .: E. | French .: R. | German .: B. | Arithmetic .: S. | French .: B. | } B. and S. |
| | 4. | Latin ...: R. | Religion .: S. | Latin ...: R. | Latin ...: R. | Religion .: S. | |
| | 5. | Arithmetic . S. | Singing | Religion .: G. | Arithmetic . S. | } Arithmetic | Religion .: S. |
| | 6. | Religion . D. | } E. and D. | German .: S. | Religion . D. | } S. and R. | Arithmetic . R. |
| 9 to 10. | II. | Drawing . F. | Arithmetic . R. | Singing .: E. | Arithmetic . R. | Ornamental Writing . M. | Singing .: E. |
| | III. | Singing .: E. | German .: B. | History .: B. | Geography . B. | Religion .: B. | History .: B. |
| | 1. | German .: B. | French .: B. | German .: R. | Singing .: E. | French .: R. | German .: R. |
| | 2. | French ..: R. | } Arithmetic | French .: B. | Arithmetic . B. | German . R. | French .: B. |
| | 3. | Geography . S. | } B. and S. | Geography . S. | Geography . S. | Singing | German .: B. |
| | 4. | German .: S. | Singing .: E. | German .: S. | German .: S. | } E. and S. | German .: S. |
| | 5. | German ..: D. | German . D. | German . D. | } Reading | German . D. | } Reading |
| | 6. | Reading . G. | Reading . G. | Reading G. and S. | } D. and G. | Reading G. and S. | } D. and G. |

274

| | | | | | | |
|---|---|---|---|---|---|---|
| 10 to 11. | II. Geometry D.<br>III. Drawing . F.<br>1. Singing .. E.<br>2. Geography G.<br>3. German . B.<br>4. Reading . S.<br>5. Writing . D.<br>6. Arithmetic R. | II. School keeping . D.<br>III. Violin ... E.<br>1. 2. 3. 4. } Geometry G. D. and S.<br>5. Reading . D.<br>6. Arithmetic R. | II. Geography B.<br>III. Arithmetic G.<br>1. French .. B.<br>2. Singing .. E.<br>3. Writing .. B.<br>4. Reading . S.<br>5. Arithmetic S.<br>6. Reading . R. | II. Theory of Arithmetic D.<br>III. Piano .... S.<br>1. Geography G.<br>2. 3. } German R. and B.<br>4. Arithmetic S.<br>5. Writing . D.<br>6. German .. S. | II. School keeping . D.<br>III. Ornamental Writing M.<br>1. 2. 3. 4. } Geometry G. D. and B.<br>5. Reading . D.<br>6. Writing . R. | II. History .. B.<br>III. Reading . D.<br>1. Geography G.<br>2. Singing .. E.<br>3. 4. 5. 6. } Writing B. S. D. & R. |
| 1 to 12 | II. Natural Philosophy .... D.<br>III. Drawing . F. | II. Singing .. C.<br>III. German . D. | II. Violin ... E.<br>III. Ornamental writing M. | II. National Philosophy .... Q.<br>III. Arithmetic G. | II. Singing .. E.<br>III. German .. D. | II. III. } Reading D. |
| 2 to 3. | II. Violin ... E.<br>III. Geometry S.<br>1. French .. B.<br>2. Reading . B.<br>3. 4. } Arithmetic S.<br>5. Reading . D.<br>6. Writing . R. | II. Violin ... E.<br>III. Piano .... S.<br>1. 2. } Botany G. and R.<br>3. Writing . B.<br>4. Arithmetic S.<br>5. Writing . D.<br>6. German . S. | | II.<br>III. Violin ... E.<br>1. 2. 3. 4. 5. 6. } Drawing F. B. S. & D. | II.<br>III. Geometry S.<br>1. 2. } Botany G. and R.<br>3. Writing . B.<br>4. Reading . S.<br>5. 6. } Singing E. and D. | I. Drawing . F. |
| 3 to 4. | II.<br>III.<br>1. History .. R.<br>2. Writing . B.<br>3. French .. B.<br>4. Writing . S.<br>5. Writing . D.<br>6. German . S. | II.<br>III. Geography B.<br>1. German .. R.<br>2. Reading . B.<br>3. Reading . S.<br>4. Writing . S.<br>5. Reading . D.<br>6. Writing . S. | | II.<br>III.<br>1. 2. 3. 4. 5. 6. } Drawing F. B. S. & D. | II.<br>III. Geography B.<br>1. History .. R.<br>2. Writing . B.<br>3. Reading . S.<br>4. 5. 6. } Writing S. and D. | I. Drawing . F. |
| 4 to 6. | I. Philosophy of Education D. | | | I. Violin<br>I. Singing } . E. | I. Singing<br>I. Violin } . E. | I. Religion . B. |

6. Arithmetic, continued through fractions and the rules of proportion;

7. Geometry—doctrine of magnitudes and measures;

8. Singing, and science of vocal and instrumental music.

IV. *Fourth part, of two years, including children from twelve to fourteen years old—six principal branches; namely:*

1. Religious Instruction in the religious observation of nature; the life and discourses of Jesus Christ; the history of the Christian religion, in connection with the cotemporary civil history; and the doctrines of christianity;

2. Knowledge of the world, and of mankind, including civil society, elements of law, agriculture, mechanic arts, manufactures, &c.;

3. Language, and exercises in composition;

4. Application of arithmetic and the mathematics to the business of life, including surveying and civil engineering;

5. Elements of Drawing;

6. Exercises in Singing, and the science of music.

We subjoin a few specimens of the modes of teaching under several of the above divisions.

I. *First part, Children from six to eight years of age.*

1. Conversations between the teacher and pupils, intended to exercise the powers of observation and expression.

The teacher brings the children around him, and engages them in familiar conversation with himself. He generally addresses them altogether, and they all reply simultaneously; but whenever necessary, he addresses an individual, and requires the individual to answer alone. He first directs their attention to the different objects in the school-room, their position, form, color, size, materials of which they are made, &c., and requires precise and accurate descriptions. He then requires them to notice the various objects that meet their eye in the way to their respective homes; and a description of these objects and the circumstances under which they saw them, will form the subject of the next morning's lesson. Then the house in which they live; the shop in which their father works; the garden in which they walk, &c., will be the subject of the successive lessons; and in this way for six months or a year, the children are taught to study *things,* to use their own powers of observation, and speak with readiness and accuracy, before books are put into their hands at all. A few specimens will make the nature and utility of this mode of teaching perfectly obvious.

In a school in Berlin a boy has assigned him for a lesson, a description of the remarkable objects in certain directions from the school-house, which is situated in Little Cathedral street. He proceeds as follows: "When I come out of the school-house into Little Cathedral street, and turn to the right, I soon pass on my left hand the Maria place, the Gymnasium and the Anklam gate. When I come out of Little Cathedral street, I see on my left hand the White Parade place, and within that, at a little distance, the beautiful statue of Frederick the Great, King of Prussia. It is made of white marble, and stands on a pedestal of variegated marble, and is fenced in with an iron railing. From here, I have on my right a small place, which is a continuation of the Parade Place; and at the end of this, near the wall, I see St. Peter's Church, or the Wall street church, as it is sometimes called. This church has a green yard before it, planted with trees, which is called the Wall Church Yard. St. Peter's Church is the oldest church in the city; it has a little round tower, which looks green, because it is mostly covered with copper, which is made green by exposure to the weather. When I go out of the school-house to the lower part of Little Cathedral street by the Coal market, through Shoe street and Carriage street, I come to the Castle. The Castle is a large building, with two small towers, and is built around a square yard, which is called the Castle yard. In the Castle there are two churches, and the King and his Ministers of State, and the Judges of the Supreme Court, and Consistory of the Church, hold their meetings there. From the Coal market, I go through Shoe street to the Hay market, and adjoining this is the New market, which was formed after St. Nicholas' Church was burnt, which formerly stood in that place. Between the Hay market and the New market is the City Hall, where the officers and magistrates of the city hold their meetings."

If a garden is given to a class for a lesson, they are asked the size of the garden, its shape, which they may draw on a slate with a pencil—whether there are trees in it—what the different parts of a tree are—what parts grow in the spring, and what parts decay in autumn, and what parts remain the same throughout the winter—whether any of the trees are fruit trees—what fruits they bear—when they ripen—how they look and taste—whether the fruit be wholesome or otherwise—whether it is prudent to eat much of it;—what plants and roots there are in the garden, and what use is made of them—what flowers there are, and how they look, &c. The teacher may then read them the description of the garden of Eden in the second chapter of Genesis—sing a hymn with them, the imagery of which is taken from the fruits and blossoms of a garden, and explain to them how kind and bountiful God is, who gives us such wholesome plants and fruits, and such beautiful flowers, for our nourishment and gratification.

The external heavens also make an interesting lesson. The sky—its appearance and color at different times; the clouds—their color, their varying form and movements; the sun—its rising and setting, its concealment by clouds, its warming the earth and giving it life and fertility, its great heat in summer, and the danger of being exposed to it unprotected; the moon—its appearance by night, full, gibbous, horned; its occasional absence from the heavens; the stars—their shining, difference among them, their number, distance from us, &c. In this connection the teacher may read to them the eighteenth and nineteenth Psalms, and other passages of scripture of that kind, sing with them a hymn celebrating the glory of God in the creation, and enforce the moral bearing of such contemplations by appropriate remarks. A very common lesson is, the family and family duties—love to parents, love to brothers and sisters—concluding with appropriate passages from scripture, and singing a family hymn.

2d. Elements of Reading.

After a suitable time spent in the exercises above described, the children proceed to learn the elements of reading. The first step is to exercise the organs of sound, till they have perfect command of their vocal powers, and

this, after the previous discipline in conversation and singing, is a task soon accomplished. They are then taught to
utter distinctly all the vowel sounds. The characters or letters representing these sounds are then shown and described to them till the form and power of each are distinctly impressed upon their memories. The same process
is then gone through in respect to diphthongs and conso-
nants. Last of all, after having acquired a definite and distinct view of the different sounds, and of the forms of the
letters which respectively represent these sounds, they are
taught the names of these letters, with the distinct understanding that the *name* of a letter and the *power* of a letter, are two very different things.

They are now prepared to commence reading. The letters are printed in large form on square cards, the class
stands up before a sort of rack, the teacher holds the cards
in his hand, places one upon the rack, and a conversation
of this kind passes between him and his pupils: What letter is that? H. He places another on the rack—What letter is that? A. I now put these two letters together, thus,
(moving the cards close together), HA—What sound do
these two letters signify? *Ha.* There is another letter—
What letter is that? (putting it on the rack.) *R.* I now put
this third letter to the other two, thus, HAR—What sound
do the three letters make? *Har.* There is another letter—
What is it? D. I join this letter to the other three, thus,
HARD—what do they all make? *Hard.* Then he proceeds in the same way with the letters F-I-S-T; joins these
four letters to the preceding four, HARD-FIST, and the
pupils pronounce, *Hard-fist.* Then with the letters E and
D, and joins these two to the preceding eight, and the pu-

pils pronounce *Hard-fisted*. In this way they are taught
to read words of any length—(for you may easily add to
the above, N-E-S-S, and make *Hard-fistedness*)—the long-
est as easily as the shortest; and in fact they learn their
letters; they learn to read words of one syllable and of
several syllables, and to read in plain reading by the same
process at the same moment. After having completed a
sentence, or several sentences, with the cards and rack,
they then proceed to read the same words and sentences
in their spelling books.

3. Elements of Writing.

The pupils are first taught the right position of the arms
and body in writing, the proper method of holding the pen,
&c.; and are exercised on these points till their habits are
formed correctly. The different marks used in writing are
then exhibited to them, from the simple point or straight
line, to the most complex figure. The variations of form
and position which they are capable of assuming, and the
different parts of which the complex figures are composed
are carefully described, and the student is taught to imi-
tate them, beginning with the most simple, then the separate parts of the complex, then the joining of the several
parts to a whole, with his pencil and slate. After having
acquired facility in this exercise he is prepared to write with
his ink and paper. The copy is written upon the black-
board; the paper is laid before each member of the class,
and each has his pen ready in his hand awaiting the word
of his teacher. If the copy be the simple point, or line *I* ,
the teacher repeats the syllable *one, one,* slowly at first,
and with gradually increasing speed, and at each repetition of the sound the pupils write. In this way they learn

to make the mark both correctly and rapidly. If the figure to be copied consist of two strokes, (thus, *ʃ* ,) the teacher pronounces *one, two, one two,* slowly at first, and then rapidly as before; and the pupils make the first mark, and then the second, at the sound of each syllable as before. If the figure consist of three strokes, (thus, *ʒ* ,) the teacher pronounces *one, two, three,* and the pupils write as before. So when they come to make letters—the letter *a* has five strokes, thus, *a* . When that is the copy, the teacher says deliberately, *one, two, three, four, five,* and at the sound of each syllable the different strokes composing the letter are made; the speed of utterance is gradually accelerated, till finally the *a* is made very quickly, and at the same time neatly. By this method of teaching, a plain, neat and quick hand is easily acquired.

4. Elements of Number, or Arithmetic.

In this branch of instruction I saw no improvements in the mode of teaching not already substantially introduced into the best schools of our own country. I need not, therefore, enter into any details respecting them—excepting so far as to say that the student is taught to demonstrate and perfectly to understand the reason and nature of every rule before he uses it.

(See Arithmetics, by Colburn, Ray, Miss Beecher and others.)

II. *Second part—Children from eight to ten years of age.*

1. Exercises in Reading.

The object of these exercises in this part of the course, is to acquire the habit of reading with accuracy and readiness, with due regard to punctuation, and with reference to orthography. Sometimes the whole class read together, and sometimes an individual by himself, in order to accustom them to both modes of reading, and to secure the advantages of both. The sentence is first gone through with in the class, by distinctly spelling each word as it occurs; then by pronouncing each word distinctly without spelling it; a third time, by pronouncing the words and mentioning the punctuation points as they occur. A fourth time, the sentence is read with the proper pauses indicated by the punctuation points, without mentioning them. Finally, the same sentence is read with particular attention to the intonations of the voice. Thus, one thing is taken at a time, and pupils must become thorough in each as it occurs, before they proceed to the next. One great benefit of the class reading together is, that each individual has the same amount of exercise as if he were the only one under instruction, his attention can never falter, and no part of the lesson escapes him. A skilful teacher once accustomed to this mode of reading, can as easily detect any fault, mispronunciation, or a negligence, in any individual, as if that individual were reading alone.

The process is sometimes shortened, and the sentence read only three times, namely—"according to the words, according to the punctuation, according to the life."

2. Exercises in Writing.

The pupils proceed to write copies in joining hand, both large and small, the principles of teaching being essentially as described in the first part of the course. The great object here is, to obtain a neat, swift, business hand. Sometimes without a copy they write from the dictation of the teacher; and in most cases instruction in orthography and punctuation is combined with that in penmanship. They are also taught to make and mend their own pens, and in doing this to be economical of their quills.

3. Religious and moral instruction in select Bible narratives.

In this branch of teaching the methods are various, and the teacher adopts the method best adapted in his judgment, to the particular circumstances of his own school, or to the special objects which he may have in view with a particular class. Sometimes he calls the class around him and relates to them, in his own language, some of the simple narratives of the Bible or reads it to them in the words of the Bible itself, or directs one of the children to read it aloud; and then follows a friendly, familiar conversation between him and the class; respecting the narrative, their little doubts are proposed and resolved, their questions put and answered, and the teacher unfolds the moral and religious instruction to be derived from the lesson, and illustrates it by appropriate quotations from the didactic and preceptive parts of the scripture. Sometimes he explains to the class a particular virtue or vice—a truth or a duty; and after having clearly shown what it is, he takes some Bible narrative which strongly illustrates the point in discussion, reads it to them, and directs their attention to it with special reference to the preceding narrative.

A specimen or two of these different methods will best show what they are:

(a) Read the narrative of the birth of Christ as given by Luke 2: 1-20. Observe, Christ was born for the salvation of men, so also for the salvation of children. Christ is the children's friend. Heaven rejoices in the good of men. Jesus, though so great and glorious, makes his appearance in a most humble condition. He is the teacher of the poor, as well as of the rich.

With these remarks compare other texts of the Bible:

"Jno. 3:16. For God so loved the world that he gave his only begotten son, that whosoever believeth in him should not perish, but have everlasting life."

"I. Jno. 4:9. In this was manifested the love of God towards us; because God has sent his only begotten son into the world that we might live through him."

"Mark 10:14, 15. But when Jesus saw it he was much displeased, and said unto them, suffer little children to come unto me, for of such is the kingdom of God: Verily I say unto you, whosoever shall not receive the kingdom of God as a little child, he shall not enter therein."

And the lesson is concluded with singing a Christmas Hymn.

Jesus feeds five thousand men: Jno. 6: 1–14.

God can bless a little so that it will do great good.

Economy suffers nothing to be lost—other texts Ps. 145: 15, 16.

"The eyes of all wait upon thee, and thou givest them their meat in due season."

"Thou openest thy hand and satisfiest the desire of every living thing." Matt. 6:31–33

Story of Cain and Abel. Gen. 4: 1–16.

*Remarks.*—Two men may do the same thing externally, and yet the merit of their acts be very different. God looks at the heart. Be careful not to cherish envy or ill will in the heart. You know not to what crimes they may lead you. Remorse and misery of the fratricide—other texts. Matt. 15: 19. Heb. 11: 4. I. Jno. 3: 12. Job. 34: 32.

"19. For out of the heart proceed evil thoughts, murders, adulteries, fornifications, thefts, false witness, blasphemies."

"4. By faith Abel offered unto God a more excellent sacrifice than Cain, by which he obtained witness, that he was righteous, God testifying of his gifts; and by it he, being dead, yet speaketh."

"12. Not as Cain *who* was of that wicked one, and slew his brother. And wherefore slew he him? Because his own works were evil, and his brother's righteous."

Story of Jesus in the Temple. Luke 2: 41–52.

Jesus in his childhood was very fond of learning—(he heard and asked questions;) God's Word was his delight, he understood what he heard and read—(men were astonished at his understanding and answers.) He carefully obeyed his parents—(he went with them and was subject to them.) And as he grew up his good conduct endeared him to God and man—other texts. Eph. 6: 1–4. Prov. 3: 1–4.

"1. Children obey your parents, in the Lord: for this is right.

"2. Honor thy father and thy mother, (which is the first commandment with promise:)

"3. That it may be well with thee, and thou mayest live long on the earth.

"4. And, ye fathers, provoke not your children to wrath: but bring them up in the nurture and admonition of the Lord."

"1. My son, forget not my law; but let thine heart keep my commandments:

"2. For length of days, and long life, and peace, shall they add to thee.

"3. Let not mercy and truth forsake thee: bind them about thy neck; write them upon the table of thine heart:

"4. So shalt thou find favor and good understanding in the sight of God and man."

On the other mode of teaching, the teacher for example, states the general truth, that God protects and rewards the good, and punishes the bad. In illustration of this he reads to them the narrative of Daniel in the lion's den, and the death which overtook his wicked accusers. Dan. 6. In illustration of the same truth, the escape of Peter and the miserable death of his persecutor, Herod, may be read. Acts 12.

The teacher may impress upon the mind of his class, that diligence, scrupulous fidelity and conscientious self-control, are the surest guarantees of success in life. And in illustration of the statement, read the narrative of Joseph's conduct in his master's house in Egypt, and in the prison, and in the results of it. Gen. 39. So, also, various incidents in the life of Jesus may be used to great advantage in illustrating different virtues.

It is recommended, that the teacher employ, in his instructions, the translation of the scripture in general use among the people; but that he occasionally take the original scriptures and read to the children, in his own translation, and sometimes use simple translations from different authors, that the children may early learn to notice the diversities in different faithful translations, and see what they really amount to.

It is scarcely necessary to observe, that a teacher who understands his business, and is faithful to his trust, will scrupulously abstain from sectarian peculiarities, or from casting odium on the tenets of any christian denominations. A man who has not magnanimity or enlargement of mind enough for this, is not fit to be employed as a teacher, even in the humblest branches of knowledge.

4. Language, or Grammar.

The knowledge of the native tongue; the ability to use it with correctness, facility, and power, is justly regarded as one of the most important branches of common school instruction. It is the principal object of the *logical exercises,* or as they may be justly termed, *the exercises in thinking and speaking,* already described as the first subject of study in the first part of the course, before the child has begun to use his book at all.

In this second part of the course, grammar is taught directly and scientifically, yet by no means in a dry and technical manner.—On the contrary, technical terms are carefully avoided, till the child has become familiar with the nature and use of the things designated by them, and he is able to use them as the names of ideas which have a definite existence in his mind, and not as awful sounds dimly shadowing forth some mysteries of science into which he has no power to penetrate.

The first object is to illustrate the different parts of speech, such as the noun, the verb, the adjective, the adverb; and this is done by engaging the pupil in conversation and leading him to form sentences in which the particular part of speech to be learned shall be the most important word, and directing his attention to the nature and use of the word in the place where he uses it. For example, let us suppose the nature and use of the adverb is to be taught:—

CALVIN E. STOWE

The teacher writes upon the black-board the words "here, there, near," &c. He then says, "children we are all together in this room—by which of the words on the black-board can you express this? Children—"We are all *here*." Teacher —"Now look out of the window and see the church; what can you say of the church with the second word on the black-board?" Children—"The church is *there*." Teacher— "The distance between us and the church is not great; how will you express this by a word on the black-board?" Children—"The church is *near*." The fact that these different words express the same sort of relations is then explained, and accordingly that they belong to the same class, or are the same pare of speech. The variations of these words is next explained. "Children, you say the church is near, but there is a shop between us and the church; what will you say of the shop? Children—"The shop is *nearer*." Teacher—"But there is a fence between us and the shop. Now when you think of the distance between us, the shop and the fence, what will you say of the fence? Children— "The fence is *nearest*." So of other verbs. "The lark sings *well*. Compare the singing of the lark with that of the canary bird. Compare the singing of the nightingale with that of the canary bird." After all the different sorts of adverbs and their variations have in this way been illus-trated, and the pupils understand that all words of this kind are called *adverbs,* the definition of the adverb is given as it stands in the grammar, and the book is put into their hands to study the chapter on this topic. In this way the pupil understands what he is doing at every step of his progress, and his memory is never burdened with mere names to which he can attach no definite meaning.

The mode of teaching the subsequent branches is founded on the same general principles, and it may not be necessary to give particular examples.

5. Numbers, or Arithmetic.

6. Doctrine of space and form, or Geometry.

7. Singing by note, or elements of Music.

The method of teaching music has already been successfully introduced into our own state, and whoever visits the schools of Messrs. Mason or Solomon, in Cincinnati, will have a much better idea of what it is than any description can give; nor will any one who visits these schools entertain a doubt, that all children, from six to ten years of age, who are capable of learning to read, are capable of learning to sing, and that this branch of instruction can be introduced into all our common schools with the greatest advantage, not only to the comfort and discipline of the pupils, but also to their progress in their other studies.

The students are taught from the black-board. The different sounds are represented by lines of different lengths, by letters, by figures, and by musical notes; and the pupils are thoroughly drilled on each successive principle before proceeding to the next.

III. *Third part of two years—Children from ten to twelve.*

1. Exercises in Reading and Elocution.

The object of these exercises in this part of the course is to accustom the pupils to read in a natural and impressive manner, so as to bring the full force of the sentiment on those to whom they read. They are examined in modulation, emphasis, and the various intonations, and they often read sentences from the black-board in which the various modulations are expressed by musical notes or curved lines.

The evils of drawling and monotone are prevented in the outset by the method of teaching, particularly the practice of the whole class reading together and keeping time. Short and pithy sentences, particularly the book of Proverbs, are recommended as admirably adapted to exercises of this kind.

2. Ornamental Writing introductory to Drawing.

The various kinds of ornamental letters are here practised upon, giving accuracy to the eye and steadiness to the hand, preparatory to skill in drawing, which comes into the next part of the course. The pupils also practise writing sentences and letters, with neatness, rapidity and correctness.

3. Religious instruction in the connected Bible history.

The design here is to give to the student a full and connected view of the whole Bible history. For this purpose large tables are made out and hung before the students. These tables are generally arranged in four columns; the first, containing the names of the distinguished men during a particular period of Bible history; the second, the dates; the third, a chronological register of events; and the fourth, the particular passages of the Bible where the history of these persons and events may be found. With these tables before the pupils, the teacher himself, in his own words, gives a brief conversational outline of the principal characters and events within a certain period, and then gives directions that the scriptural passages referred to, be carefully read. After this is done the usual recitation and examination takes place. Some of the more striking narratives, such as the finding of Moses on the banks of the Nile; Abraham offering his son; the journey of the wise men to do homage to Christ; the crucifixion; the conversation of Paul, &c., are committed to memory in the words of the Bible, and the recitation accompanied with the singing of a hymn alluding to these events. The moral instruction to be derived from each historical event is carefully impressed by the teacher. The teacher also gives them a brief view of the history between the termination of the Old and the commencement of the New Testament, that nothing may be wanting to a complete and systematic view of the whole ground. Thus the whole of the historical part of the Bible is studied thoroughly, and systematically, and practically, without the least sectarian bias, and without a moment being spent on a single idea that will not be of the highest use to the scholar during all his future life.

4. Language and Grammar.

There is here a continuation of the exercises in the preceding parts of the course, in a more scientific form, together with parsing of connected sentences, and writing from the dictation of the teacher, with reference to grammar, orthography and punctuation. The same principle alluded to before, of avoiding technical terms till the things represented by those terms are clearly perceived, is here carefully adhered to. A single specimen of the manner in which the modes and tenses of the verb are taught, may be sufficient to illustrate my meaning. The teacher writes on the black-board a simple sentence, as, "The scholars learn well;" and asks the class what sort of a sentence it is. They reply that it is a direct statement of a fact. (Teacher.) Put it in the form of a command. (Class.) Scholars, learn well. (Teacher.) Put in it a question form. (Class.) Do the scholars learn well? (Teacher.) Of a wish. (Class.) May the scholars learn well! (Teacher.) Of an exclamation. (Class.) How well the scholars learn! (Teacher.) The conditional form. (Class.) If the scholars learn well; or should the scholars learn well. (Teacher.) Of necessity. (Class.) The scholars must learn well. (Teacher.) Of ability. (Class.) The scholars can learn well, &c., &c. They are then taught, that the direct statement is called the indicative mode of the verb; the command, the imperative mode; the conditional, the subjunctive mode; the wish, the potential mode, &c., &c.—and after this the book is put in their hands and they study the lesson as it stands. After this the different tenses of the several modes are taught in the same way.

5. Real instruction, or knowledge of nature and the external world, including the first elements of the natural sciences, the arts of life, geography, and history. Instruction on this head is directed to the answering of the following questions, namely:

(a) What is man, as it respects his corporeal and intellectual nature?

Here come anatomy and physiology, so far as the structure of the human body is concerned, and the functions of its several parts.

Also the simple elements of mental philosophy. In this connection appropriate texts of scripture are quoted, as Gen. 2: 7. Ps. 139: 13–16. An appropriate hymn is also sung.

"7. And the Lord God formed man of the dust of the ground, and breathed into his nostrils the breath of life: and man became a living soul."

"14. I will praise thee; for I am fearfully *and* wonderfully made: marvellous *are* thy works; and *that* my soul knoweth right well.

"15. My substance was not hid from thee, when I was made in secret *and* curiously wrought in the lowest parts of the earth.

"16. Thine eyes did see my substance, yet being unperfect; and in thy book all *my members* were written, *which* in continuance were fashioned, when *as yet there was* none of them."

(*b*) What does man need for the preservation and ·cheerful enjoyment of life, as it respects his body and mind? For his body he needs *food;* the different kinds of food and the mode of preparing them, are here brought to view; the unwholesomeness of some kinds of food; injuriousness of improper food; cooking; evils of gluttony. The different kinds of clothing and modes of preparing them; what sort of dress is necessary to health; folly and wickedness of vanity and extravagance. *Dwellings;* materials of which houses are constructed; mode of constructing them; different trades employed in their construction.

For the mind, man needs *society;* the family and its duties; the neighborhood and its duties. Intellectual, moral, and religious cultivation; the school and its duties; the church and duties. For the body and mind both, he needs *security* of person and property; the government; the legislature; the courts, &c.

(*c*) Where and how do men find the means to supply their wants, and make themselves comfortable and happy in this life?

The vegetable, the mineral, and the animal kingdoms are here brought to view, for materials; together with agriculture and manufactures as the means of converting these materials to our use. Geography, with special reference to the productions of countries, and their civil, literary and religious institutions; towns, their organization and employments. Geography is sometimes taught by blank charts, to which the students are required to affix the names of the several countries, rivers, mountains, principal towns, &c., and then state the productions and institutions for which they are remarkable. Sometimes the names of countries, rivers, &c. are given, and the pupil is required to construct an outline chart of their localities.

In respect to all the above points, the native country is particularly studied, its capabilities, its productions, its laws, its institutions, its history, &c., are investigated, with especial reference to its ability of supplying the physical, social and moral wants of its inhabitants. Under this head the pupils are taught to appreciate their native country, to venerate and love its institutions, to understand what is necessary to their perfection, and to imbibe a spirit of pure and generous patriotism. It is scarcely necessary to add, that all the instruction under this 5th head, is confined to the fundamental and simplest principles of the several branches referred to.

6. Arithmetic continued through fractions and the rules of proportion.

7. Geometry, doctrines of magnitudes and measures.

8. Singing and science of vocal and instrumental music.

IV. *Fourth part of two years—Children from twelve to fourteen.*

1. Religious instruction, in the religious observation of nature, the life and discourses of Jesus Christ, the history of the christian religion, in connection with the cotemporary civil history, and the principal doctrines of the christian system.

The first topic of instruction mentioned under this head is one of peculiar interest and utility. The pupils are taught to observe with care and system, the various powers and operations of nature, and to consider them as so many illustrations of the wisdom, power, and goodness of the Creator, and at each lesson they are directed to some appropriate passage of the Bible, which they read and commit to memory; and thus the idea is continually impressed on them, that the God of nature, and the God of the Bible, are one and the same Being.

For example, as introductory to the whole study, the first chapter of Genesis, together with some other appropriate passage of scripture, as the 147th Psalm, or the 38th chapter of Job, may be read and committed to memory. The surface of the earth, as illustrating the power and wisdom of God, may be taken as a lesson. Then the varieties of surface, as mountains, valleys, oceans, and rivers, continents, and islands, the height of mountains, the breadth of oceans, the length of rivers, remarkable cataracts, extended caverns, volcanoes, tides, &c., may be taken into view, and the teacher may impress upon the class the greatness, power, and intelligence necessary for such a creation. The whole is fortified by the application of such a passage as Psalm 104: 1–13.

"1. Bless the Lord, O my soul. O Lord my God, thou art very great; thou art clothed with honor and majesty.

"2. Who coverest *thyself* with light as *with* a garment; who stretchest out the heavens like a curtain;

"3. Who layeth the beams of his chambers in the waters: who maketh the clouds his chariot: who walketh upon the wings of the wind:

"4. Who maketh his angels spirits; his ministers a flaming fire:

"5. *Who* laid the foundation of the earth, *that* it should not be removed forever.

"6. Thou coveredest it with the deep as *with* a garment: the waters stood above the mountains.

"7. At thy rebuke they fled: at the voice of thy thunder they hasted away.

"8. They go up by the mountains; they go down by the valleys unto the place which thou hast founded for them.

"9. Thou hast set a bound that they may not pass over; that they turn not again to cover the earth.

"10. He sendeth the springs into the valleys, *which* run among the hills.

"11. They give drink to every beast of the field; the wild asses quench their thirst.

"12. By them shall the fowls of the heaven have their habitation, *which* sing among the branches.

"13. He watereth the hills from his chambers; the earth is satisfied with the fruit of thy works."

"24. O Lord, how manifold are thy works! in wisdom hast thou made them all: the earth is full of thy riches.

"25. *So is* this great and wide sea, wherein *are* things creeping innumerable, both small and great beasts.

"26. There go the ships; *there is* that leviathan, *whom* thou hast made to play therein."

The fruitfulness and beauty of the earth, as illustrating the wisdom and goodness of God, may serve as another lesson. Here may be exhibited the beauty and variety of the plants and flowers with which the earth is adorned—the manner of their growth and self-propagation, their utility to man and beast, their immense number and variety their relations to each other as genera and species; trees and their varieties, their beauty and utility, their timber and their fruit; and, in connection with this lesson, Psalm 104: 14–34, may be committed to memory:

"14. He causeth the grass to grow for the cattle, and herb for the service of man: that he may bring forth fruit out of the earth;

"15. And wine that maketh glad the heart of man, *and* oil to make *his* face to shine, and bread *which* strengtheneth man's heart.

"16. The trees of the Lord are full of *sap;* the cedars of Lebanon which he hath planted;

"17. Where the birds make their nests; as *for* the stork, the fir-trees *are* her house.

"18. The high hills *are* a refuge for the wild goats, *and* the rocks for the conies.

"19. He appointeth the moon for season: the sun knoweth his going down.

"20. Thou makest darkness, and it is night: wherein all the beasts of the forests do creep *forth*.

"21. The young lions roar after their prey, and seek their meat from God.

"22. The sun ariseth, they gather themselves together, and lay them down in their dens.

"23. Man goeth forth to his work and to his labor until the evening."

"27. These wait all upon thee; that thou mayest give *them* their meat in due season.

"28. *That* thou givest them they gather; thou openest thine hand, they are filled with good.

"29. Thou hidest thy face, they are troubled; thou takest away their breath, they die, and return to their dust.

"30. Thou sendest forth thy spirit, they are created; and thou renewest the face of the earth.

"31. The glory of the Lord shall endure forever; the Lord shall rejoice in his works.

"32. He looketh on the earth, and it trembleth: he toucheth the hills and they smoke.

"33. I will sing unto the Lord as long as I live: I will sing praise unto my God while I have my being.

"34. My meditation of him shall be sweet: I will be glad in the Lord."

In like manner, the creation and nourishment, the habits and instincts of various animals may be contemplated in connection with Proverbs 6:6–8; Psalm 104:17–22; Proverbs 30:24–31. Gen. 1:20–24; Psalms 145:15–16.

"6. Go to the ant, thou sluggard; consider her ways, and be wise:

"7. Which having no guide, overseer, or ruler,

"8. Provideth her meat in the summer, and gathereth her food in the harvest."

"24. There be four *things which* are little on the earth but they *are* exceeding wise.

"25. The ants *are* a people not strong, yet they prepare their meat in the summer.

"26. The conies are but a feeble folk, yet they make their houses in the rocks.

"27. The locusts have no king, yet they go forth all of them by bands;

"28. The spider taketh hold with her hands, and is in kings' palaces.

"29. There be three *things* which go well, yea, four are comely in going.

"30. A lion, *which is* strongest among beasts, and turneth not away for any;

"31. A greyhound; an he-goat also; and a king against whom *there is* no rising up."

"24. And God said, Let the earth bring forth the living creature after his kind, cattle, and creeping thing, and beast of the earth after his kind: and it was so.

"25. And God made the beast of the earth after his kind, and cattle after their kind, and every thing that creepeth upon the earth after his kind: and God saw that *it was* good."

"15. The eyes of all wait upon thee; and thou givest them their meat in due season.

"16. Thou openest thine hand, and satisfieth the desire of every living thing.

"17. The LORD *is* righteous in all his ways, and holy in all his works."

The phenomena of light and color, the nature of the rainbow, &c., may make another interesting lesson, illustrating the unknown forms of beauty and glory which exist in the Divine Mind, and which He may yet develope in other and still more glorious worlds; in connection with Gen. 1, 3, 5, 9, 13, 14, and other passages of like kind.

So the properties of the air, wind, and storm, Job 28, 25–28, 33, 34. Ps. 148, 8.

"33. Knowest thou the ordinances of heaven? canst thou set the dominion thereof in the earth?

"34. Canst thou lift up thy voice to the clouds, that abundance of waters may cover thee?

"35. Canst thou send lightnings, that they may go, and say unto thee, Here we *are!*

"36. Who hath put wisdom in the inward parts? or who hath given understanding to the heart?

"37. Who can number the clouds in wisdom? or who can stay the bottles of heaven."

Then the heavens, the sun, moon, planets, fixed stars and comets, the whole science of astronomy, so far as it can be introduced with advantage into common schools, can be contemplated in the same way. The enlightening, elevating, and purifying moral influence of such a scheme of instruction, carried through the whole system of nature, must be clearly oblivious to every thinking mind, and its utility, considered merely with reference to worldly good, is no less manifest.

The second topic of religious instruction is more exclusively scriptural. The life of Christ, and the history of the apostles, as given in the New Testament, are chronologically arranged, and tables formed as before, (III. 3). The discourses of Christ are examined and explained in their chronological arrangement, and in the same way the discourses and epistles of the apostles. The history of christianity, in connection with the cotemporary civil history, is taught in a series of conversational lectures. To conclude the whole course of religious instruction, a summary of the christian doctrine is given in the form of some approved catechism.

2. Knowledge of the world and of mankind, including civil society, constitutional law, agriculture, mechanic arts, manufacturing, &c.

This is a continuation and a completion of a more systematic form of the instruction commenced in III, 5. The course begins with the family, and the first object is to construct a habitation. The pupil tells what materials are necessary for this purpose, where they are to be found, how brought together and fitted into the several parts of the building. The house must now be furnished. The different articles of furniture and their uses are named in systematic order, the materials of which they are made, and the various trades employed in making them are enumerated. Then comes the garden, its tools and products, and whatever else is necessary for the subsistence and physical comfort of a family. Then the family duties and virtues, parental and filial obligation and affection; rights of property, duties of neighborhoods; the civil relations of society; the religious relations of society; the state, the father-land, &c.; finally geography, history, and travels. Books of travels are compiled expressly for the use of schools, and are found to be of the highest interest and utility.

3. Language and exercises in composition.

The object here is to give the pupils a perfect command of their native tongue and ability to use it on all occasions with readiness and power. The first exercises are on simple questions, such as—"Why ought children to love and obey their parents?"—or they are short descriptions of visible objects, such as a house, a room, a garden, &c. There are also exercises on the various forms of expressing the same idea, as "The sun enlightens the earth." "The earth is enlightened by the sun." "The sun gives light to the earth." "The earth receives light from the sun." "The sun is the source of light to the earth." "The sun sends out its rays to enlighten the earth." "The earth is enlightened by rays sent out from the sun," &c. There are exercises also of the same sort, or metaphors and other figures of speech—familiar letters are then written and short essays on themes such as may be furnished by texts from the book of Proverbs and other sentences of the kind; and thus gradual advancement is made to all the higher and graver modes of composition.

4. Application of arithmetic and mathematics to the business of life, including surveying, civil engineering, &c.

The utility of this branch of instruction and the mode of it, after what has already been said, are probably too obvious to need any further illustration.

5. Elements of Drawing.

For this the pupils have already been prepared by the exercises in ornamental writing in the previous part of the course. They have already acquired that accuracy of sight and steadiness of hand which are among the most essential requisites to drawing well. The first exercises are in drawing lines, and the most simple mathematical figures, such as the square, the cube, the triangle, the parallelogram: generally from wooden models placed at some little distance on a shelf, before the class. From this they proceed to architectural figures, such as doors, windows, columns, and facades. Then the figures of animals, such as a horse, a cow, an elephant—first from other pictures, and then from nature. A plant, a rose, or some flower is placed upon a shelf and the class make a picture of it. From this they proceed to landscape painting, historical painting, and the higher branches of the art, according to their time and capacity. All learn enough of drawing to use it in the common business of life, such as plotting a field, laying out a canal, or drawing the plan of a building; and many attain to a high degree of excellence.

6. Exercises in singing and the science of music.

The instructions of the previous parts are extended as far as possible, and include singing and playing at sight, and the more abstruse and difficult branches of the science and art of music.

## Character of the System.

The striking features of this system, even in the hasty and imperfect sketch which my limits allow me to give, are obvious even to superficial observation. No one can fail to observe its great completeness, both as to the number and kind of subjects embraced in it, and as to its adaptiveness to develope every power of every kind, and give it a useful direction. What topic in all that is necessary for a sound business education is here omitted? I can think of nothing, unless it be one or two of the modern languages, and these

are introduced wherever it is necessary, as has already
been seen in the study sheet of Dr. Diesterweg's seminary,
inserted on a preceding page of this report. I have not
taken the course precisely as it exists in any one school, but
have combined from an investigation of many institutions,
the features which I supposed would most fairly represent
the whole system. In the Rhinish provinces of Prussia, in
a considerable part of Bavaria, Baden, and Wirtemberg,
French is taught as well as German; in the schools of
Prussian Poland, German and Polish are taught; and even
English, in the Russian schools of Cronstadt and Arch-
angel, where so many English and American merchants
resort for the purposes of trade. Two languages can be
taught in a school quite as easily as one, provided the
teacher be perfectly familiar, as any one may see by visiting Mr. Solomon's school in Cincinnati, where all the instruction is given both in German and English.

What faculty of mind is there that is not developed in
the scheme of instruction sketched above? I know of none.
The perceptive and reflecting faculties, the memory and
the judgment, the imagination and the taste, the moral and
religious faculty, and even the various kinds of physical
and manual dexterity, all have opportunity for development and exercise. Indeed, I think the system in its great
outlines, as nearly complete as human ingenuity and skill
can make it; though undoubtedly some of its arrangements
and details admit of improvement; and some changes will
of course be necessary in adapting it to the circumstances
of different countries.

The entirely practical character of the system is obvious
throughout. It views every subject on the practical side,

and in reference to its adaptedness to use. The dry technical abstract parts of science are not those first presented; but the system proceeds, in the only way which nature ever pointed out, from practice to theory, from parts to demonstrations. It has often been a complaint in respect to some systems of education, that the more a man studied, the less he knew of the actual business of life. Such a complaint cannot be made in reference to this system, for being intended to educate for the actual business of life, this object is never for a moment lost sight of.

Another striking feature of the system is its moral and religious character. Its morality is pure and elevated, its religion entirely removed from the narrowness of sectarian bigotry. What parent is there, loving his children and wishing to have them respected and happy, who would not desire that they should be educated under such a kind of moral and religious influence as has been described? Whether a believer in revelation or not, does he not know that without sound morals there can be no happiness, and that there is no morality like the morality of the New Testament? Does he not know that without religion, the human heart can never be at rest, and that there is no religion like the religion of the Bible? Every well informed man knows, that, as a general fact, it is impossible to impress the obligations of morality with any efficiency on the heart of a child, or even on that of an adult, without an appeal to some mode which is sustained by the authority of God; and for what code will it be possible to claim this authority if not for the code of the Bible?

But perhaps some will be ready to say, the scheme is

indeed an excellent one, provided only it were practicable; but the idea of introducing so extensive and complete a course of study into our common schools is entirely visionary and can never be realized. I answer, that it is no theory which I have been exhibiting, but a matter of fact, a copy of actual practice. The above system is no visionary scheme emanating from the closet of a recluse, but a sketch of the course of instruction now actually pursued by thousands of schoolmasters in the best district schools that have ever been organized. It can be done, for it has been done, it is now done, and it ought to be done. If it can be done in Europe, I believe it can be done in the United States: if it can be done in Prussia, I know it can be done in Ohio. The people have but to say the word and provide the means, and the thing is accomplished; for the word of the people here is even more powerful than the word of the King there; and the means of the people here are altogether more abundant for such an object than the means of the sovereign there. Shall this object, then, so desirable in itself, so entirely practicable, so easily within our reach, fail of accomplishment? For the honor and welfare of our State, for the safety of our whole nation, I trust it will not fail; but that we shall soon witness in this commonwealth the introduction of a system of common school instruction, fully adequate to all the wants of our population.

But the question occurs, *how* can this be done? I will give a few brief hints as to some things which I suppose to be essential to the attainment of so desirable an end.

## *Means of Sustaining the System.*

1. Teachers must be skilful, and trained to their business. It will at once be perceived, that the plan above sketched out proceeds on the supposition that the teacher has fully and distinctly in his mind the whole course of instruction, not only as it respects the matter to be taught, but also as to all the best modes of teaching, that he may be able readily and decidedly to vary his method according to the peculiarities of each individual mind which may come under his care. This is the only true secret of successful teaching. The old mechanical method, in which the teacher relies entirely on his textbooks, and drags every mind along through the same dull routine of creeping recitation, is utterly insufficient to meet the wants of our people. It may do in Asiatic Turkey, where the whole object of the school is to learn to pronounce the words of the Koran, in one dull monotonous series of sounds; or it may do in China, where men must never speak or think out of the old beaten track of Chinese imbecility; but it will never do in the United States, where the object of education ought to be to make immediately available, for the highest and best purposes, every particle of real talent that exists in the nation. To effect such a purpose, the teacher must possess a strong and independent mind, well disciplined, and well stored with every thing pertaining to his profession and ready to adapt his instructions to every degree of intellectual capacity, and every kind of acquired habit. But how can we expect to find such teachers, unless they are trained to their business? A very few of extraordinary powers may occur, as we sometimes find able me-

chanics, and great mathematicians, who had no early training in their favorite pursuits; but these few exceptions to a general rule will never multiply fast enough to supply our schools with able teachers. The management of the human mind, particularly youthful mind, is the most delicate task ever committed to the hand of man; and shall it be left to mere instinct, or shall our schoolmasters have at least as careful a training as our lawyers and physicians?

2. Teachers, then, must have the means of acquiring the necessary qualifications; in other words, there must be institutions in which the business of teaching is made a systematic object of attention. I am not an advocate for multiplying our institutions. We already have more in number than we support, and it would be wise to give power and efficiency to those we now possess, before we project new ones. But the science and art of teaching ought to be a regular branch of study in some of our academies and high schools, that those who are looking forward to this profession may have an opportunity of studying its principles. In addition to this, in our populous towns where there is an opportunity for it, there should be large model schools, under the care of the most able and experienced teachers that can be obtained; and the candidates for the profession who have already completed the theoretic course of the academy, should be employed in this school as monitors or assistants, thus testing all their theories by practice, and acquiring skill and dexterity under the guidance of their head master. Thus, while learning, they would be teaching, and no time or effort would be lost. To give efficiency to the whole system, to present a general

standard and a prominent point of union, there should be at least one model-teachers' seminary, at some central point,—as at Columbus,—which shall be amply provided with all the means of study and instruction, and have connected with it schools of every grade, for the practice of the students, under the immediate superintendence of their teachers.

3. The teachers must be competently supported, and devoted to their business. Few men attain any great degree of excellence in a profession, unless they love it, and place all their hopes in life upon it. A man cannot, consistently with his duty to himself, engage in a business which does not afford him a competent support, unless he has other means of living, which is not the case with many who engage in teaching. In this country especially, where there are such vast fields of profitable employment open to every enterprising man, it is not possible, that the best of teachers can be obtained, to any considerable extent, for our district schools, at the present rate of wages. We have already seen what encouragement is held out to teachers in Russia, Prussia, and other European nations, and what pledges are given of competent support to their families, not only while engaged in the work, but when, having been worn out in the public service, they are no longer able to labor. In those countries, where every profession and walk of life is crowded, and where one of the most common and oppressive evils is want of employment, men of high talents and qualifications are often glad to become teachers even of district schools; men who in this country would aspire to the highest places in our colleges, or even our halls of legislation and courts of justice. How much more

necessary, then, here, that the profession of teaching should afford a competent support!

Indeed, such is the state of things in this country, that we cannot expect to find male teachers for all our schools. The business of educating, especially young children, must fall, to a great extent, on female teachers. There is not the same variety of tempting employment for females as for men, they can be supported cheaper, and the Creator has given them peculiar qualifications for the education of the young. Females, then, ought to be employed extensively in all our elementary schools, and they should be encouraged and aided in obtaining the qualifications necessary for this work. There is no country in the world where woman holds so high a rank, or exerts so great an influence, as here; wherefore, her responsibilities are the greater, and she is under obligations to render herself the more actively useful. I think our fair countrywomen, notwithstanding the exhortations of Harriet Martineau, Fanny Wright, and some other *ladies* and *gentlemen,* will never seek distinction in our public assemblies for public discussion, or in our halls of legislation; but in their appropriate work of educating the young, of forming the opening mind to all that is good and great, the more they distinguish themselves the better.

4. The children must be made comfortable in their school; they must be punctual, and attend the whole course. There can be no profitable study without personal comfort; and the inconvenience and miserable arrangements of some of our school-houses are enough to annihilate all that can be done by the best of teachers. No instructor can teach unless the pupils are present to be taught, and

no plan of systematic instruction can be carried steadily through, unless the pupils attend punctually and through the whole course.

5. The children must be given up implicitly to the discipline of the school. Nothing can be done unless the teacher has the entire control of his pupils in school hours, and out of school too, so far as the rules of the school are concerned. If the parent in any way interferes with, or overrules the arrangements of the teacher, he may attribute it to himself if the school is not successful. No teacher ever ought to be employed to whom the entire management of the children cannot be safely entrusted; and better at any time dismiss the teacher than counteract his discipline. Let parents but take the pains and spend the money necessary to provide a comfortable school-house and a competent teacher for their children, and they never need apprehend that the discipline of the school will be unreasonably severe. No inconsiderable part of the corporeal punishment that has been inflicted in schools, has been made necessary by the discomfort of school-houses and the unskilfulness of teachers. A lively, sensitive boy is stuck upon a bench full of knot-holes and sharp ridges, without a support for his feet or his back, with a scorching fire on one side of him and a freezing wind on the other; and a stiff Orbilius of a master, with wooden brains and iron hands, orders him to sit perfectly still, with nothing to employ his mind or his body, till it is *his turn to read*. Thus confined for hours, what can the poor little fellow do but begin to wriggle like a fish out of water, or an eel in a frying-pan? For this irrepressible effort at relief he receives a box on the ear; this provokes and renders him still more uneasy, and next

comes the merciless ferule; and the poor child is finally burnt and frozen, cuffed and beaten into hardened roguery or incurable stupidity, just because the avarice of his parents denied him a comfortable school-house and a competent teacher. [On the subject of school discipline, I solicit attention particularly to the answers to question 3, in Appendix B, to this report.]

6. A beginning must be made at certain points, and the advance towards completeness must be gradual. Every thing cannot be done at once, and such a system as is needed cannot be generally introduced till its benefits are first demonstrated by actual experiment. Certain great points, then, where the people are ready to co-operate, and to make the most liberal advances in proportion to their means, to maintain the schools, should be selected, and no pains or expense spared, till the full benefits of the best system are realized; and as the good effects are seen, other places will very readily follow the example. All experience has shown, that governmental patronage is most profitably employed, not to do the entire work but simply as an incitement to the people to help themselves.

To follow up this great object, the legislature has wisely made choice of a Superintendent whose untiring labors and disinterested zeal are worthy of all praise. But no great plan can be carried through in a single year; and if the Superintendent is to have opportunity to do what is necessary, and to preserve that independence and energy of official character which is requisite to the successful discharge of his duties, he should hold his office for the same term and on the same conditions, as the Judges of the Supreme Court.

Every officer engaged in this, or in every other public work, should receive a suitable compensation for his services. This justice requires, and it is the only way to secure fidelity and efficiency.

There is one class of our population for whom some special provision seems necessary. The children of foreign immigrants are now very numerous among us, and it is essential that they receive a good ENGLISH EDUCATION. But they are not prepared to avail themselves of the advantages of our common English schools, their imperfect acquaintance with the language being an insuperable bar to their entering on the course of study. It is necessary, therefore, that there be some preparatory schools, in which instruction shall be communicated both in English and their native tongue. The English is, and must be, the language of this country, and the highest interests of our State demand it of the Legislature to require that the English language be thoroughly taught in every school which they patronise. Still, the exigencies of the case make it necessary that there should be some schools expressly fitted to the condition of our foreign immigrants, to introduce them to a knowledge of our language and institutions. A school of this kind has been established in Cincinnati by benevolent individuals. It has been in operation about a year, and already nearly three hundred children have received its advantages. Mr. Solomon, the head teacher, was educated for his profession in one of the best institutions of Prussia, and in this school he has demonstrated the excellencies of the system. The instructions are all given both in German and English, and this use of the two languages does not at all interrupt the progress of the children in their respective studies. I cannot but recommend this philanthropic institution to the notice and patronage of the Legislature.

In neighborhoods where there is a mixed population, it is desirable, if possible, to employ teachers who understand both languages, and that the exercises of the school be conducted in both, with the rule, however, that all the reviews and examinations *be in English only.*

These suggestions I have made with unfeigned diffidence, and with a sincere desire that the work which has been so nobly begun by the Legislature of Ohio, may be carried forward to a glorious result. I should hardly have ventured to take such liberty had not my commission expressly authorized me to "make such practical observations as I might think proper," as well as to report facts. I know that I am addressing enlightened and patriotic men, who have discernment to perceive, and good feeling to appreciate, every sincere attempt, however humble it may be, for the country's good; and I have therefore spoken out plainly and directly the honest convictions of my heart; feeling assured that what is honestly meant, will, by highminded men, be kindly received.

All which is respectfully submitted.

C. E. STOWE.

*Columbus, Dec.* 18, 1837.

---

NOTE.—I cannot close my report without acknowledging my special obligations to some gentlemen whose names do not occur in it. To Professor Dorner of the University of Tuebingen, I am particularly indebted for his unwearied kindness and assiduity in directing me to the best schools, and introducing me to the teachers. To Dr. Bowring of London, and Professor Pryme and Henslow of the University of Cambridge, I am under particular obligations. Dr. Drake of Cincinnati, and Hon. W. C. Rives, and Hon. Henry Clay of the United States Senate, also rendered me timely aid. Hundreds of teachers, and other gentlemen interested in education, whose sympathies I enjoyed, I shall always remember with pleasure and gratitude.

# INDEX

# INDEX

## Q

*Quarterly Review,* 119

## R

Raikes, Robert, 22 *(see also* Sunday schools).
Russell, William, 3

## S

*Spectator,* 119
State school supervision, first established in United States, 5
Stowe, Calvin E., 4, 5
    selections from "Report on Elementary Public Instruction in Europe," 248-316
    biography of, 243–247
Sunday schools, 22 *(see also* Raikes).
Surveys, educational, 2

## T

Teachers, appointment of, in Prussia, 173 *ff.*
training, 6, 7
    early, in United States, 6, 7
    in Prussia, 167 *ff.*

## W

Wiley, Calvin H., 2
Woodbridge, William C., 3

## Y

"Year in Europe," Griscom, selections from, 16-111
Yverdun, 64

## Z

Zion Parnassus, 6